INDEPENDENT CITIES
Rethinking U.S. Urban Policy

Robert J. Waste
California State University, Sacramento

New York   Oxford
OXFORD UNIVERSITY PRESS
1998

Oxford University Press

Oxford   New York

Athens   Auckland   Bangkok   Bogotá   Bombay   Buenos Aires
Calcutta   Cape Town   Da res Salaam   Delhi   Florence   Hong Kong
Istanbul   Karachi   Kuala Lumpur   Madras   Madrid   Melbourne
Mexico City   Nairobi   Paris   Singapore   Taipei   Tokyo   Toronto   Warsaw

and associated companies in
Berlin   Ibadan

Library of Congress Cataloging-in-Publication Data

Waste, Robert J.
   Independent cities : rethinking U.S. urban policy / Robert J.
Waste.
      p.   cm.
   Includes bibliographical references and index.
   ISBN 0-19-510829-9 (cl.) — ISBN 0-19-510830-2 (pb.)
   1. Urban policy—United States.   2. Cities and towns—United
States.   3. Social problems—United States.   I. Title.
HT123.W35   1998
307.76'0973—dc21   97-27328
                                                                      CIP

1 3 5 7 9 8 6 4 2

Printed in the United States of America
on acid-free paper

To the late
Robert G. Thompson

Bob Thompson—my teacher, mentor, friend, and later
(all too briefly) my colleague at California State University,
Sacramento—was a teacher with a capital T.

Contents

List of Tables

Preface

This book is both a history of national and sub-national urban policies, and a prediction of the trajectory that those polices will need to take in the future if, as a society, we are to solve the mounting crisis in America's cities. Since at least 1990, American cities have been stuck in a seemingly *permanent crisis*, involving high levels of poverty, hunger, homelessness, crime, and low levels of funding for infrastructure needs, mass transit, and education. Perhaps unsurprisingly, metro voters are more alienated and less likely to participate in elections and civic affairs than at any time since the late 1950s. Worse, if there needed to be anything worse for America's cities, cities and their surrounding metro areas have become virtually "invisible" in American national and presidential politics.

Is there a way out of the permanent crisis and the invisibility problem for American cities? I think so, but the "answers" I have arrived at are bound to alienate both traditional academic and political readers. The academic world and the political world are in many respects polar opposites. Academics are wholesalers, while politicians are in the retail business. Politicians are looking for a few good, "big" ideas. Academics, on the other hand, distrust any analysis that does not have numerous levels, multiple causalities, and a complex multi-tiered set of intervention strategies. For such scholarly readers this analysis may strike some—but not all—ears as reductionist or simplistic. For readers primarily from the political world, there will probably still be too many causes and interventions reviewed and suggested in the text.

A final source of discomfort for many readers—but, hopefully, not for all— is a certain lack of ideological consistency in a book that argues that the two most effective urban aid interventions in the past fifty years are the Head Start program created under the liberal War on Poverty/Great Society Administration of Lyndon Johnson, and the Revenue Sharing program created under the aegis of the conservative New Federalism administration of Richard Nixon. After a good deal of reflection, I have opted to abandon ideological consistency in favor of trying to put together a set of programs and policies that, if they were really given a fair trial at the national level, might actually solve the current crisis in American cities.

Every fifteen minutes a child in an American city is wounded by guns. Every two hours an American child is killed by gunfire. Every night thirty million Americans go to bed hungry. Twenty percent of the bridges in metro areas are functionally obsolete, yet Americans continue to resist car pools and mass transit, choosing instead to spend 15 to 19 percent of the gross national product simply getting to work or going somewhere else to play. Voter turnout nationally and in metro areas has declined about a quarter from the 1960s to the 1990s, as voter alienation, poverty, and crime now have moved from the center city to also occupy stage-center in the suburbs and *edge cities*. The costs, both financial and in starker human terms, of this mounting permanent crisis in American cities is staggering—the pathologies of the Permanent Crisis now consume more than $585 billion annually, a figure that is over 8 percent of the gross domestic product, a per capita cost of over $2,000, every year.

Thankfully, there is a way out of the permanent crisis; in fact, two ways out. We can either pursue the modest Safe Streets, Safe Cities progressive and revenue-neutral policy package that I outline in Chapter 6—a program that would result in the creation of strong, healthy, *Independent Cities*—or we can opt for the far stronger, more expensive and more radical medicine outlined in Chapter 7. Either way, it is well past time to begin the effort. The problems of cities are solvable, but not by those who would stay within the narrow tribal walls of ideological purity, academic neutrality, or by those who remain wedded to the failed programs and policies of the past. I am reminded of a wonderful painting of two street masons, "The Street Menders," by Vincent Van Gogh at the Phillips Gallery in Washington, D.C. That, I think, is what American cities will need in the late 1990s and in the early part of the next century; not grandiose city attackers or civic boosters, not antiseptically clean academic scholars or ideologically pure and consistent politicians—rather, what the city needs are "menders," a few folks willing to roll up their sleeves and get their hands dirty building the streets and the civic life that American metro areas so desperately need. My single greatest wish is that we had a Michael Harrington—the gifted social critic of the 1960s whose book on poverty in America, *The Other America* (1962), moved Presidents Kennedy and Johnson, and an entire generation of Americans to embark on a War on Poverty—capable of persuading them to do so.

R.J.W.
Sacramento, California

Acknowledgments

A number of friends and colleagues have aided me in the course of this study, and it is a pleasure to publicly acknowledge my debt, and my gratitude, to them. This book was a long time in the making, involving some five years of research and significant financial assistance from Cleveland State University and California State University, Chico. In 1994–95, I had the distinct honor of serving as the Albert A. Levin Chair of Urban Studies and Public Service in the Maxine Goodman Levin College of Urban Affairs at Cleveland State University. During that time, I was able to research and produce a rough draft of the first three chapters of this book. My debts to my colleagues at the Maxine Goodman Levin College of Urban Affairs are almost too numerous to list. I am deeply grateful to: Jennifer Alexander, William Bowen, Mittie Olin Chandler, Claire Felbinger, Ned Hill, Sandra Kaufman, Norman Krumholz, Julie Rittenhouse, Michael Spicer, and Larry Terry. I would particularly like to thank, for constant inspiration, goading, and fellowship in the specific service of this book project several other Levin College scholars, including: Dick Bingham, Dennis Keating, Larry Ledebur, Roberta Steinbacher, and Levin College Dean, David Sweet. Finally, the assistance and partnership of Maxine Goodman Levin and Morton Levin in believing in my scholarship, and in supporting it in countless ways during my tenure as the 1994–1995 Albert A. Levin Chair of Urban Affairs and Public Service, are deeply appreciated.

I have a special debt of gratitude to my long-time friend, co-editor (along with another friend, supporter, and co-editor, Margaret Wilder of the University of Delaware) of a Book Series on *Cities and Planning,* and long-suffering roommate at Urban Affairs Association Annual Meetings, Roger W. Caves of San Diego State University. Thanks also to David Ames of the University of Delaware; William Barnes of the National League of Cities in Washington, D.C.; Robyne Boyle of Wayne State University; Mary Helen Callahan of the University of Delaware; Scott Cummings of the University of Louisville; Robert A. Dahl of Yale University; Judith Garber of the University of Alberta; Woodrow Jones, Jr., of Texas A&M University; Kenneth Ornstein of Providence, Rhode Island; Dan Rich of the University of Delaware; David Rusk of Washington, D.C.; Clarence Stone of the University of Maryland; Todd Swanstrom of SUNY, Albany; Fritz Wagner of the University of New Orleans; Rob Wassmer of California State University, Sacramento; and Hal Wolman of the University of Maryland, Baltimore County. I would like to include a special note of thanks to two friends and accomplished urban scholars, Myron Levine of Albion College and Bernie Ross of American University. Their friendship over a number of years, and their indispensable urban textbook, now in its 5th edition—Ross and Levine (1996), *Urban Politics*, 5 (Itasca, Ill.: F. E. Peacock Publishers, Inc.)—have been of inestimable comfort and assistance over the years.

I would like to thank Nancy Lane, former Social Science Editor at Oxford University Press, for her support and belief in this book. Nancy, the third editor I have had the pleasure of collaborating with at Oxford, continues in a tradition set earlier by Susan Rabiner and Valerie Aubry, to manage to be both directive and supportive. I am deeply grateful for what appears to be an in-house Oxford tradition of mixing editorial direction with editorial encouragement.

Finally, I am grateful to my wife, Kathrine, and my son, John, for enduring a year apart when our family was spread out between Ohio and California; for enduring a husband and a dad sometimes more involved with a computer and a book project than is healthy for any family; and for being the two kindest, wisest, and most loving people that I think that I shall ever know.

1

Permanent Crisis

The New Ecology of American Cities

In the Middle Ages the city was said to represent the *plenum mundi*, the pulse of the world. One thing that seems to have drained out of American politics is a sense of cities as vital organs whose health is essential to the survival of the social body . . . woes betide us if we have a national policy to let our cities become scenes from "Escape from New York" or "Blade Runner," the city of dreadful night. You can't have a policy that lets cities decline, because in the decline of cities comes the decline of everything.

KEVIN STARR (Applebome, 1991: A12)

Sometime around 1990, the basic fabric of American cities changed dramatically. The new post-1990 ecology of American cities is characterized by a seemingly *permanent crisis* involving persistently high levels of poverty, hunger, homelessness, violent crime, infrastructure deterioration, fiscal stress, and—perhaps understandably given the elements that accompany it—voter alienation and a decline in civic participation. Fully *8 percent* of our gross national product is consumed annually by the pathologies of this permanent crisis. Cities, and particularly their impoverished inner-city neighborhoods, have become isolated urban reservations where an ever-expanding number of American children grow up hungry, poor, and—increasingly—as victims of violence.

This book argues that there are three basic approaches to fighting the permanent crisis of American cities: the *status quo* programs and policies already in place, progressive and *revenue-neutral* programs and policies to stem the tide of the current permanent crisis, or radical policy responses. We examine the status quo programs put in place from the Reagan administration in 1980 to the Clinton-era 1990s programs in Chapter 4. While many of the status quo programs have been modestly successful, they have not prevented the current permanent crisis in American cities. Ironically, for about the price

1

set aside by Congress to solve the Savings-and-Loan crisis, the permanent crisis in American cities can be solved, and solved in a bipartisan and good-government fashion. Chapter 6 presents a progressive plan for saving America's cities and their children, a plan that is bipartisan, revenue-neutral, and readily achievable.[1] Chapter 7 explores far more radical policy responses to the permanent crisis, responses that may grow in popularity or necessity if the progressive policies outlined in Chapter 6 are ignored, and if the status quo policies described in Chapter 4 continue to fail.

As Chapter 6 argues, Americans can have cities that are financially stable and adequately policed and protected, with safe and sufficient housing, well-financed public schools, greater financial stability at the local level, and higher turnout elections at half the current cost. America can accomplish this in a way that is *revenue-neutral*, that is, a way that does not add one cent to the national debt or reduce current spending for alternative programs such as health care, social security, national defense, or deficit reduction.

America *needs* to act to head off the permanent crisis, a crisis costing the American soul and the American pocketbook staggering sums each year. It may do so by: (1) staying the course with the current policies that have had only modest success against the permanent crisis, (2) adopting the progressive bipartisan *independent cities* approach outlined in Chapter 6, or (3) using the more radical medicine for cities discussed in Chapter 7. Before turning to a discussion of each of these three policy options it is first necessary to spell out in more detail the scope of the current, seemingly *permanent*, crisis in American cities.

THE SCOPE OF THE PERMANENT CRISIS

Poverty and Hunger

The permanent crisis is a threat America's metro areas can no longer afford. American cities are losing valuable social capital. Americans are joining, trusting, and voting in far smaller numbers than ever before. American elections have lost nearly a quarter of the electorate since 1960 (Putnam, 1995). The American economy has lost $585 billion annually since 1990 in costs directly attributable to the permanent crisis. While voter turnout has declined from the anemic 30% level typical of the 1960s to turnouts in the high teens in many American cities (Alford & Lee, 1963; Putnam, 1995c, 1995d), every other indicator of the permanent metro crisis has risen. The number of Americans living in poverty has increased from over 11 percent in 1979 to over 14 percent in 1996, while the number of America's poor living in metropolitan areas has skyrocketed from 62 percent in 1979 to 74 percent in 1995 (U.S. Bureau of the Census, 1996. See also, Ames et al., 1992; U.S. Department of Housing and Urban Development [cited hereafter as HUD], 1995).[2]

Hunger in America has reached epidemic proportions in the 1990s. Thirty million Americans will go to bed hungry tonight (1996 Second Harvest

TABLE 1.1
Changes in U.S. National Rates of Poverty, 1959–95

Year	Percent of U.S. population below poverty line
1959	22.4
1960	22.2
1965	17.3
1966	14.7
1967	14.2
1968	12.8
1969	12.1
1970	12.6
1971	12.5
1972	11.9
1973	11.1
1974	11.4
1975	12.3
1976	11.8
1977	11.6
1978	11.4
1979	11.7
1980	13.0
1981	14.0
1982	14.7
1983	15.2
1984	14.4
1985	14.0
1986	13.6
1987	13.4
1988	13.1
1989	12.8
1990	13.5
1991	14.2
1992	14.5
1993	15.1
1994	14.5
1995	13.8

Source: U.S. Bureau of the Census (1996) (available on the Internet from the U.S. Census Bureau Web Page at: census.gov/hhes/poverty/hstpov6).

Study, see Appendix); most of them are city-dwellers, and the vast majority of the metro poor are, unfortunately, children.[3] Children are 27 percent of the U.S. population, but are 40 percent of the American poor (U.S. Bureau of the Census, 1996a). Whereas 14 percent of all Americans live below the official poverty level, 22 percent of all American children live in poverty—a dramatic

TABLE 1.2
Percent of the Nation's Poor Living in Metropolitan Areas

Year	Percent in Metropolitan Areas
1979	62
1985	70
1990	73
1995	74

Source: U.S. Bureau of the Census (1995). See Historical Poverty Table 8, "Poverty of Persons, by Residence," and Table 4, "Poverty Status of Families, by Type of Family, Presence of Related Children," available on the Internet from the U.S. Census Bureau Web Page at: gov/ftp/hhes/poverty/histpov/hstpov4.html. The author is indebted to Ms. Jean E. Tash of the Housing and Economic Statistics Division, Bureau of the Census, for assistance in identifying the location and the prevailing methodology for performing this calculation.

increase from the 15 percent and 18 percent levels of poverty for children in 1970 and 1980 (Albelda & Folbre, 1996: 27). Worse, over 50 percent of the chronically poor persons in the United States—people who fall below poverty-level income for two or more consecutive years—are children (U.S. Bureau of the Census, 1996b).[4]

A recent Annie E. Casey Foundation annual report found that one out of every four African-American children lives in a severely distressed neighborhood. Add to this the fact that one out of every ten Hispanic or Latino children, and one out of every sixty-three white children, currently live in a severely distressed metro neighborhood, and the stakes for the well-being of America's children in resolving the permanent crisis in America's cities becomes painfully clear (Annie E. Casey Foundation, 1994: 11).[5]

A War against Children

The permanent crisis in cities has produced a violent war in which America's children have been drafted as both combatants and victims. The juvenile crime arrest rate for youths aged ten through seventeen increased 50 percent between 1985 and 1991.[6] Drug use among teenagers has skyrocketed in the 1990s. A recent annual survey of illicit drug use among teenagers by the U.S. Department of Health and Human Services ([cited hereafter as HHS], 1996) found that drug use among teens more than doubled from 1992 to 1996. Marijuana use is up 109 percent since 1992, and up 37 percent from 1994 to 1995 alone. LSD use increased 183 percent since 1992, and rose 54 percent in one year from 1994 to 1995. Cocaine use among teens increased by 163 percent in just one year, from 1994 to 1995.

The story gets worse, particularly for children. Every day, 8,493 U.S. children are reported abused or neglected, and three die of it. *Every two hours, an American child is killed by gunfire.*[7] A survey conducted by University of Maryland pediatrician Jack Gladstein and published in the *Journal of Adolescent Medicine* (1992) indicated that 50 percent of inner-city youth have lost a friend to slayings. Statistically, for every ten inner-city youths, by the time that they would have reached age eighteen, five of the youths will know someone who has been the victim of armed robbery, two will have witnessed a murder, and four will have viewed a shooting. One of the youths will have been the victim of an assault with a weapon, one will have been raped, and two more will have had their lives threatened. By way of contrast, suburban youth will also be at risk, but substantially less so. Fourteen percent of suburban youth (as opposed to 50 percent for inner-city youth) will lose a friend to murder, and 14 percent (as opposed to more than 42 percent for inner-city youth) will witness a shooting before reaching age eighteen.

A February 1995 report by the City of Los Angeles Mayor's Committee on Children, Youth and Families (*LA4KIDS*, 1994; p. 23) traced a statistically average week in the life of Los Angeles children. During 1993, over the course of an average week, 1 child was murdered, 3 children were kidnapped, 9 children were raped, 6 were victims of other sex offenses, 97 children were robbed, 130 children were assaulted with a deadly weapon, and 664 were reported as victims of domestic violence.

Transportation Woes

The new ecology of American cities is a *permanent crisis* for airports, city streets, and bridges. A recent Heritage Foundation study found that almost 20 percent of all the bridges in the National Highway system are "function-ally obsolete," and the Federal Aviation Administration, by late 1996, had completed only 36 of the 200 upgrades that will be needed for the nation's air traffic control system by the year 2000 (Hodge, 1996). Many city streets are dangerously congested, as suburban commuters clog center-city business districts to commute to work or use the educational, entertainment, sports, and cultural facilities of center cities, gridlocking metro traffic with steadily increasing demands on city streets, bridges, and thoroughfares.

Americans now spend 15 to 19 percent of the gross national product on transportation costs simply getting to work or, alternately, going somewhere to play. Is this level of expenditure rational or desirable? Consider, for example, that by way of contrast Japan spends less than 9 percent of its gross national product on transportation and that per-capita vehicle travel in the United States is almost twice that in Europe or Japan (Richmond, 1994: 24).[8] Worse, the transportation problem, as part of the permanent crisis in American cities, is due to escalate dramatically between now and the year 2005. As one expert has noted: "Between 1990 and 2005, traffic congestion is expected to more than quadruple, resulting in an estimated productivity loss of $58 billion per year" (Richmond, 1994: 24. See also HUD/NUPR, 1995: 19).

Declining Voter Turnout

Increased traffic congestion is a byproduct of the fact that we have gone from a nation of urban dwellers to a nation of suburbanites, from a dependence on center-city development and jobs to the creation of "edge-city" meccas and suburbs (Garreau, 1991)[9]—from a connection to and with each other civically to a retreat from civic duty and responsibility (Putnam, 1995).[10] Even those who have not retreated to the suburbs have seen their electoral participation drop from an anemic voter participation level of 30 percent in the 1960s to electoral turnouts in the teens in local elections in America's cities. As Putnam has noted, voter turnout nationally has declined twenty-five percent from 1960 to the 1990s (1995c, 1995d).

THE CHANGED ENVIRONMENT OF CITIES IN THE 1990s

Finally, in addition to the elements of the permanent crisis that have led to a changed ecology for American cities in the 1990s, the ecology of American cities has also changed in six additional respects, each with major consequences for the American city. Just at a time when cities have reached a seemingly permanent crisis in terms of levels of crime, poverty, fiscal stress, decaying infrastructure, and a lack of civic participation—and at a time when cities are facing the uncertain consequences of the August 1996 Welfare Reform Act—cities have been cut off from the rest of the sociopolitical world in six key respects. A recent symposium of top urban experts (Ames et al., 1992: 214) noted that the urban problems of the 1990s contain important new elements that differ from the problems of American cities in the 1960s;

- Urban problems are no longer confined to the inner city, but are regional in nature.
- The federal government has largely withdrawn from the urban policy arena, thereby leaving cities and states to develop their own solutions to local problems.
- The economy of cities is no longer organized around a central business district, but is dispersed throughout a metropolitan region.
- The national economy has experienced a fundamental reorganization and many cities have experienced the direct effects of deindustrialization and disinvestment.
- The fiscal crisis within the public sector is unprecedented and has seriously negative effects for the provision of services at all levels of government.
- The nature of work itself has changed within cities as more women enter the labor market; the changing nature of work has affected the urban family in numerous ways, many of which have direct ramifications for social welfare and family policies.

Whereas each of the new elements of the permanent crisis of cities in the 1990s noted above is important and well documented in several volumes of scholarly academic work,[11] it is worth noting that the permanent crisis in American cities is showing signs of expanding into the permanent crisis of American metropolitan areas, or—to put the issue bluntly—into the permanent crisis of American central cities *and* suburbs. The English poet, John Donne, was right when he wrote centuries ago that "No man is an island . . . apart from the main." Neither, as it turns out, are suburbanites. Far from being safe in their suburban enclaves from the ravages of the permanent crisis in American cities, suburbanites are watching the slow march of the permanent crisis out to the suburbs. The permanent crisis is slowly extending into the suburbs, and the stakes of suburban dwellers—and suburban voters— are necessarily changing with that changing reality. The suburban "share" in the permanent crisis, and the suburban stake in solving the permanent crisis— as Table 1.3 illustrates—has increased dramatically from the 1990s to the present time.

THE SUBURBAN SHARE AND STAKE IN THE PERMANENT CRISIS

Americans in metro areas are fleeing the center city in record numbers, resulting in what former Clinton Secretary of Labor and Harvard professor Robert Reich has labeled a "secession of the successful" (1991). Many of the relocated suburbanites believe, incorrectly, that they have left the permanent crisis of the urban center city far behind them. The reverse is actually the case as the permanent crisis slowly spreads out to the suburban enclaves. Unless checked by vigorous government action, the most probable result of the current permanent crisis in America's cities is that, far from subsiding, the crisis will move out into the suburbs. Indeed, as Table 1.3 illustrates, it has already done so.

If center cities are increasingly isolated because of suburban flight and the "secession of the successful," the suburban "successful" should give some thought to their very real share of the problems of the permanent crisis, and their stake—the stake for all suburbanites—in solving the permanent crisis in American cities.[12] First, it should be admitted that, on one level, suburbanites have escaped the worst of the center-city war stories, and that, secondly, there are, regrettably, more than enough such war stories to go around. Consider, for example, the fact that Chicago as of 1995 contained seven of the nation's ten poorest urban neighborhoods[13]—New York City, which in 1996 had the dubious distinction of containing seventy-nine of the eighty-seven poorest-performing schools in the entire state of New York (Hernandez, 1996)—or, South Central Los Angeles, the scene of the 1992 Rodney King riots, with a median household income of only $20,357 (compared with $37,904 for Los Angeles County as a whole). Thirty-two percent of the families in South Central Los Angeles fall below the officially established poverty line, a figure that is 112 percent higher than the poverty level for the rest of the nation

TABLE 1.3
The Suburbanization of Inner-City Issues, 1980–90

Traditional Inner-City Problem Area	Suburban "Share" of Problem (1980–90)
Decline in median family household income[a]	Income declined 35%
Population flight to outer-ring suburbs[b]	Loss of 8% of population to outer-ring suburbs by inner-ring suburbs
Poverty[c]	42% of all metro poor
White Metro Poor[d]	51.2% reside in suburbs
Hispanic-Latino Metro Poor[d]	40% reside in suburbs
African-American Metro Poor[d]	23.7% reside in suburbs
Suburban office markets	
Vacancy square feet[e]	54.7% vacancy rate
Commercial growth absorption pace[e] (Years to absorb current vacant space at 5 year average absorption rate)	4.3 years in suburbs versus 5.3 years for central business districts

[a] Estimate based on study by Paul Glastris in *U.S. News & World Report*, cited in Peirce (1993a), "Cities' blight now extends into suburbia," *Sacramento Bee*, October 11, p. B15.

[b] Estimate based on multiplier developed in study by Rob Gurwitt in *Governing*, cited in Peirce (1993, B15).

[c] U.S. Bureau of the Census (1991), "Metropolitan Areas and Cities," *1990 Census Profile*, No. 3, September, p. 1.

[d] 1990 census data reported in Ames, Brown, Callahan, Cummings, Smock, and Zeigler (1992), "Rethinking American Urban Policy," *Journal of Urban Affairs*, 14: 205–206.

[e] TCW Realty Associates, summary includes data for 1988 for 46 largest metropolitan office markets in the United States. Estimate based on a recalculation of data cited in E. J. Blakely and D. L. Ames (1992), "Changing Places: American Planning Policy for the 1990's," Table 1, "Comparison of Central Business District and Suburban Office Markets: 1988," *Journal of Urban Affairs*, 14: p. 42.

(Alin & Davila, 1993). Or, consider the staggeringly high unemployment in cities such as Detroit, with unemployment rates twice the national average, or the extreme-poverty neighborhoods of America's largest 100 cities in which "more than 40 percent of working age men are not working, compared to just over 19 percent in non-poverty neighborhoods in the central city" (HUD/NUPR, 1995: 15).[14]

Whatever else the retreat of the New Suburbanites from such center-city problems means, ultimately cities will be facing increasing problems with less people, a smaller tax base, and less support from both suburban and national political institutions than ever before. Ironically, as we have argued in this chapter, the New Suburbanites should reassess their presumed safety and "distance" from the problems of the center city, since, as Table 1.3 illustrates, they have not left the permanent crisis of the center city in the rear-view mirrors of their commuter cars and vans. Quite the reverse. The suburban "share" of the permanent crisis has grown exponentially from 1980 to 1990 (see Table 1.3). The suburbs are now the destination of choice for a majority of every major ethnic group in America except blacks and Hispanics (Blakeley & Goldsmith, 1994). With this emigration wave also comes the permanent crisis and its attendant problems. As of 1990, 42 percent of all poor persons in metro areas lived not in the center city but in suburban, predominately inner-ring suburbs. Over 50 percent of the white metro poor live in suburban addresses, as do 40 percent of the Hispanic-Latino poor, and 24 percent of the African-American poor. Accordingly, the suburban "successful" have begun their own secession in which the inner-ring suburbs from 1980 to 1990 lost 8 percent of their population to outer-ring suburbs. The permanent crisis, a feature of central cities since at least 1990, has now moved out to the "burbs." With this change in address it has become a problem not simply for urban America but for America in general. In the 1990s the old "urban problem" of past decades has become the "national problem." Like it or not, from the 1990s on, it is indisputably the case that suburbanites and city-dwellers have "interwoven destinies" (Cisneros, 1993; Peirce, 1993a).

SUMMARY AND CONCLUSION

Beginning earlier but statistically evident since at least 1990, is a changed ecology for major American cities—an ecology in which cities and their suburban rim communities are plagued by a seemingly *permanent crisis* featuring persistently high levels of poverty, hunger, homelessness, violent crime, gridlocked highways, fiscal stress, and correspondingly low levels of voter turnout and civic participation. This phenomenon of cities locked into a permanent crisis is compounded by social, political, and economic trends that, collectively, have forced the American city to "go it alone" without the hope of significant assistance from either neighboring suburbanites or—with only a few notable exceptions such as the Clinton-era Crime Bill, Empowerment Zone, and minimum wage legislation—the national political process.

The permanent crisis is costing American cities mightily, both in human terms including high levels of poverty, hunger, homelessness, and crime, and in terms of sheer dollars-and-cents. The pathologies of the permanent crisis consume more than $500 billion dollars annually—over 8 percent of the gross domestic product each year, over $2,000 per capita annually.[15]

Children are paying a far higher price. *Every two hours an American child is killed by gunfire.* Unlike the Savings and Loan tragedy, which struck primarily at adult-aged savers and investors, the primary victims of the permanent crisis in America's cities are children. A nation that has acted to save its banks must now decide if it also wants to save its children. As Chapter 2 illustrates, it is not simply the children that are at risk from the permanent crisis in American cities. Thirty-seven percent of all Americans—nearly four out of every ten Americans—live in an *adrenaline city*—a metro area experiencing extreme long-term stress from the 1980s to the present day. Chapter 2 names names, identifying the 44 adrenaline cities in the United States, and catalogs the challenges facing residents of these high-stress metro areas.

2

Need More Proof?

Forty-four Adrenaline Cities

Then she sprays them. She shakes an aerosol can and sprays their heads, their tiny out-stretched hands. She sprays them back and front to protect them as they go off to school, facing bullets and gang recruiters and a crazy, dangerous world. It is a special religious oil that smells like drugstore perfume, and the children shut their eyes tight as she sprays them long and furious so they will come back to her, alive and safe at day's end.

ISABEL WILKERSON, from a Pulitzer Prize–winning 1994 *New York Times* article describing the efforts of an inner-city mother to protect her family from harm and fear as she sends her children to school.

ADRENALINE CITIES: HIGH-STRESS CITIES STUCK ON "FIGHT OR FLIGHT"

We are a nation of cities, and many of our cities are in trouble. Eighty percent of all Americans live on two percent of America's land surface, squeezed into one of the seventy-two largest cities designated in Census terms as Metropolitan Statistical Areas (MSAs). Unfortunately, forty-four U.S. cities, *containing four out of every 10 Americans*, are *adrenaline cities*—MSAs experiencing severe chronic stress due to the permanent crisis of American cities in the 1990s. These forty-four cities have, since at least 1990, been stuck in a prolonged state of acute stress. The word stress derives from the Latin word meaning "to be drawn tight" and for the forty-four American adrenaline cities and their residents, they have been drawn far too tight, far too long—to the point where chronic stress has become a dangerously routine way of life.[1]

Psychologists traditionally describe the response to stress as having four stages. In the first stage, a general alarm is sounded as the organism learns of a stressful condition or threat. In the second stage, the organism rapidly mobilizes energy and resources to prepare to respond to the threat(s) posed by the environment. Adrenaline is released in Stage 2 to facilitate Stage 3 activity. The third stage is characterized by vigorous physical movement as the organism makes the decision to respond to the threat with either "fight or flight," and acts on that choice. The fourth stage is a return to equilibrium as the organism returns to the quieter life of an environment now without either the threat or the adrenaline that helped to power the successful response to the threat.

The adrenaline state is meant to be a temporary adrenaline-powered surge of hyper-alertness and activity in response to a potentially life-threatening situation. No healthy organism can long sustain the temporary adrenaline state without incurring serious and potentially life-threatening psychological and physiological costs. The implications of stretching out the fight-or-flight adrenaline state into a long-term permanent crisis are profound—both for the cities themselves, and for the residents within them trying to live out otherwise normal lives within the confines of the chronic stress syndrome produced by the permanent crisis in America's adrenaline cities.

The forty-four adrenaline cities have been stuck in prolonged acute stress since at least 1990, due to a number of reasons, including: economic restructuring and job loss, population loss, the increasing racial isolation of America's nonwhite minority population into substandard and dangerous urban reservations, a decline in center-city resident incomes vis-à-vis suburban household incomes, and epidemic levels of violent assaults, drive-by shootings, and homicides. American *adrenaline cities* are facing grave dangers, but they can be saved if we act decisively and quickly. This book is a blueprint for that action. There is a way out for cities but not unless adrenaline cities—and American metro areas in general—are redesigned or *reinvented* as strong, self-reliant *independent cities*. Before examining the remedies that cities might pursue, let's examine the challenges facing America's most severely distressed cities, cities that one top expert has suggested are already beyond the point of no return.

The Thirty-four *No-Return* Cities: Economically Devastated and Racially Segregated

David Rusk, an experienced and cautious observer of the American city scene, recently described thirty-four American cities as "beyond the Point of No Return" (1994).[2] Rusk uses three key indicators for severely distressed *no-return* cities. No-return cities have lost population, increasingly isolated their nonwhite minority populations, and decreased the incomes of city residents vis-à-vis their suburban counterparts. As Table 2.1 illustrates, the thirty-four no-return cities have typically lost 20 percent or more of their population since peak population periods of the 1950s. Second, no-return cities have increasingly isolated nonwhite minority populations in the central cities, ranging in isolation-concentration mixes from a 28 percent nonwhite minority population in Saginaw, Michigan to 98 percent in East St. Louis, Illinois.

Finally, no-return cities have seen a dramatic decline in the purchasing power of center-city residents, as the incomes of city residents fell to 70 percent or less of the suburban incomes.

Some of these cities are more troubled than others: East St. Louis, for example, saw its population decline from 82,295 in 1950 to 40,944 in 1990, its minority population soar to 98 percent from 35 percent, and the incomes of city residents decline to 39 percent of the incomes of suburban residents

The Five Urban-Reservation Cities: Concentrations of Extreme-Poverty Neighborhoods

As Table 2.2 illustrates, three cities—Los Angeles, San Francisco, and New York City—need to be added to Rusk's "No Return" list. These cities, as well as no-return cities Chicago and Philadelphia, are *urban-reservation* cities, meaning that they have the highest concentrations of extreme-poverty neighborhoods (those with 40 percent or more of residents below the official poverty line) in the nation.[3] Extreme-poverty neighborhoods have been concentrated in these cities so heavily from 1980 to the 1990s, that these five urban-reservation cities have accounted for over 25 percent of the national total of extreme-poverty neighborhood residents.[4] Further, as Table 2.2 illustrates, these five cities are caught in an urban-reservation "double-bind," in which staggeringly high poverty rates (when compared with the already high national poverty rate), are combined with—particularly in the non-Western cities—a high percentage of older and presumably substandard housing stock, much of it dating back to 1939 and earlier.

It seems fitting to add the five urban-reservation cities to the list of thirty-four no-return cities complied by Rusk. See, for example, the descriptions of urban reservations in Los Angeles and New York City, below, in Tables 2.3 and 2.4. While Rusk knowingly overstates the case that these cities are beyond the "Point of No Return,"[5] it is not an exaggeration to claim that *all thirty-four of these cities and the five extreme-poverty urban-reservation cities are adrenaline cities*—cities desperately in need of intervention and aid. If anything, Rusk's analysis *understates* the number of large American cities stuck in "fight or flight." The thirty-four no-return or adrenaline cities identified by Rusk (see Table 2.1) are undergoing great stress, but other cities—including the urban-reservation cities discussed above—need to be added to the list. Since two of the five urban-reservation cities already overlap with the thirty-four cities on the no-return list by Rusk, we have at this juncture in our analysis a grand total of thirty-seven adrenaline cities identified thus far. We turn next to *shooting-gallery* cities—fourteen cities collectively responsible for over 30 percent of all homicides in the United States annually during 1994 and 1995.

The Fourteen Shooting-Gallery Cities: High Crime–High Danger

Several large cities have become macabre *shooting galleries*—grim vectors of violence in which America's most defenseless and most disadvantaged

TABLE 2.1
The Thirty-four Cities Past the "Point of No Return"

	Population Loss 1950–90 (%)	Non-White Population in 1990 (%)	City-to-Suburb Income Ratio (%)	MSA Designation	1990 Population
Holyoke, Mass.	26	35	69	Springfield, MA	529,519
Birmingham, Ala.	22	64	69	Birmingham, AL	907,810
Flint, Mich.	29	52	69	Flint, MI	951,270
Buffalo, N.Y.	43	37	69	Buffalo, NY	1,189,288
St. Louis, Mo.	54	50	67	St. Louis	2,444,099
Chicago, Ill.	23	60	66	Chicago CMSA	8,065,633
Saginaw, Mich.	29	28	66	Saginaw, MI	399,320
Baltimore, Md.	23	60	64	Baltimore, MD	2,382,172
Dayton, Ohio	31	36	64	Dayton, OH	951,270
Philadelphia, Pa.	23	45	64	Phil PMSA	4,856,881
Youngstown, Ohio	44	35	64	Youngstown, OH	492,619
Kansas City, Kan.	11	38	63	Kan.Cty, MoKs	1,566,280
Petersburg, Va.	07	74	63	Richmond, VA	865,460
New Haven, Conn.	21	47	62	New Haven, CT	530,180
Milwaukee, Wis.	15	39	62	Mlk, WI PMSA	1,566,280
Atlantic City, N.J.	43	69	61	Atlantic City	319,416
East Chicago, Ill.	41	81	60	Chicago CMSA	
Gary, Ind.	25	85	59	Gary, INPMSA	604,526
Bessemer, Ala.	17	59	58	Birmingham, AL	
Chicago Heights, Ill.	19	50	57	Chicago CMSA	
Pontiac, Mich.	17	52	55	Detroit CMSA	4,665,299
Elizabeth, N.J.	04	60	54	NY-NJ CMSA	18,087,251
Cleveland, Ohio	45	50	54	Cleveland, OH	2,759,823
Perth Amboy, N.J.	04	65	53	NY-NJ CMSA	
Hartford, Conn.	21	66	53	Hartford PMSA	767,841
Detroit, Mich.	44	77	53	Detroit CMSA	
Trenton, N.J.	31	59	50	Trenton PMSA	325,824
Paterson, N.J.	03	72	47	NY-NJ CMSA	
Benton Harbor, Mich.	33	93	43	Benton Harbor	161,378
Newark, N.J.	38	83	42	NY-NJ CMSA	
Bridgeport, Conn.	11	50	41	Bridgept PMSA	443,722
North Chicago, Ill.	26	47	39	Chicago CMSA	
Camden, N.J.	30	86	39	Phil PMSA	
East St. Louis, Ill.	50	98	39	Chicago CMSA	
Totals: 34 Cities				**23 MSAs**	**51,489,161***

Source: David Rusk (1994), "Bend or Die: Inflexible State Laws and Policies Are Dooming Some of the Country's Central Cities," Table A.1 The 34 cities past the statistical 'point of no return,' p. 7 *State Government News* (February), Rusk's original table has been modified to include MSA populations for each of the 34 central cities analyzed in Rusk (1994).

* The total population in the MSA's described by Rusk as beyond the point of no return is 51,489,161, or 20.70% of the census figure for the 1990 U.S. population, which is 248,709,873.

TABLE 2.2

The Urban Reservation Double-Bind: High Growth in Poverty, Low Growth in New Housing

Cities	Percentage of Population Below Poverty Line (1989)	Percentage of Housing Units Built 1939 or Earlier (1990)
1. New York City	19.3	40.9
2. Los Angeles	18.9	17.4
3. Chicago	21.6	44.6
4. San Francisco	13.6[a]	32.8[a]
5. Philadelphia	20.3	51.6
For purposes of comparison:	12.8	
	Percentage of U.S. population in poverty in 1989	

Source: U.S. Bureau of the Census (1996), Table 3: "Cities with 200,000 or More Population Ranked." This information and a wealth of census data is available from the Census Bureau Internet Home Page Web Site (ww.census.gov/ftp/pub/statab/ccdb/ccdb3112.txt).

[a] Because the unit of analysis in this section of the book is the CMSA (Consolidated Metropolitan Statistical Area), the Census Bureau figures for San Francisco in Table 2.2 are combined with those of San Jose and Oakland to reflect CMSA rather than MSA figures for both the poverty level and for the percentage of housing stock built in 1939 or earlier.

TABLE 2.3

Selected Demographic Profile of an Urban Reservation: South Central Los Angeles (1990)

Demographic Characteristic	1990 Data
Total population	523,156
African-American population	55%
Latino population	45%
People per household	3.48
Population earning high school diploma	47.8%
Non-English speakers	43.5%
Median household income	$20,357
Poverty	32.9%
Rent 35% of income	47.9%
Median home value	$113,400

Sources: Data from 1990 U.S. Census, reported in Fahizah Alin and Robert D. Davila (1993), "South Central's Woes Still Burn," *Sacramento Bee*, April 18, p. 1.

populations are subjected to probabilities of violent harm far higher than that faced by residents of America's suburbs. In 1993, Dr. David Satcher, Director of the Center for Disease Control, went so far as to describe violent crime in U.S. cities as an "epidemic" on the order of AIDS or breast cancer. Dr. Satcher

TABLE 2.4
Selected Demographic Profile of an Urban Reservation:
New York City (1990)

Demographic Characteristic	1990 Data
Population	18,087,532[a]
Poverty line	19.3%[a]—1 in 5 New Yorkers
Schools	Almost 91,000 of New York City's 1,000,000 public school students do not have desks[b]
	New York City schools will need $7 billion in the next 5-to-10 years to cover basic repairs of aging buildings[c]
	79 of the 87 poorest-performing schools in New York state are in New York City[d]
	90 New York City schools failed to meet minimal academic standards and have been placed on the state Education Department list of "Schools Under Registration Review"[e]
Job/Skill Mismatch	New York City lost 135,000 jobs in industries where workers average less than 12 years of education, and gained 300,000 jobs in industries where workers average 13 or more years of education"[f]

[a] Data from U.S. Bureau of the Census (1990).

[b] George Will (1996), "Education in Harlem," Washington Post Writer's Group, September 16.

[c] Harold Levy (1996), "Opinion: The Schools Need $7 Billion," *New York Times*, September 15, Op-Ed page.

[d] Hernandez, 1996.

[e] Sol Stern (1990), "The Catholic School Miracle," *New York Times* September 25, p. A19.

[f] William Julius Wilson (1996), *When Work Disappears: The New World of the Urban Poor* (New York: Alfred A. Knopf).

argued that: "If you look at the major cause of death today, it's not smallpox or polio or even infectious diseases. Violence is the leading cause of lost life in this country today."[6]

This violence is, surprisingly, concentrated in a small number of cities and, within those cities, a small number of high-danger or *kill-zone* neighborhoods. According to the 1994 and 1995 FBI Uniform Crime Reports, over 80 percent of all U.S. murders occurred in Metropolitan Statistical Areas (MSAs), and only a handful of cities consistently account for approximately 30 percent of all homicides in the nation each year. Rusk pointed to thirty-four no-return cities and their economic and demographic troubles. Equally troubling are the fourteen shooting-gallery cities—cities that have developed grim killing fields where city residents in general, and city children and nonwhite residents in particular, face a high probability of death or injury by violent assault (see Table 2.5). In fact, these grim shooting galleries have transformed coming-of-age in inner-city America. For half of all inner-city youth, coming-of-age means losing a friend to slayings. As the Maryland study illustrates, the risk of death by slaying is far from randomly distributed in the United States as a whole. There are whirlpools of violent crime in the United States, narrow vectors in which danger and homicide gather strength and spread. The worst intersections for this violence and danger are the streets and homes of inner-city kill-zone neighborhoods in the fourteen shooting-gallery cities listed in Table 2.2.

Kill Zones in America's Adrenaline Cities

Both journalistic accounts and scholarly studies[7] are making it increasingly clear that violent crime is not randomly distributed. Instead, violent crime is highly concentrated, often more grimly evident in what local police refer to as *kill zones* (Marinucci & Zamora, 1995)—high-poverty/high-crime neighborhoods such as the Double Rock section of the Hunter's Point neighborhood in San Francisco, the Robert Taylor high-rise public-housing project in downtown Chicago, or the former *kill zone* at Williams Avenue in East New York City/Brooklyn. Double Rock, a housing project, apartment and industrial building sector located close to San Francisco's 3 Com Park baseball stadium, has one small intersection at the corner of Griffith and Fitzgerald that San Francisco police call the "kill zone." Six people were murdered in separate incidents at this locale in 1994—more than at any other single location in San Francisco—and almost one in ten of the ninety-eight homicides recorded for

TABLE 2.5
The Fourteen Shooting-Gallery Cities

Cities	Cumulative Percentage of all U.S. Murders, 1994	Cumulative Percentage of all U.S. Murders, 1995
1. New York City	7	5
2. Los Angeles	11	9
3. Chicago	15	13
4. Detroit	17	15
5. New Orleans	19	17
6. Philadelphia	21	19
7. Washington, D.C.	23	21
8. Houston	25	23
9. Baltimore	26	25
10. Dallas	27	26
11. St. Louis	28	27
12. Phoenix	29	28
13. San Antonio	30	29
14. Atlanta	31	30

Source: Table constructed from data reported in the FBI *Uniform Crime Report: 1995 Preliminary Annual Release* (Washington, D.C.: U.S. Department of Justice, Federal Bureau of Investigation). The 1995 Preliminary Report is available on the Internet at the following location: www.fbi.gov/ucr/95preprl.htm.

the year in 1994 for the entire city of San Francisco were slain within blocks of the Griffith and Fitzgerald intersection. It is this level of *concentrated danger* that I call a *kill zone*—a label I have borrowed from the police officers in San Francisco working the homicide beat in 1994.[8]

In another, now infamous, MSA kill zone, the Robert Taylor low-income housing project in Chicago, 300 shootings were reported in one two-week period during the summer of 1994. Still other Chicago kill zones on the South and West Sides are home to an estimated 2,000 to 10,000 members of street gangs such as the Black Disciples, the Latin Kings, and the Simon City Royals.

New York City police refer to a similar high murder area on Williams Avenue as the "dead zone."[9] In 1993, this one-block area was the site of 3 drug-related murders and 500 drug-trafficking arrests. This particular zone is unique in that it no longer exists. A multi-year effort dating back to the administration of Edward I. Koch in 1986 through the current Giuliani administration reclaimed this formerly high-crime zone and others as a result of creating 50,000 new apartments and houses in some of New York City's most troubled sections, including Bedford-Stuyvesant, Brownsville, Crown Heights, East New York, and the South Bronx.

As the New-York-City Williams Avenue kill-zone story illustrates, the kill zones in America's shooting-gallery cities can be dismantled, but only with sustained effort by local leadership, and the commitment of substantial funds by both local and national authorities. Chapter 6 outlines a plan for helping to turn around life in America's kill zones, providing increasing funding and police officers for community policing efforts to combat the crime-wave part of the *permanent crisis* in America's cities.

PUTTING IT ALL TOGETHER: AMERICA'S FORTY-FOUR ADRENALINE CITIES

Rusk's argument that thirty-four cities are approaching the point of no return needs to be amended. Several cities in America are experiencing prolonged and traumatic stress. Thirty-four of these adrenaline cities are the cities identified by Rusk—cities experiencing population loss, income disparities, and racial isolation. An additional 5 extremely high-poverty urban-reservation cities (CMSAs or Consolidated Metropolitan Statistical Areas in Census Bureau terminology)—Chicago, Los Angeles, New York, Philadelphia, and San Francisco—were also added to the no-return cities List. This results in the growth of the adrenaline-city list from the original thirty-four cities identified by Rusk to now include Los Angeles, New York City, and San Francisco—a total of thirty-seven adrenaline cities (two urban-reservation cities, Chicago and Philadelphia, not surprisingly, were already included on Rusk's no-return list earlier). This total of thirty-seven adrenaline cities and their MSAs grows again to include forty-four adrenaline cities/MSA areas due to the addition of seven new adrenaline shooting-gallery cities—Atlanta, Dallas, Houston,

TABLE 2.6
The Forty-four American Adrenaline Cities and MSA Regions

	MSA Designation	1990 Population
1. Atlanta, Ga.	Atlanta, Ga.	2,883,511
2. Atlantic City, N.J.	Atlantic City	319,416
3. Baltimore, Md.	Baltimore, MD	2,382,172
4. Benton Harbor, Mich.	Benton Harbor	161,378
5. Bessemer, Ala.	Birmingham, AL	*
6. Birmingham, Ala.	Birmingham, AL	907,810
7. Bridgeport, Conn.	Bridgept PMSA	443,722
8. Buffalo, N.Y.	Buffalo, NY	1,189,288
9. Camden, N.J.	Phil PMSA	*
10. Chicago, Ill.	Chicago CMSA	8,065,633
11. Chicago Heights, Ill.	Chicago CMSA	*
12. Cleveland, Ohio	Cleveland, OH	2,759,823
13. Dallas, Tx.	Dallas-Ft. Worth CMSA	3,885,415
14. Dayton, Ohio	Dayton, OH	951,270
15. Detroit, Mich.	Detroit CMSA	*
16. East Chicago, Ill.	Chicago CMSA	*
17. East St. Louis, Ill.	Chicago CMSA	*
18. Elizabeth, N.J.	NY-NJ CMSA	18,087,251
19. Flint, Mich.	Flint, MI	951,270
20. Gary, Ind.	Gary, INPMSA	604,526
21. Hartford, Conn.	Hartford PMSA	767,841
22. Holyoke, Mass.	Springfield, MA	529,519
23. Houston, Tx.	Houston-Gal-Braz CMSA	3,711,043
24. Kansas City, Mo.	Kan.Cty,MoKs	1,566,280
25. Los Angeles, Ca.	LA-Ana/Rvs CMSA	14,531,529
26. Milwaukee, Wis.	Mlk, WI PMSA	1,566,280
27. New Haven, Conn.	New Haven, CT	530,180
28. New Orleans, La.	New Orleans	1,238,816
29. Newark, N.J.	NY-NJ CMSA	*
30. New York City, NY	NY-NJ CMSA	*
31. North Chicago, Ill.	Chicago CMSA	*
32. Paterson, N.J.	NY-NJ CMSA	*
33. Perth Amboy, N.J.	NY-NJ CMSA	*
34. Petersburg, Va.	Richmond, VA	865,460
35. Phoenix. Ariz.	Phoenix, AZ	2,122,101
36. Philadelphia, Pa.	Phil PMSA	4,856,881
37. Pontiac, Mich.	Detroit CMSA	4,665,299
38. Saginaw, Mich.	Saginaw, MI	399,320
39. San Antonio, Tx.	San Antonio, TX	1,302,099
40. San Francisco, Ca.	SF/Oakland/San Jose	6,253,311
41. St. Louis, Mo.	St. Louis	2,444,099
42. Trenton, N.J.	Trenton PMSA	325,824
43. Washington, D.C.	Washington DC-MD-VA	3,923,574
44. Youngstown, Ohio	Youngstown, OH	492,619
Totals: 44 Cities	**33 MSAs**	**91,340,560**
		(37% of 1990 U.S. Population)[d]

* Population for cities designated with an asterisk is included in the larger CMSA figure given, respectively, for Birmingham, Chicago, Detroit, Philadelphia, or New York–New Jersey CMSA.

[d] The total population in the adrenaline city MSAs is 91,340,560—37% of the official census figure for the 1990 U.S. population, which is 248,709,873 (U.S. Bureau of the Census, 1990).

New Orleans, Phoenix, San Antonio, and Washington, D.C. The presence of violent crime is also a key indicator of traumatic stress for cities. *Any city* on the shooting-gallery list—each with deadly kill zones located within MSA boundaries—is also, by any reasonable criteria, if not a city beyond the point of no return, then, at the very least, an adrenaline city. As Table 2.6 illustrates, by adding up all the adrenaline cities we have now identified 44 separate cities/MSA areas as *adrenaline cities*—cities and regions stuck in a prolonged state of acute stress.

CONCLUSION: HELP WANTED FOR AMERICA'S ADRENALINE CITIES

Forty-four cities in the United States are *adrenaline cities.* These cities and their corresponding thirty-three MSAs are experiencing severe prolonged stress due to the *permanent crisis* in American cities in the 1990s. These forty-four Adrenaline Cities/MSA's have a combined population of over 91 million residents, meaning that *nearly four of every ten Americans live in an adrenaline city* subject to stress levels, dangers, and expenses that are no longer tolerable either for American cities or the American economy. These forty-four no-return, urban-reservation, and shooting-gallery MSAs are the worst-case metro scenarios, but it should be emphasized that *most American cities are adrenaline cities—experiencing prolonged severe stress as a direct result of the permanent crisis in American cities.* The forty-four adrenaline cities are, in this respect, only the tip of the *permanent crisis* iceberg. Nevertheless, it is important to stress that this book is a hard-headed look at both urban problems *and* urban solutions. In Chapter 3, we will take one more look at the problems before concentrating on three alternative strategies for salvaging America's adrenaline cities. Chapter 4 onward is a blueprint for salvaging these cities before Rusk's intentionally provocative "no-return" label changes from a timely call for action into a bald and irreversible statement of fact.

3

The Political Invisibility
of American Cities

As much as [former HUD Secretary] Cisneros talks about cities,
President Clinton rarely breathes the word. Most likely it's because
his political instincts suggest that in a suburban nation, there's
no payoff in talking about cities or using the word "urban." But
in reality, many of the answers to poverty, homelessness, crime,
and credit shortages will have to be forged in the "real" cities of
the 1990s—the metropolitan regions, or citistates, where the vast
majority of Americans live.

NEAL PEIRCE, 1993b

Three problems exist simultaneously for American cities. First, as Chapter 1
illustrates, most major American cities have—since at least 1990—endured
a seemingly *permanent crisis* involving persistently high levels of poverty,
hunger, homelessness, violent crime, infrastructure deterioration, fiscal stress,
voter alienation, and a decline in civic participation. Fully 8 percent of our
gross national product is consumed by the problems of this permanent crisis
at an annual cost of over $2,000 per capita.

Second, as Chapter 2 argues, forty-four American cities are special cases—
adrenaline cities— cities that since at least 1990 have been stuck in a prolonged state of acute stress, drawn far too tight, far too long in response
to economic restructuring, job loss, population loss, the increasing racial
isolation of America's nonwhite minority population into substandard and
dangerous urban reservations, a decline in center-city resident incomes vis-
à-vis suburban household incomes, and epidemic levels of violent assaults,
drive-by shootings, and homicides. These forty-four adrenaline cities were
subdivided in Chapter 2, above, into thirty-four *no-return* cities, five *urban-
reservation* cities, and fourteen *shooting-gallery* cities.

Third, as we shall argue in the present chapter, American cities and
American city voters are curiously *invisible* in American politics. This problem

of virtual political invisibility is the third key problem facing American cities in the late twentieth and early twenty-first centuries. This chapter examines the problem of the political invisibility of America's cities and shows how the invisibility of cities has only partially decreased in recent times. Serious efforts to raise the visibility of American cities, to link the fortunes of center-city residents and suburbanites into a larger pattern of "interwoven destinies" (Peirce, Johnson, & Hall, 1993; Cisneros, 1993) and to mobilize inner-city voters have been waged of late. Few of these ventures have succeeded in raising the visibility or importance of cities or city voters in American national politics. We turn next to a detailed account of efforts to decrease the political invisibility of American cities.

OUR DISAPPEARING, REAPPEARING "OLD FRIEND"—THE NATIONAL URBAN CRISIS

One of the great ironies of life in metropolitan America is that despite the fact that eight out of ten Americans live in *metropolitan statistical areas* (MSAs), the political needs and key concerns of urban areas have—absent an occasional "mega-event" such as the 1992 Rodney King riots in South Central Los Angeles—never really managed to stay on the national political radar screen for any sustained length of time. This on-again, off-again appearance and disappearance of the "urban problem" in American politics, accompanied far more often than not by the sheer invisibility of American cities as urban concerns typically sink below the waterline of American national politics, is one of the most curious and durable features of American national political life.

THE POLITICAL INVISIBILITY OF AMERICAN CITIES

A quick glance at voting patterns in U.S. presidential elections and the 1990 Census illustrates two structural reasons why cities lack clout in American national politics, and why status-quo policies have failed to stop the permanent crisis in America's cities. Neither the presidency nor the Senate can accurately be characterized as "urban" political institutions. The U.S. presidency is, in the 1990s, a *suburban* institution. In contrast, the U.S. Senate in the 1990s is distinctly *rural* in character. In many important respects, cities are invisible in contemporary American national politics.

The core battleground for the past four presidential elections has been the American suburb, not the American urban center or inner city. Kevin Phillips—political commentator and author of *The Emerging Republican Majority* (1969)—a book that chronicled the winning Sunbelt/Southern strategy of the 1968 presidential campaign and signaled a major shift in regional voting habits for the presidency, bringing white male Southern voters and nationally bringing white ethnic middle-class Democrats into the Republican presidential fold—has written of a more recent shift to a suburban presidential electorate in *Boiling Point: Anger and Middle Class Politics in the American Suburbs* (1994).

The emerging importance of, first, the South and, later, the suburbs was not lost on strategists in the Reagan or Bush campaigns. As Table 3.1 illustrates, as recently as 1988, President Bush won the election *without the support of traditional center-city voters.* While Presidents Reagan and Bush enjoyed political support in the American South and Sunbelt regions generally, and in newer Sunbelt *"technocities"* and *"technoburbs"* (Fishman, 1987: 184) such as Austin, Phoenix, and San Jose, Reagan-Bush and Republicans generally drew far less support from central cities and the large cities of the frostbelt and Northeast. As William Barnes has documented:

> In 1988, the total presidential vote split 53.4% for the Republican ticket and 45.6% for the Democratic. The central areas that contain the 32 largest cities, in contrast, reversed that split: 45.5% Republican and 53.5% Democratic. . . . [In contrast,] suburbs and the new cities created in the image of the suburban ideal are the main constituency of the Reagan-Bush coalition. Their lack of interest in urban policy is essential to their definition. (Barnes, 1990: 568–69)

By the 1992 presidential election the rise of the suburbs and the political demise of the traditional large urban center was complete. Arkansas Governor

TABLE 3.1
1988 Presidential Voting Patterns by Selected Cities

City[a]	Percentage Voting Republican	Percentage Voting Democratic[b]	Percentage of Black Voters[c]	Percentage of Hispanic Voters[c]
New York City	32.8	66.2	25.23	19.88
Chicago	29.8	69.2	39.83	14.05
Philadelphia	32.5	66.6	37.84	3.77
Baltimore	25.4	73.5	54.80	.97
San Francisco	26.1	72.8	12.73	12.28
Washington	14.3	82.6	70.32	2.77
Boston	33.2	65.2	22.42	6.41
New Orleans	35.2	63.6	41.12	1.34
Denver	37.1	60.7	12.03	18.76
St. Louis	27.0	72.5	45.55	1.22
United States total	*53.4*	*45.6*	*12.2[d]*	*6.45*

[a] Large cities for which vote totals are reported by municipal jurisdiction.

[b] Data furnished by Alice McGillivary, Election Research Center.

[c] Data furnished by U.S. Bureau of the Census.

[d] Unpublished data from the Bureau of the Census.

Source: William Barnes, (1990), "Urban Policies and Urban Impacts After Reagan," Table 1:1988 Presidential Voting Patterns by Selected Cities, *Urban Affairs Quarterly* 4 (June): 569.

William Clinton became the first American president of "a nation more suburban than urban" (Applebome, 1991: 1), a president who owed his electoral victory to suburban voters. The net result of this shift in political demography in favor of suburban voters is that the term *urban*—missing from much of the vocabulary of the Reagan and Bush administrations—is also noticeably absent from the Democratic Clinton administration.

In contrast to the suburban presidency, the U.S. Senate has a rural bias that stems from the original constitutional compromise allowing each state to have two U.S. senators. Writing in the 1980s, America's preeminent democratic theorist, Robert A. Dahl, lamented the rural policy bias of the U.S. Senate, noting that in the 1980 Census an absolute voting majority in the Senate—fifty-one votes from the twenty-six smallest states—could be drawn from only 14 percent of the U.S. population (Dahl, 1980). The demographics of representation in the U.S. Senate have changed only slightly since Dahl noted the inequities of urban politics in the Senate in the 1980s. The 1990 Census demonstrates that urban policies may be blocked by a coalition of the twenty-six smallest states, which currently constitute 40,958,248 persons, or 16.5 percent of the total population of the United States (U.S. Bureau of the Census, 1990).

Given the suburban nature of the presidency and the structural rural bias of the Senate, it is easy to see the ways in which—despite the fact that they hold a majority of the nation's citizens—American cities have become over time the "stepchildren" of American national politics. Urban problems and urban politics have become so sublimated in the American political psyche that no consistent national urban policy has been attempted in Washington since the Carter administration. Indeed, since the failed attempt by the Carter administration to construct an urban policy, urban problems and coherent national urban policies have been largely written-off by Washington, D.C., policymakers. The conventional wisdom of Washington-watchers augurs for more of the same as cities move into the late 1990s largely invisible on the national political stage. Barnes (1990: 567) described the problem for cities in these words:

> A recent *National Journal* article summed up the situation as "more prob-
> lems, less clout" for big cities (Kirschten, 1989: 2026). A similar report in
> *Governing* leads with a headline declaring that "a shrinking urban bloc in
> Congress plays defense" (Ehrenhalt, 1989: 21).

This decline in the role of urban problems and urban politics in the national political arena has resulted in a paradoxical action-reaction response to the problems of America's cities. Despite the fact that urban politics is structurally shut out from the presidential and Senate policymaking arenas, urban problems—the problems taking place within the immediate living space of over 77 percent of all Americans—occasionally make their way into the national political limelight via such tragedies as the videotaped police beating of Rodney King and the resultant riots in South-Central Los Angeles in 1992, the hosting by Jesse Jackson of a Washington, D.C., Conference on

Urban Crime and Violence in 1994, or the 1994 Los Angeles earthquake. In such moments, in the words of Senator Daniel Patrick Moynihan (D-NY): "Suddenly we're back to our old friend, the urban crisis" (Toner, 1992: 13).

Even in cases of an obvious urban mega-event such as a riot or an earthquake, the national policymaking arenas respond remedially to the specific problems raised by such dramatic crises (e.g., police brutality, poverty, an epidemic spike in the rate of violence and murderous crime in American cities, and a potentially disastrous reliance on automobile transit in place of genuine mass transit in Los Angeles and other large cities), and, rather quickly (absent a second urban triggering event), the national political equilibrium reasserts itself, and the "urban crisis" goes into remission waiting only for the next crisis to be "discovered" yet again. Cities, and with them a majority of Americans, return to their accustomed state of political invisibility. Indeed, in the absence of urban mega-crises bringing with them the periodic rediscovery of the urban crisis, the major "urban" policy that most Americans can come to expect from national policymaking circles are not urban programs at all but, rather, the indirect benefits of national policies on such issues as health care and employment policy. Lacking any structural pressure to produce an urban policy, the best that most city dwellers can expect from national policymakers in most administrations is to benefit from policies that indirectly affect the metro areas.

The only way to change this equation would be to somehow bring cities back into national politics and policymaking by changing either the political resources of city residents or the way in which cities are viewed in American national politics. Efforts to do both—to empower city residents and to change the view of cities in American political life—have been attempted. Several of these efforts—notably the Motor Voter Law of 1993 and the CityVote presidential primary effort of 1995, both of which tried to increase the turnout of urban voters and both of which failed miserably—we will reserve for discussion somewhat later in the present analysis. Better to start with the efforts to change the *invisible status quo* position of cities that has been, even if only marginally, more successful. These successful attempts involve an effort to recast "the city" (read: center cities and impoverished center-city residents, notably the nonwhite center-city poor) in terms likely to strike a more resonant chord with the predominately white and middle-to-upper-middle-class residents of America's suburbs.

THE NEW REGIONALIST LANGUAGE OF URBAN POLITICS: CITISTATES, COMMON MARKETS, AND INTERWOVEN DESTINIES

Professor Todd Swanstrom of the State University of New York, Albany, has described the work of several noted urbanists as comprising a "New Regionalism" school of thought (1994). Two of the leading New Regionalists, William Barnes and Larry Ledebur (1997: 44), have described their approach: "The core thesis of this somewhat eclectic group is economic inter-dependence, or mutual dependence of all parts of the [metropolitan] region. Distinctions within this camp relate primarily to methodology and framework. We and others frame the issue in terms of a single regional economy or labor market." The New Regionalists divide into two distinguishable camps. The first group, *citistate* scholars following the direction set by Neal Peirce and Associates (Peirce, Johnson, & Hall, 1993) in their pioneering 1993 study, *Citistates*, examines center-city–suburban issues and interdependency focus-ing on the center-city–suburb as comprising a larger citistate "region" (Drier, 1995; Hill, Wolman, & Ford, 1995; Peirce, 1995; Savitch, 1995; Savitch et al., 1993; Voith, 1992). Other New Regionalists, most notably Barnes and Ledebur (1993, 1997), view "regional" in even broader perspective. The most sweeping of the latter is the new work by Barnes and Ledebur (1997) in which the authors demonstrate that the United States "national" economy is more accurately viewed as a series of interlocking regional economies; that local economies, in the largest view, are *regional economic commons* (RECs) linking up at the largest or macro level to comprise the "United States common mar-ket of local economic regions." In this view, cities (both center cities and their suburbs) are small political economic units making up larger RECs, which, in turn, make up the larger common market of U.S. regional economies.

Vocabulary is important to such scholars. Note, for example, the political differences that might flow from reframing the problem(s) of center cities as a shared tragedy in which all community members have a joint responsibility for maintaining the overall strength of the city. In the largest sense the effort of the New Regionalists is to change the ways in which academics and Americans in general both describe and relate to metropolitan areas. Interestingly, not only does the New Regionalist effort make political sense, it makes sense descriptively.

The vocabulary of the New Regionalists fits the demographic changes of the past several years rather well. A nation that slowly became urban after World War II has suddenly become suburban at the close of the Cold War (Schneider, 1992). Demographers have documented the suburbanization of the American population (U.S. Bureau of the Census, 1991a; Blakely & Ames, 1992: 430; Frey & Speare, 1988), and urban scholars have attempted to understand and explain the changes resulting from increased suburbaniza-tion in America's urbanized areas in the late 1980s and early 1990s (Kling, Olin, & Poster, 1991; Garreau, 1991; Peirce, 1993a). Urban scholars de-veloped phrases such as "edge cities" (Garreau, 1991), "technoburbs" (Fish-man, 1987: 184), "multinucleated metropolitan regions" (Gottdiener, 1985), "citistates" (Peirce, 1993), "postsuburban" regions (Kling, Olin & Poster, 1991; Baldassare, 1994, 1995), and the new "polycentric metropolitan form" (Blakely & Ames, 1992: 436) to describe the large cities of the 1990s in which—as Table 1.1 illustrates—both a majority of the population *and* a large share of the traditional "urban" and "inner-city" problems have now made their way out to the suburbs.

By the early 1990s—as the proliferation of new labels illustrates (Gott-diener, 1985; Fishman, 1987; Kling, Olin, & Poster, 1991, Garreau, 1991; Blakely & Ames, 1992)—the older term *urban* no longer accurately describes life, growth, and politics in America's large cities. Most Americans now live in *citistates*—(Peirce, Johnson, & Hall, 1993)—combined central-city and *edge-city* social ecosystems in which escape from problems formerly associated primarily with inner-city living is no longer possible. In these vast citistates, inner-city blight now extends into suburbia, the earlier "white flight" from the city to the inner-ring suburbs has been replaced by a flight of nonwhites from the inner city to inner-ring suburbs, and there has been a corresponding flight of whites to newer outer-ring suburban rings located further outside the core metro area. Blakely and Ames (1992: 430–31) described these brave new metro regions in the following terms:

> Suburbs are not merely bedrooms but a way of living that is preferred by a majority of Americans of every race and social class. In fact the rate of suburbanization of African-Americans in the 1970–1980 decade exceeded that of whites. In that decade, the African-American central city population increased by 5.1%, while the comparable rate for the suburbs was 4.61%. In the 1980s, African-American central city growth actually declined, whereas suburban growth increased in most major metropolitan areas. However, racial distribution in suburbs is not at all even. The majority of African-Americans moving to the suburbs are relocating in the inner ring suburbs, in areas like Long Island in New York, New Jersey, San Francisco's East Bay, and inner suburban Chicago, which are rapidly becoming minority suburbs themselves. The outer suburbs are predominately inhabited by upper income households and whites. In essence, the suburban pattern is only a redistribution of the patterns of discrimination previously practiced in the cities with new income gradations among minority groups.

Citistates—a term that, thanks to the pioneering work of Neal Peirce is already widely used (although unscientifically, since it lacks a widely accepted definition) by urban scholars, but that can be differentiated from the technical term *metropolitan area* used by the U.S. Census Bureau—captures the new social and political ecology of large cities far better than earlier terms such as *city* or *urban*. For purposes of our discussion, we will give *citistates* the following working definition: As used in this chapter, a *citistate* refers to a combined center-city and suburban-fringe political and social system that has become the living space of a majority of the American population.

Strictly speaking, citistates are neither urban or suburban, neither inner-city nor semi-rural outer-ring suburban locales. Citistates are both, simul-taneously. As a label, *citistate* is preferable to *urban* both descriptively and politically. Descriptively, the term citistate is superior to urban because the former captures the ecology of large cities more accurately than does the latter. The crucial defining components of citistate as a term are that large American cities of the 1990s: (1) have a majority of the nation's population; (2) have interrelated core and suburban areas; and (3) have *area-wide* problems of poverty, population flight, eroding tax bases, and growth management. The problems of large cities are, as Table 1.3 illustrates, problems now shared by both inner-city residents and suburbanites. Poverty plagues both locations. The *urban-reservation* inner-city poverty neighborhood has, in the 1990s, an *edge-city* poverty neighborhood counterpart located in the older suburban ring, housing—however inadequately—42 percent of those below the poverty line for the entire citistate region, including 51.2 percent of the white poor, 40 percent of the African-American poor, and 23.7 percent of the metro Hispanic-Latino poverty population.

CREATING A LANGUAGE OF EMPATHY AND SHARED RESPONSIBILITIES: CAN LANGUAGE BIND THE SUBURBS TO CENTER CITIES?

Politically, *citistate* is superior to *urban* for two reasons. First, citistate accurately ties together the descriptive problems and the political futures of the center-city and the suburban ring. Just as the problems of these two areas are now joined, so is their political future. As former HUD Secretary Cisneros observed: "Interwoven destinies tie the fate of the inner cities to their entire metropolitan areas. . . . Upon the shoulder of these citistates rests the future of our nation's competitiveness on the global economic marketplace" (Peirce, 1993b). Second, citistate encompasses the suburbs as well as the center city, and where, as Peirce notes: "in a suburban nation . . . there's no payoff in talking about cities or using the word 'urban,' " it may be politically easier for a suburban president to construct policies aimed at city problems by referring to "citistate problems" and "citistate ghettos" (e.g., the combined inner-city poverties of urban reservations and the parallel poverties of the edge-city poverty neighborhoods).

The term *citistate* by the New Regionalists—both the notion of *interwoven destinies* (Peirce, Johnson, & Hall, 1993; Cisneros, 1995) and of the "U.S. common market of local economic regions" (Barnes & Ledebur, 1997: 000)—has been adopted by the Clinton Administration, as witnessed in both the National Urban Policy Report (HUD/NUPR, 1995) and by frequent public pronouncements by former Housing and Urban Development Secretary Cisneros. Typical of this attempt to create a new language of empathy between the city and its suburbs is the argument by Cisneros in his HUD study, *Interwoven Destinies*, that:

> Central cities and their suburbs are clearly "joined at the hip" in the structure and functioning of interrelated economic activities, stretching from the older downtown central business districts to the new "edge city" suburban office and retail centers and from inner city manufacturing plants to suburban industrial parts. (1993, p. 24)

The suggestion by the New Regionalists that suburban and center-city residents are linked by "interwoven destinies," and the power of such an idea to change the role of cities—particularly center cities—in American national politics is, as yet, an under-tested concept. Clearly, one HUD Secretary has advanced the idea markedly. Whether the idea itself is one of those crucial "big ideas" that resonate in American politics, and whether the idea succeeds in attracting more prominent, including presidential, sponsors, remains to be seen.

Former Harvard Kennedy School political economist and Clinton Administration Secretary of Labor, Robert Reich has written persuasively of *The Power of Public Ideas* (1988; Moore, 1988). Some ideas have the capacity to advance political dialogue, whereas other ideas, other phrasing will impede or slow down public debate. For example, scholars such as Marmor, Mashaw, and Harvey (1990) and Tom W. Smith (1987), long-time Director of the National Opinion Research Center at the University of Chicago, have shown persuasively that, on the topic of social welfare expenditures, Americans have a deep and long-term commitment to aid the American poor but that such commitment weakens when psychologically loaded terms such as *welfare* or *bureaucracy* or *welfare state* are introduced into the discussion. As Smith describes it in the title to his classic article on the subject, "That Which We Call Welfare by Any Other Name Would Smell Sweeter" (1987: 75). To twist Smith's twisting of Shakespeare only a little, that which we call "urban" may not only be descriptively more accurate if labeled citistate, it may also create a political opportunity, a political space in which a suburban nation and a suburban president may address the problems of America's cities, and do so in a way that does not threaten the lot of suburban voters but— by addressing area-wide concerns such as *citistate ghettos*, rather than inner-city ghettos—the metro label promises to improve the lives of all Americans by addressing the ties that bind the fate of the inner city to the entire metropolitan region.

USING POLITICAL AND ACADEMIC LANGUAGE TO ACHIEVE POLITICAL GAINS FOR CITIES

This, then, is the part of the dialogue that "urban" scholars and policy advocates have advanced. By electing to use *citistate* in place of *urban* as a term, scholars of city life and politics have simultaneously replaced a less-accurate term with a descriptively superior alternative, and the continued use of the terms *citistate* or *interwoven destinies* or *regional economic commons* may help to foster a public and political climate in which city problems may be addressed in a suburban nation, and by a suburban presidency.

In a similar vein, William Julius Wilson has argued for replacing the descriptively and normatively weaker term *urban underclass* with the term *ghetto poor* (1991b) for many of the same reasons, that the terms *city* and *urban* have been replaced by *citistate* and *regional economic commons* in the vocabulary of the New Regionalists.

Changing the vocabulary of urban (read: citistate) researchers has improved descriptive accuracy and created a marginally larger "political space" for addressing metro problems in a suburban nation. However—even granting Reich's "power of public ideas" (Reich, 1988; Moore, 1988) and the gains that flow from altering public perceptions associated with popular terms— vocabulary changes alone will not create sufficient political space or sufficiently change the existing rules of the game in American national politics to produce political equity for the vast majority of Americans residing in cities but seemingly permanently stuck below the water-line of the American political iceberg. Making urban politics more central to the national political and policymaking process requires changing the national political equation so that city problems are visible and city voters are significant, numerous, and empowered. Two recent efforts to do exactly this—the Motor Voter Act of 1993 and the CityVote presidential primary effort of 1995—failed miserably. A third effort, however—the increasing use of "mail ballot elections" by state and local jurisdictions at the city and county levels in California and statewide in Oregon—appears far more promising.

TARGETING VOTER REGISTRATION RATHER THAN TURNOUT: THE 1993 MOTOR VOTER BILL STEERS FOR THE BREAKDOWN LANE

The Motor Voter Bill, officially enacted as the National Voter Registration Act of 1993, was widely supported by Democrats and a number of grass-roots and organized labor groups, including the AFL-CIO and the Human Service Employees Registration and Voter Education Fund (Human SERVE)—the registration activist group led by Richard Cloward and Francis Fox Piven (Piven & Cloward, 1995) that lobbied hard for the passage of Motor Voter and monitors its implementation. Motor Voter was opposed by Republicans, including a number of Republican governors like Michigan's John Engler and California's Pete Wilson, who refused to implement the Act, even after enacted by Congress and signed into law by President Clinton. While a few lawsuits from these refusals remain, most have been resolved in the Courts in favor of the legality of the Motor Voter legislation.

What is the Motor Voter law? What effect will it have, and why did it draw the ire of Republican officeholders? The law requires that states offer on-site voter registration at convenient state offices, including state departments of motor vehicles. Motor Voter was believed by Republicans to be a threat, since nonvoters are typically more poor and nonwhite (thus, less likely to vote Republican) than regularly participating primary election voters in general. Democrats anticipated a boost in the numbers of their natural constituency of nonwhite, poorer, urbanized voters. Human SERVE

estimates that 20 million voters have registered as a result of Motor Voter—
9 million new voters, and 11 million voters re-registering or updating their
registration using the Motor Voter law (Ganz, 1996: 49; 1996b). According
to a study prepared by Human SERVE for the League of Women Voters and
the National Association for the Advancement of Colored People (NAACP),
these figures represent 17 percent of the approximately 54 million persons
eligible to vote but currently unregistered to vote in states covered by the new
Motor Voter law. The Human SERVE October 1996 study (cited in Ganz,
1996: p. 41) found that due to the new Motor Voter law 8.8 million new
registrants (44 percent) registered at departments of motor vehicles, 5 million
(24 percent) registered via the mail, with the remaining new registrants
registering at government bureaus such as libraries, military recruitment
offices, or unemployment offices. Finally, it should be noted that the Motor
Voter law only applies to forty-three states and the District of Columbia, since
six states, which have either same day, Election Day registration laws or no
organized voter registration procedures at all are exempt from the law. (*New
York Times,* Oct. 10, 1996, p. A2).

What, if any, difference will this flood of 20 million newly registered or
newly reregistered voters make for presidential elections, and for introducing
city issues and city voters into the national presidential election process? The
answer, at this early point in the implementation of Motor Voter, is that it
appears to be a wash, registering voters for both major parties but mobilizing
few newly registered *and newly voting* election participants.

Both parties have been somewhat surprised by the results of Motor
Voter to date. The primary effect as of this writing has been to increase the
registration numbers not of the poor but of those voters who were otherwise
inclined to vote but who were put off by the procedural or logistical difficulties
of registering to vote—typically persons under the age of thirty or people
who move frequently, or both. And, what of the voting preferences of this
new group of voters? Are they predominately Democratic, Republican, or
undeclared?

As Marshall Ganz (1996: 42) notes: the results are mixed. The partisan
orientation of the "thirty-something" voters

> do not differ substantially from that of the electorate as a whole. What's
> more, these new voters will have a disproportionate impact in states where
> Democrats [and, thus, presumably urban-oriented candidates and issues]
> already struggle—states like Florida, Georgia, and Arkansas, all of which
> have long histories of restrictive registration laws.

In short, although Motor Voter may produce more *registered voters*, it may
not favor one political party over the other in terms of increased registration,
nor may it, in the end, actually mobilize voters to participate (as opposed
to merely register) in presidential elections. Note, for example, that increased
registration efforts in 1984 increased registration by 2 percent to 71.8 percent

of voting-age population, but turnout that year increased by only 0.7 percent (Ganz, 1996: 43). Despite such registration increases, voting turnout in presidential elections did not increase substantially until 1992, rising by 5 percentage points to 55.2 percent due primarily to the highly contested race between Bill Clinton and George Bush (Ganz, 1996: 43).

MOBILIZATION VERSUS REGISTRATION

The key group affected by Motor Voter has, thus, been people otherwise motivated to vote but not voting due to a recent move or the logistical complexity of the act of registering itself. What about those persons not motivated to vote in the first place, persons for whom politics and elections may not seem to make a difference in their lives? Such persons, notably the very poor and persons of color, are the tip of the iceberg of the unregistered and nonvoting urban electorate. Motor Voter cannot mobilize such an urban electorate unless they are engaged by the political process itself, meaning actively brought into elections with the belief that they have a stake in the outcome that is real and meaningful. In such cases, the key to mobilization, beyond simply making it easier to register to vote via Motor Voter or similar programs, is (1) personal contacts with unregistered nonparticipants by activists, (2) partisan mobilization of key electorate groups by political parties, and (3) get-out-the-vote (GOTV) efforts that, again, are personal in nature, by "people that they know rather than by pieces of direct mail, telemarketers, and television commercials" (Ganz, 1996: 46).

Bottom-Line Assessment: The jury is still out on the 1993 Motor Voter Act. In all likelihood, despite the fact that 9 million new voters registered, most of them will be concentrated in states where registration has been historically designed to be purposely difficult (i.e., in Florida, Georgia, and Arkansas) to produce low-turnout elections favoring established political parties. Second, most newly registered voters may choose not to vote unless *engaged and personally contacted* by campaign workers, a difficult process at best for most campaigns. Third, several states—including California, Connecticut, Massachusetts, Michigan, New Hampshire, New York, Ohio, Pennsylvania, Rhode Island, South Carolina, and Virginia—have actively resisted implementing Motor Voter. Governors of such states resisted placing ballot registration in the hands of the poorest state citizens. By early 1997, for example, Connecticut had registered less than 3 percent of persons applying for public assistance. Few other states have registered more than 7 percent of the welfare population of their state (Ganz, 1996). Without higher percentages of the poor and persons of color registering and actually voting, Motor Voter, far from being a radical vehicle to mobilize city electorates, is far more likely to end up in the breakdown lane or wrecking yard of creative but, ultimately, ineffective ideas for mobilizing the American urban electorate.

INTRODUCING "URBAN" TO IOWA AND NEW HAMPSHIRE: THE 1995 CITYVOTE PRESIDENTIAL PRIMARY ELECTION EFFORT

Larry Agran, the former mayor of Irvine, California, started CityVote, a non-binding "urban primary," in an effort to bring urban issues and American cities into the Presidential primary election season of 1995–96. In a nutshell, CityVote placed twenty announced or prospective candidates for president on ballots in local elections in seventeen cities in the United States, including: Boulder, Colo.; Burlington, Vt.; Couer d'Alene, Idaho; Fayette, Mo.; Lacey, Wash.; Minneapolis, Minn.; Moscow, Idaho; Newark, N.J.; New Britain, Conn.; Olympia, Wash.; Rochester, N.Y.; St. Paul, Minn.; Spokane, Wash.; Tacoma, Wash.; Tucson, Ariz.; Tumwater, Wash.; and Wenatchee, Wash.

With the exception of the Reverend Jesse Jackson, no major political figure of the 1995–96 presidential campaign season endorsed the CityVote effort, and CityVote was actively opposed by the Chairs of both the Democratic and Republican parties. Nevertheless, Agran aggressively sold the idea to almost twenty American cities and sought to raise the visibility of city issues and cities themselves in the presidential primary election season by conducting an "urban primary" on November 7, 1995. The event was, at best, a mixed success. While it did draw over 200,000 participants in seventeen cities nationwide on their November 7th urban primary (see the results reported in Table 3.2), the vote was non-binding since there were, in fact, no delegates at stake for the presidential nominating process.

In short, while CityVote was a creative attempt to raise the role of cities in American politics and American presidential elections, it failed to do so. Iowa and New Hampshire still remain far more important in the presidential nominating process than are large American cities. CityVote was a creative effort to change the political equation in which cities might, for once, be brought back into American national politics. Despite Agran's efforts at shepherding over 200,000 city voters nationwide into local voting booths in 17 cities over 100 days before the Iowa and New Hampshire presidential primaries, it is obviously going to take stronger medicine than the CityVote effort to bring America's cities squarely into the political mainstream of the presidential nomination process. Still, CityVote may have a role in future presidential elections. It is worth remembering that the CityVote effort represented urban areas with a cumulative population of over 4 million, a figure far exceeding the population of all of the early primary states, including New Hampshire, Iowa, Maine, and South Dakota. Also, it is worth noting that the CityVote line was kept off the ballot in Boston only at the last moment. Had Boston been a CityVote location with its potential for print, radio, and television coverage distributed or broadcast to New Hampshire during the CityVote urban primary, CityVote might have had more impact than the resoundingly dull thud made in 1995.

TABLE 3.2
CityVote: The November 8, 1995 *Urban Primary* Results

Candidate	Percentage
Bill Clinton	43.8
Colin Powell	18.2
Robert Dole	11.8
Ross Perot	3.6
Pat Buchanan	3.0
Phil Gramm	2.9
Bill Bradley	2.7
Jesse Jackson	2.0
Alan Keyes	1.3
Lamar Alexander	*
Harry Browne	*
Charles Collins	*
Robert Dornan	*
Arthur Fletcher	*
John Hagelin	*
Lyndon LaRouche	*
Richard Lugar	*
Arlen Specter	*
Lowell Weicker	*
Total Votes:	**209,436**

* A candidate receiving less than one percent of the CityVote urban primary total.

Note: Cities participating included: Boulder, Burlington, Couer d'Arlene, Fayette (Mo.), Lacey (Wash.), Minneapolis, Moscow, Newark, New Britain, Olympia, Rochester, St. Paul, Spokane, Tacoma, Tucson, Tumwater (Wash.), and Wenatchee (Wash.).

Bottom-Line Assessment: CityVote failed miserably in 1995 but may be back in future presidential elections—again, most likely with minimal impact. Don't count CityVote out completely yet, even after the poor showing in the 1995–96 presidential election season. It is worth noting that in 1995 CityVote won an endorsement from the National Conference of Mayors, and received funding from a number of sources, including a $500,000 contribution from the Carnegie Corporation of New York.

WAIT A MINUTE, A REFORM THAT WORKS? MAIL-BALLOT ELECTIONS CUT COSTS IN HALF AND DOUBLE THE TURNOUT

Mail balloting is the practice of voting at home rather than requiring voters to ballot at traditional precinct polling places. In jurisdictions that have tried mail-ballot elections, the costs of local elections have decreased by as much as 50%, while voter participation has increased markedly, ranging from a rise of 10% to a record turnout increase of over 60% in the case of San Diego.

Turnout in local elections in the United States has, since the 1960s, been "relatively and consistently low" (Hamilton, 1971), generally averaging no more than "one-third of the electorate" (Alford & Lee, 1968: 796). Nationally, turnout in presidential elections has remained relatively constant at between 50 and 52 percent of the eligible voters voting, an average that invariably dips down to the 44 to 46 percent range in off-year congressional elections. The most recent figures, contained in a study released by the Census Bureau in June of 1995, indicate a troubling trend in which affluent voters are voting more while poorer voters are dropping off in record numbers. As the report shows: 60.1 percent of voting-age Americans with incomes of $50,000 or more voted in Fall '96, up from 59.2 percent four years earlier. Those with incomes under $5,000 declined from a 32.2 percent turnout to 19.9 percent. The drop was from 30.9 percent to 23.3 percent for those making $5,000 to $10,000.

MAIL BALLOTING: CALIFORNIA AND OREGON LEAD THE WAY

In May of 1981, the city of San Diego, which has experienced local elections ranging from 18 to 30 percent since the 1960s (Waste & Sparrow, 1985: 58), pioneered the large-scale use of mail-ballot local elections. On May 5, 1981, San Diego conducted the largest mail ballot ever attempted in the United States. Ballots were mailed to all 430,211 registered voters in the city for a special election to determine the fate of a proposed bond issue for a new convention center. Voters were instructed to mail their completed ballots within fifteen days to the County Registrar of Voters. The response rate was 60.77 percent or 261,433 voters—the largest number of people ever participating in a San Diego election, the highest percentage turnout for a special election, and the highest percentage turnout of all but six citywide elections in the thirty-year period preceding the 1981 vote. The San Diego County Registrar of Voters estimated the cost of a regular walk-in election, using precinct polling places, at $550,000. The actual cost of the mail-in 1981 ballot was $327,000—a reduction of 40.5 percent (Ortiz, 1981: 2). Although the San Diego election was the largest-scale attempt at municipal mail balloting to date, other cities, including Rochester, New York, and Berkeley, California, have experienced similar success.

More recently, in the presidential primary of 1995, the state of Oregon pioneered the successful use of mail-ballot elections in a statewide United States Senate election. Oregon, which has experimented with mail-in ballot elections in school bond issues and statewide ballot initiatives for over fifteen years, recently conducted a mail-in election to fill the then-vacant U.S. Senate seat of Bob Packwood. The turnout for the January, 1996 election was

66 percent, a figure far higher than the 40 percent of Oregonians who voted in the 1994 midterm congressional elections. Oregon voters were given three weeks in which to return their ballots, a process that resulted in considerable savings for local governments. Multnomah County (serving a large portion of metropolitan Portland), for example, which had spent $266,000 for comparable traditional polling place elections in the past, spent only $100,000 for the 1996 election—a savings of over 50 percent. Participation appears to have increased by 20 percent or more depending on location. Turnout was 57.9 percent statewide as opposed to 38.25 percent in the May 1994 primary election season in Oregon.

Considering the track record of Oregon, San Diego, Rochester, Berkeley, and numerous other jurisdictions—Stanislaus County in California, for example, held a mail-ballot election in 1994 that only slightly increased turnout but that markedly decreased election costs—that have experimented with mail-ballot elections since the early 1980s, widespread adoption of mail balloting by both state and metro jurisdictions seems probable in the foreseeable future. There are several advantages to jurisdictions adopting mail balloting. First, the legal questions, at least in California, have been resolved in favor of mail balloting. The California Supreme Court, in *Patterson v. City of San Diego* (1981), upheld the use of mail balloting by California cities. While a state-by-state legal determination would be necessary to establish the local legality of balloting by mail, the outcome in California suggests that the outcome would be favorable.

Second, the increased participation and decreased costs associated with mail ballots are a rare and welcome reform, especially to states and cities living within the severe fiscal constraints that have characterized the 1980s and 1990s (Clark, 1994; Mollenkopf, 1983, 1992).

Third, in a democratic political system, increased participation leads to two salutary ends—increased legitimacy for elected governmental officials and acts, and an increase in the democratic quality of city life that comes from not simply an increase in numbers of voting participants but, also, in the number of times that voters participate in local elections.

There are three additional reasons why local and state jurisdictions may increasingly elect to adopt mail balloting. First, "absentee voting" has lost much of its traditional meaning. A recent innovation in the use of the now-misnomered "absentee" local and congressional elections has been the increased use of absentee ballots by both major political parties, whereby in California fully 20 percent (Endicott, 1993) of the electorate now votes using an absentee ballot. Increasingly, this represents fewer shut-ins and out-of-state business persons than it does supporters successfully identified by political consultants for both major parties, who want to have those votes "in the bag" for their candidate before the actual day of the election. The Registrar for Sacramento County, for example,—having grown tired of the increasingly thin fiction of the "absentee ballot" label—has even suggested that the name "absentee" ballot be changed due to the high numbers of voters requesting mail-in ballots for reasons more of convenience than necessity. Voter registrars in jurisdictions where mail balloting has been tried, registrars elsewhere hoping to cut back on expenses and increase turnout, as well as good government groups such as Common Cause, support the overall shift to mail balloting in California (Endicott, 1993).

Second, the possibilities of voter fraud that in the 1980s were considered a major roadblock to widespread adoption of mail ballot elections are, ironically, *actually lower* in a mail-ballot election than in regular precinct polling booth elections. Endicott (1993) sums up the California experience this way:

> As for the argument that vote-by-mail will invite fraud, California officials say just the opposite is true. All return envelopes [in a recent 1994 Stanislaus County election, for example] are bar-coded to automatically pull up a voter's signature and get instant verification. When's the last time anybody verified your signature when you signed in at a polling place?

Finally, mail-ballot elections are not simply a way of increasing local voter turnout and decreasing the costs of local elections, although that alone would warrant their widespread adoption by state and local governments. Mail-ballot elections, with their potential for greatly increasing the turnout of metropolitan voters, should act to ensure the increased representation of traditionally under-represented groups at the local level as well as increase the influence of traditionally lower turnout city voters in state and national elections. By doing so, mail balloting acts to "increase the public space" for raising metro issues in local, state, and national elections, and to decrease the enormous gap between those who presently participate in American local, state, and national politics, and those who do not. A recent Ford Foundation study illustrates the depth of that gap. The study concluded that a person with a graduate degree making over $70,000 is twice as likely to vote, 6 times as likely to protest, 9 times more likely to write elected officials, and 100 times more likely to contribute to political campaigns than are less-educated, less-wealthy citizens (Ford Foundation, 1990).

Bottom-Line Assessment: Many partisan groups, notably some Republicans, are not going to like the effects of mail-ballot elections, but an idea that has generally resulted in less corrupt elections with double the average turnout and half the average costs associated with traditional in-place, precinct elections is probably here to stay. The mail-ballot election technique is one of the very few bright spots in the mixed track record of progressives and others who have attempted to increase the "political space" available to city voters and city issues in American national politics. In some respects, mail-ballot elections and the changed vocabulary—*interwoven destinies, citistates,* and *regional economic commons*—of the New Regionalists are, at least for the late 1990s, the cutting edge of whatever increased political space is available to cities nationally in the 1990s and early in the twenty-first century. By use of these meager means, perhaps cities will grow somewhat less invisible politically in American national politics. If so, as Chapter 4 illustrates, cities will still have a long way to go before their voters and their problems—the *permanent crisis* in America's cities—are genuinely placed on the front-burner of American national politics. As Chapter 4 demonstrates, status quo policies have been as instrumental in exacerbating the permanent crisis, as in attempting to alleviate it.

4

Washington's Cities
Status Quo National Policies for American Cities

It is probable that at this time we are about to make great changes in our social system. The world is ripe for such changes and if they are not made in the the direction of greater social liberality, in the direction forward, they will almost of necessity be made in the direction backward, of a great social niggardliness. We all know which of these directions we want. But it is not enough to want it, not even enough to work for it—we must want and work for it with intelligence. Which means that we must be aware of the dangers which lie in our most generous wishes.

LIONEL TRILLING

Self-help groups across the country are fond of saying, with a large grain of truth, that it's not our worst efforts but our best efforts that have landed us exactly where we are today. The story is much the same for the relationship between America's cities and policymakers in the federal government. Washington's best efforts, or, in the words of Lionel Trilling, Washington's most generous wishes—and we will describe several of these generous wishes ranging from the years 1946 to 1996 in this chapter—have resulted in exactly what Americans would have created for their cities if, ironically, we had been putting forward our *worst efforts* and our *least generous wishes*. Explaining this paradox, explaining the mixed legacy that Washington has bequeathed to American cities, is the central task of this chapter.

The point, to return to this chapter's opening self-help story, is not that our worst efforts get us in trouble and our best efforts keep us out. Rather, that, as the earlier self-help quote suggests, the world is more complicated than it appears at first glance. Until we really examine our actions, *both* our worst efforts *and* our best efforts are almost equally likely to end up getting us in trouble. So it is, also, with cities. Until as a nation we carefully examine what has worked and what hasn't in terms of urban policy (both national urban policy and local city policy variants), we are destined to keep making the same mistakes over and over again. Until we know what it is that isn't working *and stop doing it*, both our best efforts and our worst, ironically, are likely to fail. And, as this chapter argues, what hasn't worked, what isn't working, and what will continue not to work if we keep trying to do it, is to micro-manage cities from the nation's capital, turning local jurisdictions into, in effect, *Washington's cities*, and turning local policymakers into little more than local colonial administrators of Washington's "generous wishes."

From 1946 to the present, Washington enacted numerous programs for the cities, provided vast amounts of monies, and began again and again to fight wars on poverty, hunger, crime, slums, transportation needs, and health problems. Regrettably, the net result of much of this legislation has not been to free cities, or to make them stronger, or to make them any more vital, or more independent. Rather, it has created an almost neo-colonial system of dependency in which cities increasingly became *Washington's cities*, as American cities began after the early 1950s to increasingly rely on Washington's largess, programs, and policies. While it is probably fair to say that the federal government's best efforts have, time and again, been genuine efforts to ameliorate the plight of those living in the cities, Washington has instead created a crazy quilt of urban programs and policies that, in their collective totality, have sown a legacy of some real assistance, some despair, and considerable confusion.

This chapter documents the best and the worst in the growth of Washington's policies toward cities, arguing that only two federal programs have been clear successes—the 1964 War on Poverty-era Head Start program enacted under President Lyndon Johnson, and General Revenue Sharing enacted under President Richard Nixon's New Federalism plan in 1972. In fact, alone of all federal-urban programs from 1946 to the present, only Revenue Sharing has ever tried to foster independent cities by turning revenues back over to local jurisdictions and allowing those jurisdictions and local officials the power to spend the money in the way that local politicians, local citizens, and local preferences deemed wisest.

Fortunately, a large number of independent and local initiatives (non-Washington, D.C.–based initiatives) have also succeeded—initiatives generated from local governments, public-private partnerships, foundations, court actions, think tanks, and urban specialists in the field and in academe. Several of these initiatives—ranging from the Gautreaux experiment in Chicago, successful implementation of community policing in the New York City, the Sandtown development in Baltimore, the Unigov city-county consolidated government in Indianapolis, regional tax sharing in Minneapolis, "reinventing government" efforts at the state, national, and local levels, as well as the progressive planning (Region 2040) practices in Portland, Oregon—are also part of the urban policy status quo, and, what's better, are clear status quo urban success stories. This chapter describes *national* urban policy, as that policy has been created in Washington, D.C., from World War II to the present. Chapter 5 describes describes *status quo decentralized* approaches to urban public policy.

Here, then, is the urban public policy story from 1946 to the present. It stars, as we have said, two successful Washington-based national urban policy efforts, Revenue Sharing and Head Start—the former terminated in 1986 during the Reagan administration, the latter continuing to the present even if continuing to be significantly under-funded at the moment. Note, for example, that as recently as 1994, "only 62 percent of four-year-olds and 28 percent of three-year-olds who could have benefited from Head Start in 1994 actually got spaces in the program" (Harris, 1996: 75). In addition to the success of these two Washington-based national urban programs, the *status quo* urban policy story, as we noted earlier, also stars several locally based programs up and running successfully in locales as diverse as Baltimore, Chicago, and Portland. In-between the two Washington-based programs and the locally based urban policy success stories are several policies and programs from 1946 to 1996 that are, at best—literally, figuratively, and qualitatively—in between.

RAPIDLY CHANGING NATIONAL URBAN POLICIES: NEW ADMINISTRATIONS, NEW APPROACHES TO URBAN PROBLEMS

Even more troubling for the cities than the dependency inherent in their new post-1950 role as Washington's cities, was the problem of rapidly changing national-urban rules and programs in Washington, D.C., from 1950 to the later 1990s (Brown, Fossett, & Palmer, 1984). Cities had to strategize in those years for their share of rapidly changing grant programs under, first, the New Frontier of John F. Kennedy, and next, the War on Poverty and Community Action Programs of Lyndon B. Johnson. This, in turn, was succeeded by the need of cities to gear up to participate in and compete for programs in the New Federalism of Richard Nixon, the later Creative Federalism of Jimmy Carter, yet another round of New Federalism under Ronald Reagan, which in turn was followed by the HOPE Partnership of the Bush administration, and, finally, by the Clinton administration New Covenant programs such as community policing and empowerment zones.

FDR AND THE BEGINNINGS OF MODERN NATIONAL URBAN POLICY (1932–46)

While some early grants-in-aid went from the national government to local governments during the FDR Great Depression era, national urban policy toward the cities and federal programs aimed at spending federal money to aid local problems are largely a post–World-War-II phenomenon. Grants-in-aid to localities were federal-local aid programs in which Washington provided *formula grant* funds to states and local governments according to formulas developed by Congress and the administering federal agencies. *Project grants* were also available, but not to all jurisdictions. Instead, project grants were restricted to a limited number of jurisdictions (i.e., low-income neighborhoods or cities, urban jurisdictions, or agricultural locations) in which local governments usually competed for project grant funding. Project grants, in turn, were subdivided into *categorical grants* targeted for narrow specific purposes such as vocational education, and in the late 1960s and early 1970s, block grants in which local jurisdictions had less "strings" attached to the federal grant money, and in which several governmental objectives such as public safety, urban redevelopment, and employment programs would typically be combined into one large block grant program.[1]

Expansion of Grants-in-Aid and "Alphabet Soup" Programs

The early grants-in-aid system grew rapidly. One measure of this growth in federal policymaking toward cities, and in the flow of federal money to cities, is, as Ross, Levine, and Stedman (1991: 338) have pointed out, the sharp increase in aid available to localities in the late 1950s and early 1960s compared to the prewar level of aid. As Ross, Levine, and Stedman acknowledged: "The year 1932 serves as an important benchmark for cities and the grant-in-aid system. In that year about $10 million were transferred in grants from the federal government to cities. During the next three decades that figure increased dramatically. By 1960, federal aid to state and local governments reached $7 billion" (1991: 338), a figure amounting to 7.6 percent of all federal expenditures and 14.5 percent of state and local governmental budgets.

Grants-in-aid assistance by the federal government continued to rise to a historic high of $91 billion or 16 percent of all federal spending, and 25.8 percent of all state/local spending in 1980, the final year of the Carter administration. Grants-in-aid dropped dramatically during the Reagan administration (1981–88), with federal grants-in-aid expenditures declining in 1982 from $94.8 billion (15.5 percent of all federal outlays, 25.8 percent of all state/local outlays) to $88.2 billion (11.8 percent of federal outlays, 21.6 percent of state/local outlays). The Reagan years marked continued decreases in federal grants-in-aid expenditures, reaching twenty-year lows of 10.8 percent of the federal budget in 1987 and 1988, and 10.5 percent in 1989. By way of comparison, the 1968 level of federal grants-in-aid was 10.4 percent of the federal budget, the 1969 level was 11%, and *all intervening years from 1969 to 1980 had remained constant at least 15 percent of the federal budget.* Under Presidents Bush and Clinton, grants-in-aid began once more to rise, growing from 10.8 percent of the federal budget (19.4 percent of state/local outlays) to 1993 levels of $203 billion, or 13.8 percent of federal outlays, and over 20 percent of state/local expenditures in 1993 (Ross & Levine, 1996: 18).

By comparison with contemporary federal expenditures for grants-in-aid to state and local governments, the early FDR years constituted important but modest expenditures by the federal government. Thus, the aid that cities received during the FDR New Deal program was limited to a few grants-in-aid programs, and the primary assistance to cities during this period was largely indirect. Cities did benefit indirectly, for example, from some of the "alphabet soup" programs of the New Deal, notably the Works Progress Administration (WPA) and the Public Works Administration (PWA), which aimed primarily at providing jobs to the unemployed but which also resulted in the construction of large numbers of parks, schools, bridges, streets, sewers, and recreational facilities.

The Rise of the FHA and the FSLIC

A second urban aid legacy of the New Deal was the creation of the Federal Housing Administration (FHA) and the Federal Savings and Loan Insurance Corporation (FSLIC) in the National Housing Act of 1934. The 1934 Housing Act was intended to prop up the ailing banking industry, to stop bank foreclosures on family homes, to coax hard-earned family saving back into banks and savings-and-loans by insuring the deposits of individual savers, and to jump-start the then-floundering home building industry. The logic of the FHA program contained in the Housing Act was to provide government insurance for home mortgages of new or existing one-to-four unit homes so that lenders would be encouraged to loan more, require smaller down payments, and charge lower interest rates. A sweetener was added to induce more home loans from financial institutions. The attraction for financial institutions to loan increased amounts of money to home purchasers was that, in the event that an FHA-insured home purchaser were to default on the home loan, under the new law the federal government agreed to pay the lender 80 percent of the agreed house purchase price.[2]

FHA Program Consequences and the Policy Road Not Taken

The FHA program did accomplish these ends, but by building-in a programmatic preference for assistance to purchasers of single-family homes and new homes over apartment dwellers, the FHA program also resulted in increasing the segregation of America's inner cities by encouraging out-migration to new homes in suburban bedroom communities. As Edward Banfield observed over two decades ago in *The Unheavenly City, Revisited* (1974: 32), the FHA assistance and later similar home-buying assistance in the Veteran's Administration went primarily for the purchase of new homes. These were located almost exclusively in suburban locations or in outer locations still within the city limits of large metro areas, where vacant land was still available for housing developments.

A 1940s/1950s Urban Policy Path Not Taken: Subsidizing Existing Center-City Housing Stock

A policy option not taken would have been for the FHA program to subsidize the renovation of exiting housing stock or to encourage the construction of new homes (both recently encouraged in a Clinton administration homeownership program) in America's center cities, thus delaying or perhaps entirely reshaping what would later become the out-migration housing boom. Of course, to have done so would have meant a very different set of winners and losers in terms of who gets what, when, where, and how, as Harold Lasswell once (1966) formulated—the essential political question involving any public policy. Instead of favoring middle-class, predominately white home-buyers, had the FHA home subsidy program emphasized rehabilitating and refurbishing existing center-city housing stock—the national urban policy path not taken—"it would have assisted many of the not well-off, a category that included most Negroes as well as other minority group members" (Banfield, 1974: 32). In fact, the FHA program opted for the beginnings of a great "land race" to the American suburbs, a race that accelerated by quantum leaps after World War II, checked only by the amount of space of land available to housing developers.

Not only did FHA policies and programs favor white home buyers until the late 1950s and early 1960s, it explicitly worked against black home-buyers. First, the FHA accepted bank "redlining" practices that made it difficult, and in some cases impossible, for center-city African-American families to secure loans for center-city housing stock. Second, the FHA allowed and encouraged the use of *restrictive covenants*, agreements that prohibited the deed of a house from being sold to a member of a minority ethnic group. Finally, as Ross and Levine illustrated, the Agency's own *Underwriting Manual* stated that: "If a neighborhood is to retain stability, it is necessary that properties shall continue to be occupied by the same social and racial classes." These practices led to such severe ethnic discrimination in the FHA home-loan program that only 2 percent of the FHA subsidized housing built after World War II was sold to nonwhite home buyers, and half of this total was provided by the FHA to minority families seeking home loans to move into housing built in exclusively minority subdivisions (Ross & Levine, 1996: 35. See also Schneider, 1980; Jackson, 1985).

URBAN POLICY IN THE TRUMAN AND EISENHOWER ADMINISTRATIONS (1946–60)

Many of the "urban" programs of the Truman and Eisenhower administrations also aided the great American land race out to suburban home sites. During the Truman and Eisenhower presidencies, Congress appropriated funds for hospital construction (1946), slum clearance and urban renewal (1949), waste treatment facilities (1956), water pollution control (1956), and highway construction (1956). By far, the most influential of these policies involved the 1949 Housing Act, and, later, the Highway Act of 1956. In the 1949 Housing Act, "the Truman Administration created Urban Renewal, the first Federal program to make a strong commitment to restoring cities to some kind of past glory" (Lemann, 1994: 2).

The 1949 Housing Act attempted to provide assistance to low-income-rental families, to provide monies for slum clearance and urban removal—an approach that quickly became controversial and that was described by opponents as "Negro removal" (Jacobs, 1961; Gans, 1962; Anderson, 1964; Lowi, 1969; Listokin & Casey, 1979; Hirsch, 1983; Ross, Levine, & Stedman, 1991; Lemann, 1994; Ross & Levine, 1996)—and to support the continued growth of the private real estate market.

The newly created Housing and Home Finance Agency (HHFA), established by the Housing Act of 1949, was given the task of providing grants-in-aid to local redevelopment agencies—agencies that, in turn, had been or were to be created by state legislatures—to encourage the acquisition and clearance of blighted areas in cities. Federal funds were used to help private developers acquire the slum sites, clear them, and market the new sites at below market costs to private developers. The politics of such slum clearance quickly became acrimonious. Cities such as Chicago and San Francisco became dominated by slum clearance controversies in which fights over a given project would drag on for ten or more years (Jacobs, 1961; Gans, 1962; Hirsch, 1983; Browning, Marshall, & Tabb, 1984).

Urban Renewal Turns into "Negro Removal" and the "Federal Bulldozer"

The 1949 federal slum clearance and urban renewal program, a program begun with the best of intentions, became in the end, in the words of economist Martin Anderson, "the federal bulldozer" tearing down over 126,000 sub-standard housing units across the nation from 1950 to 1960, but replacing them with only 30,000 housing units, most of which were low-income public housing units (Anderson, 1964: 6–8; Herson & Bolland, 1990: 299). As Nicholas Lemann has observed, the "federal bulldozer" charge was "wholly justified":

> The rap on it, wholly justified, was that it bulldozed neighborhoods, especially black neighborhoods (hence its nickname, "Negro Removal,") and replaced them with highways, sterile housing developments and municipal office complexes that looked wonderful when planners presented them at Chamber of Commerce meetings but, when built, only hastened the city's decline." (Lemann, 1994: 3)

Thus, the Housing Act of 1949 and the slum clearance and urban renewal effort the Act initiated actually intensified urban poverty by removing vast numbers of substandard but low-priced rental housing units and greatly concentrating the urban poor into high-rise low-income public housing projects, and into existing but uncleared poverty neighborhoods. As Scott Greer has noted: "At a cost of more than three billion dollars, the Urban Renewal Agency (URA) has succeeded in materially reducing the supply of low-cost housing in American cities" (1965: 3). The 1949 Housing Act and URA had the net effect of "Negro removal"—the increasing "ghettoization" of America's urban poor, particularly poor people of color, a trend that, unfortunately, continues up until the present day.

GI Bill of Rights and the VA Home Loan Program

The "GI Bill of Rights" passed by a grateful nation in 1944 extended earlier home buying and mortgage insurance programs originally established in the 1934 Housing Act. The 1944 GI Bill authorized the Veterans Administration (VA) to insure home mortgages for millions of World-War-II-era vets. Like the 1934 Housing Act before it, the federal government guaranteed or insured the home mortgages, but, unlike the 1934-era program, World War II veterans were entitled by the GI Bill to purchase homes *without a down payment*. The 1944 GI Bill of Rights, in combination with the earlier 1934 and 1949 Housing Acts, added to the increasing ghettofication of inner cities, creating what in some respects amounted to a "Caucasian removal" program by insuring that veterans would be able to take advantage of home loan provisions offering them favorable, below-market interest rates on new, typically suburban, homes.[3] The VA program worked with the FHA to help millions of new home-buyers purchase housing at a rate never before experienced in the history of the United States. This explosion of home-buying in the American suburbs by white American veterans, in combination with the earlier exodus from the center cities promoted by the Housing Acts of 1934 and 1949, the pent-up housing demand from people who deferred new home acquisition during the World War II war effort, and massive construction of freeways during the 1950s (stemming from the Highway Act of 1956—an Act arguing that American national defense required an extensive set of freeways connecting major cities so that troops and material might be rapidly moved from place to place in the event of a national emergency), helped produce a giant emptying out of large American cities.

As Banfield (1974) noted, there were few checks on this outward migration except the supply of vacant land and the fact that the new suburban "Levit-towners" (Vidich & Bensman, 1958) were able to afford large lots, often a half acre or more, on land zoned for single-family houses; a process that resulted, in the case of outward migration from New York City—which experienced some of the greatest out-migration in the country at the time—in six million people taking "as much land as the previous sixteen million took" before them (43). Thus, not only did the postwar national urban policies encourage outward migration, but the same policies also foreshadowed the need for area-wide metropolitan governance in the years to come on issues such as managed growth, tax-base sharing, and traffic congestion.

A Postwar Urban Aid Summary: The Creation of Doughnut Cities, Out-Migration, and Concentrated Poverty

In this combination of post–World-War-II urban policies and programs, the federal government did some good and considerable harm. The net effect of the combined programs was to greatly concentrate the very poor in America's cities into intensified ghetto areas by removing large numbers of inexpensive housing stock; by crowding old low-income neighborhoods with even more low-income residents, this time newly and governmentally displaced persons in poverty, creating the legacy that remains today of high-rise newer poverty ghetto neighborhoods—now governmental in their origins; and encouraging the vast outward migration that has helped to empty-out American cities and produce *doughnut cities*—impoverished inner-city neighborhoods surrounded by more affluent bedroom suburban communities serviced by state and federally supported freeways, subways, and transit systems.

George Sternlieb (1971) has argued that what we are describing as the "doughnut city process" has over time turned many American central cities into the Great American "sandbox"—a place where suburbanites can work, or seek sports, cultural, or entertainment experiences and then, at the end of the day or the end of the play, leave the center-city sandbox, taking their high incomes and tax monies to gated suburban jurisdictions, taking their children to predominately white and upper-income suburban schools, and taking their sales tax dollars and spending to suburban shopping malls.

This outward migration to the suburbs, already exacerbated by the policies of the HFA and GI Bill, was accelerated by federal highway policy. Beginning with the enactment of the Highway Act of 1944, the federal role in encouraging the expansion of state and local highways loomed large. In fact, the 1944 Act earmarked 25 percent of federal highway funds for assisting city highway construction. Reframed in 1956 as a national defense imperative, the 1956 National Defense Highway Act created a boom in highway construction because, under the new law, 90 percent of highway construction costs would be borne by the federal government. Large-scale highway construction projects resulting from the 1956 Highway Act often accelerated center-city decay by building new freeways in center-city neighborhoods. The Cross-Bronx Expressway in New York City, which literally cut in half the largely Jewish Bronx neighborhood, and the building of Interstate 95 through the middle of the primarily black Overtown neighborhood in Miami are prominent examples—as is the Central Freeway complex in San Francisco that accelerated the deterioration of the South of Market/Mission District. Acting with newly available federal highway construction funds, cities built freeways that not only facilitated the rise of doughnut and sandbox cities, but freeways that, because of their placement, divided and weakened minority neighborhoods, in many cases greatly accelerating neighborhood decline—in all cases, greatly accelerating the concentration of center-city poverty by forcing residents to relocate either outside the city or placing increased demands on existing poorer neighborhoods not otherwise impacted by the freeway construction such as Liberty City in Miami, and the Mission District and the Tenderloin in San Francisco.

CITIES UNDER THE JFK AND LBJ ADMINISTRATIONS (1961–68)

The next round of urban aid programs, this time in the Kennedy and Johnson administrations, were "animated by a backlash against [the] Urban Renewal" of the Truman-Eisenhower years (Lemann, 1994: 3) and animated by an enthusiasm for a small number of successful experimental city programs such as the Ford Foundation financed Gray Areas Project in New Haven and (also financed by the Ford Foundation) the Lower East Side (Manhattan) Mobilization for Youth Program. These prototype programs became the policy template for what later became the War on Poverty and the Community Action Program (CAP). Before turning to a description of the CAP federal urban aid program, it is important to note that some of the aid to urban areas during the Kennedy–Johnson era came about as a result of *indirect* rather than *direct* urban aid.

A great deal of national urban policy, much of it indirectly aimed at cities, much directly aimed at cities, took place in the Lyndon Johnson years. The indirect effects are most visible in the Civil Rights Act of 1964 and the Voting Rights Act of 1965. As Stanley (1987), Herson & Bolland (1990), and Browning, Marshall, & Tabb (1984) have documented, the Civil Rights acts aided in mobilizing the urban poor and black city voters by legally insuring their rights to vote, by encouraging black political leaders to seek and secure local elective office, by guaranteeing blacks access to public accommodations, lodging, and transportation, and by guaranteeing free and fair elections and equal employment opportunities.

More indirect aid to American cities during the Johnson years came in the form of 1963-to-1967-era Great Society programs, including Medicare, Medicaid, and food stamps. Direct aid to cities was provided by the creation of regional economic development councils, aid to elementary and secondary education, and the two central urban programs of the Great Society effort—the War on Poverty and the Model Cities program. The War on Poverty, enacted as the Economic Opportunity Act of 1964, began the contemporary food stamp and school lunch programs, as well as Head Start, Upward Bound, the Adult Workshops Program, Volunteers in Service to America (VISTA), and the Legal Services Program. Head Start was assigned the task of preparing three- and four-year-old children in poverty for kindergarten and early elementary school education, stressing a range of skills from early reading and math skills to health care screening, nutrition, peer-group interaction, social skills, and the encouragement of active parent participation in each child's education. Upward Bound was designed to encourage teenage children in poverty to eventually attend college by means of counseling, special programs, and visits to college campuses. Adult Workshops encouraged adults to develop skills useful in the job market via workshops and study sessions. Finally, VISTA was LBJ's domestic equivalent to the popular Kennedy Peace Corps New Frontier program.

While food stamps, Head Start, Medicare, and school lunches have continued to enjoy both popular and legislative support from the Johnson Great Society War on Poverty Years until the present, much of the remainder of the War on Poverty, including the CAPs—Legal Services, VISTA, Upward Bound, and Model Cities—came under fire. In later years, these more controversial programs were either eliminated completely or remain today in only scattered sites, funded with local monies, public-private partnerships, and foundation grants, and existing more-or-less in only a skeleton form of the halcyon days of the War on Poverty, Model Cities, and the Great Society. Much of this controversy, which resulted in the eventual dismantling of the LBJ Great Society programs by the Nixon administration (1968–74), arose as a result of the CAP and the Model Cities Program.

Despite the fact that the CAP approach to urban aid and neighborhood revitalization was largely dismantled by the Nixon administration, the early 1960s CAP program contained the genesis of contemporary policy and thinking about urban aid and ghetto intervention programs. As Nicholas Lemann noted: "The early 1960s, then, were the starting point for the current phase of thinking about ghettos. For fully 30 years, the reigning ideas about Government policy in poor city neighborhoods have been essentially the same—even though these ideas are still being referred to as new" (1994: 3). The ideas are:

> *Bottom up, not top down.* The people who know the most about the needs of poor neighborhoods are the residents themselves; therefore, poverty programs should be designed and implemented by them, not imposed from above by mayors, members of Congress, social workers, intellectuals, federal bureaucrats, or other authority figures.
>
> *Comprehensive and coordinated.* Antipoverty programs are a confusing morass, run by competing, byzantine bureaucracies. Rather than being operated "categorically" by different agencies in Washington (Welfare and Medicaid are examples of "categorical" antipoverty programs because each addresses a single problem in isolation), these programs should be, on a local level, housed under one roof and reorganized so that all the problems of poor people are addressed together systematically.
>
> *Revitalize the neighborhood.* Ultimately, the theory goes, the health of a neighborhood depends on its economic base. The only real long-term answer to the problems of an inner-city ghetto is for good jobs to be

available there. Anyone interested in helping poor neighborhoods must primarily focus on economic development.

This three-fold theoretical legacy—bottom-up planning, coordination of programs, and neighborhood revitalization—bequeathed an almost instantaneous controversial quality to the LBJ War on Poverty CAP approach. CAP was controversial with local elected officials from the outset, since it attempted to deliver services *directly* to the poor in poor neighborhoods by creating Local Community Action Agencies (LCAAs) in each poverty neighborhood or in each city, and funneling federal aid to the LCAA agencies rather than directing such aid to established city agencies, via the supervision of elected and appointed city officials. This approach, in effect, set up a competing patronage and political support system *outside* the jurisdiction of local city halls.

Second, the LCAA approach was anything but "comprehensive and coordinated." Described by LBJ officials in the Office of Economic Opportunity as an effort to create "maximum feasible participation" by the poor—and designed, as one scholar has described it, as an effort to provide the poor with a "greater sense of involvement and commitment" (Henig, 1985: 103)—the LCAA approach resulted instead in what Senator Daniel Patrick Moynihan described as *Maximum Feasible Misunderstanding* (1969), a three-sided political war of poverty neighborhood activists against local and congressional officials against, in turn, federal officials from the Office of Economic Opportunity.

"Maximum feasible misunderstanding" via LCAAs changed the highly charged urban political landscape, a landscape already literally charred from urban riots and strife, into the national urban policy equivalent of a Hobbesian "war of all against all." City officials were angered that federal funds were not flowing through their channels, and more angered that local LCAA officials were running competing patronage empires in poverty neighborhoods, and running, in some cases, for elective political office against incumbent local office holders. LCAA officials, in turn, were angered that, as one scholar has estimated, by 1968 only 25 percent of the federal funds spent by the Office of Economic Opportunity were channeled directly to LCAAs, "the remainder going to private organizations, including universities, churches, civil rights groups, settlement houses, family service agencies, United Funds, or newly established nonprofit groups" (Judd, 1988: 316).

Early Eisenhower- and Truman-era slum clearance and urban renewal were, indeed, guilty of concentrating urban poverty, promoting "Negro removal," and exacerbating outward suburban migration from the inner city to suburban bedroom communities. The LBJ CAP national urban programs, on the other hand, were guilty of what might be labeled "City Hall removal," and what Moynihan has accurately described as "maximum feasible misunderstanding."

A third problem with the CAP War on Poverty is far more subtle but far more lasting in its consequences; namely that *neighborhood revitalization—a* key element in the CAP and subsequent urban aid policies—might itself be suspect as a national urban policy goal. Economic revitalization of urban neighborhoods, the key assumption implicit in virtually every urban aid program from 1960 to the present, passes, as Nicholas Lemann (1994) acidly observed, "every test but one, the reality test." Lemann went on to explain that economic revitalization efforts

> are popular among all the key players in antipoverty policy; they sound good; they have bipartisan appeal; they are based on tax breaks rather than spending and so are easier to pass. The only problem is so far they haven't worked— which creates a larger problem.
>
> Think for a minute about *why* most people believe that the Great Society was a failure. What's the evidence? It is the enduring physical and social deterioration of poor inner-city neighborhoods. The Government promised to turn these places around, and instead they got worse; ipso facto, Government can't do anything right."

As we shall argue later in this chapter, Lemann's criticism is correct, but only partially so. Washington has failed repeatedly at large-scale and dramatic attempts to physically and economically revitalize neighborhoods, particularly poor inner-city ghetto neighborhoods. The LCAA community action program from the War on Poverty is, unfortunately, a case in point. That is not to say, however, that all urban programs are *necessarily* failures, or even that all economic revitalization programs are implicitly bound to fail. Rather, again as we shall argue throughout this chapter, only that neighborhood and economic revitalization programs directed primarily from Washington, D.C.—creating or perpetuating, in effect, a vast reservation system of *Washington's cities* micro-managed from the nation's capital—have failed since the early urban renewal and CAP days, and continue to fail until the present day.[4]

To anticipate a later argument, just because Washington has been unsuccessful in dramatic economic revitalization of America's neighborhoods and cities does not mean that such cities and neighborhoods cannot be revitalized successfully on a more limited scale by public-private partnerships, foundation-funded demonstration projects, and local community development corporations (CDCs). Indeed, the evidence of the 1980s and 1990s, particularly in the area of providing housing for the poor, is precisely that CDCs are so successful that the "implications of an existing replicable formula for running subsidized housing for the poor are immense" (Lemann, 1994: 54). The key success story in revitalizing neighborhoods in American cities in the 1980s and 1990s has, in fact, been the progress of hundreds of local economic development corporations—often funded in whole or part by private foundations—such as the New Community Corporation in Newark, New Jersey. Founded in the 1980s, New Community Corporation currently provides 2,500 housing units to over 6,000 low-income Newark residents; a large supermarket, day care, nursing home, and job search facilities; a restaurant; and even a newspaper for area residents. Paradoxically, CDCs, the key urban policy success story of the 1980s and early 1990s (Vidal; 1992;

Keating, 1994a), were available as an option for national policymakers as early as the 1960s, but remained a policy path, regrettably, not taken.

A 1960s Policy Path Not Taken: CDCs and the Economic Development Corporation Approach

As noted earlier, the CDC economic development corporation policy option was available to national urban planners as early as the 1966 demise of the CAP program, but early signs of the success of local development corporations were largely ignored at that time and during the 1967 rise of the next national urban policy approach, Model Cities. The economic development urban aid approach lost national prominence and visibility with the 1968 assassination in Los Angeles of its major proponent, then-presidential candidate and U.S. Senator Robert F. Kennedy (D-NY). Kennedy, who had supported an early CAP prototype program, the President's Council on Juvenile Delinquency, as Attorney General, later criticized CAP and the successor Model Cities program, advocating instead an early CDC prototype program, the Bedford-Stuyvesant Restoration Corporation.

This early support for the CDC approach was little recognized and not enacted as national urban policy. Instead, policymakers opted for the final urban antipoverty effort of the Johnson Administration—Model Cities, which was designed to significantly include local elected officials and members of Congress and to eliminate some of the "maximum feasible misunder-standings" of the CAA-CAP administrative format. Unfortunately, unlike the ignored CDC approach, Model Cities approached America's cities as *Washington's* cities—cities and neighborhoods to be socially and economically revitalized via micro-management from the nation's capital. Thus Model Cities contained the seeds of its own demise; it simultaneously raised unrealis-tic expectations about revitalizing entire neighborhoods and American cities while continuing with prevailing but unrealistic assumptions that neighbor-hood economic revitalization, large or small, could successfully be managed and directed from the nation's capital.

The Demise of CAP and the Rise of Model Cities

Even leaving aside the unrealistic hopes for neighborhood revitalization that have accompanied most urban programs from CAP to the present, the addi-tional problems of bottom-up instead of top-down and comprehensively co-ordinated but, in fact, "maximum feasible misunderstanding," spelled doom for the LBJ CAP approach. Given the array of forces that quickly began to oppose the LBJ CAP urban aid approach, national urban policy, once more, was poised for a dramatic shift in direction. And change it did with the advent of the Model Cities program.

With Congress, the United States Conference of Mayors, LCAAs, and a Presidential Task Force on Urban Problems (1965–66) all voicing dissat-isfaction with the CAP approach, Congress attempted a targeted urban aid approach, the Model Cities program. Created in the Model Cities Act of 1967, Model Cities grew quickly to encompass $1 billion in grants for over sixty cities by 1967, a program that Congress ensured would be required by law to be run by a local agency supervised by local elected officials, and in which local officials had few strings on how the money, intended to aid poverty neighborhoods and residents, needed to be spent.

Model Cities suffered from several flaws. A key structural problem inherent in its design was the effort to continue the strong earlier CAP emphasis on community and neighborhood participation and involvement and, at the same time, restore the legitimate overseer role played by elected and appointed local officials. If anything, this structural unity of opposites (empowerment of local community groups and individual citizens and the restoration of supervisory and patronage interests of local elected officials) was to produce even more "maximum feasible misunderstanding" than had been witnessed in the earlier CAP programs. Second, Congress itself compromised the design of the Model Cities intervention strategy in the process of enacting the enabling legislation. Originally designed as a highly selective, highly targeted intervention program aimed at only a small number of high-need cities that presented the worst examples of urban decay—an intervention designed in these limited cases to "completely eliminate blight in the designated area, and to replace it with attractive, economical shelter" (Haar, 1975: 296)—Congress, expanded the program to allow virtually every city in the United States to apply for Model Cities grants. With $1 billion stretched out over more than sixty cities, and with built-in tensions between citizen participation and significant program and patronage supervision by elected officials, Model Cities was fatally flawed as an urban aid intervention strategy.

True, in the first three years of Model Cities, Congress did appropriate $1 billion dollars for projects and services to assist the poor, but cities had considerable leeway on such expenditures. The Model City money spent by some locales on specific services and improvements to poverty neighborhoods was counterbalanced by the choices of elected officials in other jurisdictions, instead, to spend the funds for larger citywide services such as "schools, police, sewage, and sanitation" (Herson & Bolland, 1991: 305). As Herson and Bolland noted, despite the small number of scholars who have argued that Model Cities was a success (Levitan & Tagart, 1976, 1981; Levitan, 19; Lockhart, 1986), most authorities view Model Cities as a program that "promised much but delivered relatively little" (1990: 305). In sum, "Urban services were assisted, and targeted areas were improved. But slums remained slums, and the quality of life in inner cities was not much altered" (Herson & Bolland, 1991: 305).

The lack of a clear urban aid success story to show for the Model Cities effort doomed the Model Cities approach, as did the unresolved combination of both enthusiasm for and antipathy toward citizen participation at the heart of the Model Cities program design. David Caputo has argued that both the Model Cities and the earlier CAP programs displayed an inability of Congressional representatives to decide whether poverty-neighborhood residents and elected city officials ought to be bound by a *negotiating* or an *expert* relationship:

> In a negotiating relationship, the participants (experts and citizens) attempt to reach a compromise acceptable to both sides. If such a compromise cannot be reached, then subsequent policy decisions cannot be made because of the stalemate. In a consulting relationship, the expert requests information from and considers the views of the members of the affected group, but is not bound to abide by their requests or information. (Caputo, 1976: 212)

The Model Cities legislation attempted to have it both ways, to create extensive citizen participation by mandating citizen involvement on decision-making boards but also requiring the involvement of experienced elected local officials and trained city-planning staffs. In the end, the Rube Goldberg–style, top-heavy, citizen-inclusion/citizen-exclusion Model Cities framework proved unworkable.

Federal-Urban Policy in the LBJ Years: A Summary

The LBJ national urban policy record is a study in contrasts. Spectacularly unsuccessful with large-scale direct urban aid programs such as LCAA/CAP and Model Cities, the LBJ years were nonetheless significant for the creation of Head Start and successful large-scale indirect aid programs such as food stamps, the School Lunch program, Medicare, Medicaid, the Civil Rights Act of 1964, and the Voting Rights Act of 1965. Thus, one of the ironies of analyzing the Lyndon Johnson domestic record in terms of aid to American cities is that spectacular large-scale failures were mixed with equally spectacular large-scale successes.

It is worth noting that the LBJ administration did have another urban policy success story, one easy to overlook in light of the more high-profile urban programs of the time such as LCAA/CAP and Model Cities. In 1965 and 1966 Congress and the LBJ administration helped set the stage for metropolitan area-wide governance and the contemporary New Regionalism debate (analyzed in Chapter 3). The Johnson administration had slightly more success mandating government cooperation than mandating citizen participation. The passage in 1965 of Section 710(g) as an amendment to the Housing Act of 1954, and the passage the next year of Section 204 of the Model Cities Act, encouraged the creation of Councils of Government (COGs)—regional cooperative associations of elected officials and local governments seeking to establish a regional framework for analyzing and, eventually, governing the key shared concerns of a large metropolitan area.

The 1965 Amendment to the Housing Act attempted via federal planning grants to expand regional cooperation and professional staffing and resources for COGs. The 1966 Model Cities legislation went further by requiring that either a state or *regional* agency must comment on and judge "the application's consistency with regional planning goals" for over thirty federal grant and loan programs through which local jurisdictions might apply to Washington for federal monies (Ross, Levine, & Stedman, 1991: 293). While the authority of COGs (until the "Ice Tea" ICSTA Highway Act of the 1990s) was to remain voluntary, consultative and advisory in nature, COGs did multiply in number as a result of the LBJ-era encouragement, growing from 126 COGs nationally in 1963 to 253 in 1973, and over 600 in the 1980s (Ross, Levine, & Stedman, 1991: 293).

In terms of direct aid programs to American cities, the 1965–66 emphasis on regional cooperation via an expanded COG network and the widely popular Head Start program, established in the Economic Opportunity Act of 1964, remain, today, as the primary successful direct urban aid legacy of the Lyndon Johnson years.

Cutting Poverty in Half: The Single Greatest Indirect Urban Aid Success of the LBJ Years

In fairness to the larger Lyndon Johnson social welfare policy record, it should be emphasized that while direct urban aid programs such as Head Start and an increased proliferation of COGs resulting from the Model Cities legislation may seem a slight national urban policy legacy when contrasted with the rising and later falling expectations that accompanied much-heralded Great Society urban aid programs such as CAP and Model Cities, in the largest sense they are not. The totality of the LBJ-era urban and policy package—combining both the direct and indirect aid programs—was staggeringly successful. (The debate about this success continues in some quarters [see Murray, 1984], versus the compelling refutation by Lockhout, 1986; as well as Schwarz and Vogly, [1992]; and Jencks, 1992).

Lyndon Johnson presided over a period in American history when official U.S. poverty levels were reduced by nearly half, dropping 45% from an inherited high tide of 22.2% of Americans in poverty in 1960 to a low of 12.1% by the time that LBJ left office in January of 1969. No modern American president, with the possible exception of Franklin Delano Roosevelt—with his WPA and related "alphabet soup" Great Depression–era anti-poverty programs—can match such a record.

By way of comparison, bear in mind the example of presidents since LBJ. Despite the example of Johnson's success in reducing poverty, *no president since Johnson has succeeded in reducing poverty by more than 1.5 percent.* LBJ's accomplishment in reducing poverty by 45 percent is underlined by a quick accounting of the lack of success in fighting poverty of presidents who succeeded Johnson. For example, poverty declined by .7 percent in the Nixon years from 1968 to 1974, increased .2 percent under the brief presidency of Gerald Ford, increased 2.4 percent under President Carter, decreased by 1.2 percent under President Reagan, increased 2.3 percent in the Bush presidency, and decreased 1.3 percent from 1993 to 1995 in the first term of the Clinton administration. Thus, while the legacy of successful direct urban aid policies such as Head Start and COGs under LBJ looms surprisingly small, the result of his indirect urban aid package was an was an unprecedented decrease in American poverty during his administration unparalleled from the close of World War II to the present day.

NIXON AND NEW FEDERALISM (NEW FEDERALISM I)

New Federalism (Reagan & Sanzone, 1981) is the key Nixon administration contribution to national urban policymaking. The key to New Federalism was the division of the country into ten federal regional councils (FRCs) in 1969, and the passage of Revenue Sharing in 1972. Announced in Executive Order 11647, "Standard Federal Regions," the FRC decision divided the country into ten regional councils, with each FRC located in a large city within the region (e.g., in Boston, San Francisco, Seattle, Albuquerque, or Chicago), and was only partially successful. The federal regional councils languished under President Carter and were eventually disbanded by executive order by President Reagan in February of 1983. Federal regional offices for various federal departments such as the U.S. Department of Housing and Urban Development (HUD) still exist in cities such as San Francisco, but the attempt to return power to regions of one or more states, and to devolve national spending, oversight, and policymaking authority from Washington, D.C., to these regional centers was, in the end, a failure.

The Rise and Fall of Revenue Sharing (1972–86)

Revenue Sharing (RS) was formally introduced by President Nixon in August 1969 and enacted after much debate and modification by Congress as the State and Local Fiscal Assistance Act of 1972. According to Nixon, RS was to be a key aspect of the second American revolution; the state and local governments would be provided with the fiscal resources they needed to meet and, it was hoped, solve their pressing problems (Caputo, 1976: 144). The key to the second revolution was to be the return of both local and regional decision-making authority via FRCs, and the return of tax dollars from Washington, D.C., to the local units of government. Prior to its enactment in 1972, RS had been discussed in policy circles in Washington, D.C., with prominent advocates in both the Democratic and Republican parties. Walter Heller, Chairman of the Council of Economic Advisors under President Kennedy, was influential in shaping the early conceptualization of RS. According to him, the federal government, because of its income-taxing capability, would have a budgetary surplus at the conclusion of the Vietnam War (this foreshadows, of course, a later discussion of how to spend the "Peace Dividend" following the close of the Cold War), whereas state and local governments would continue to have considerable difficulties meeting their financial responsibilities because of an inadequate resource base and the unavailability of the tax mechanisms (especially the income tax) necessary to raise funds. Heller advocated that the federal government "share" a portion of the revenue it received from income taxes with the states and localities and permit these localities to decide how to spend the funds and what additional resources they would need to meet their needs. The Heller proposal assumes the existence of a three-tiered federal system consisting of national, state and local levels of government as well as the availability to the local governments of the necessary revenues (Caputo, 1976: 145).

Heller's proposal, based on the notion that the federal government would have surplus federal revenues following the Vietnam War, and that a percentage of this surplus should be returned to the states with few or no strings attached, continued to be debated during and after the war. Due to the prolonged timeframe of American involvement in the Vietnam War and a host of congressionally enacted social programs, the projected surpluses originally envisioned by Heller never materialized.[5] Nevertheless, Revenue Sharing was eventually enacted in October 1972 as the State and Local Fiscal Assistance Act, allocating $30.2 billion to state and local governmental units for a five-year period ending in 1977 (Dommel, 1980; Reagan & Sanzone, 1981). RS was extended in 1976 with the support of both President Gerald Ford when he ran for reelection, and his opponent, Georgia Governor Jimmy Carter. Extended for a second life during the 1976 presidential election season and allocated $26 billion over a three-and-one-half-year period, the new lease on life for RS was purposely set by Congress to expire during the next presidential election cycle in 1980. Renewed again, despite increased opposition in Congress, for three years (until 1983) in 1980, this time the money for the state share of RS was not appropriated. Extended again in 1983 for three years (until 1986), RS was eliminated by a combination of a hostile President Reagan, Democratic leaders in Congress, and a coalition of "deficit hawks" that combined to kill the RS program.

Contradictory Studies on RS Expenditures

Although an ambitious national study indicated that RS was widely supported by both the general public and by 95 percent of the city managers and mayors in the United States (Caputo & Cole, 1974: 108–116), RS became controversial, both in Congress and in policy analysis circles for several reasons. Some states were showing fiscal surpluses rather than deficits in the early 1980s, and this put pressure on Congress to eliminate the state component of RS—a move with which Congress agreed in 1980. Second, several academic studies, including a national study of RS expenditures by the Brookings Institution (Caputo & Cole, 1975; Lovell & Korey, 1975; Juster, 1976; Nathan & Adams, 1977), indicated that local governments spent most of their RS monies on existing programs. Richard Nathan and Charles Adams found that local governments spent slightly more than 50 percent of their RS funds on new programs, capital expenditures that were new, or pay increases for local government employees, choosing instead to use the funds to lower existing taxes or maintain old programs.

States were even less innovative with RS funds, spending only 37 percent of RS monies on new programs, capital expenditures, or salary/benefits increases. A second study found that cities were spending 60 percent of their RS funds for existing programs in such areas as police and fire protection, environmental measures, streets, and parks and recreation (Caputo, 1976: 146). Two further studies by the General Accounting Office (GAO) in 1974 and the National Science Foundation (NSF) in 1976 found that capital expenditures were higher than reported by the Brookings and Cole/Taebel studies, and that local jurisdictions were far more likely to use RS money to maintain or expand existing programs than, somewhat more cynically perhaps, to use the funds to reduce or stabilize taxes.

Given these contradictory findings on how local jurisdictions were or were not spending RS money, and given the outright hostility to RS that had developed at the Congressional and Reagan White House levels, RS fell victim to the congressional budgetary axe. While not a major blow to states that, since 1983, had seen virtually no RS monies flow to their level of government, the demise of RS for cities was another matter entirely. In the estimation of one Urban Institute expert, by 1979 RS money had grown to comprise 4 percent of all city revenues in the United States.

Revenue Sharing Revisionism: A Contrarian View

The conventional view of RS is that, as an urban intervention and aid program, it was problematic at best or, at worst, fatally flawed. The Brookings and Caputo/Taebel studies suggest, as noted, that local governmental jurisdictions were slow to fund new or innovative programs with RS money. Second, the Brookings study demonstrated that rich and poor jurisdictions alike were aided by RS funds that were dispersed on a per-capita basis rather than on the basis of the demonstrated *need* of various jurisdictions. Cities such as Oakland, Newark, Chicago, Detroit, and St. Louis received RS funding, but so, too, did wealthier locales such as Scarsdale, New York, and Palm Beach, Florida (Ross & Levine, 1996: 419).

Third, since RS was a "no-strings" program, Congress had little say in how cities ultimately decided to spend RS funds. This incurred the wrath of members of Congress, who quickly grew hostile to a program many within the Washington, D.C., beltway began to view as a runaway "Santa Claus" program—the implication being that no one, would have the courage, especially close to election time, to "shoot Santa Claus" (read: the RS program).

Indeed, in an instructive, if hardly scientific anecdote that may capture the flavor of the times in terms of hostility to RS, this author was once standing in a vending line behind a former senior member of Congress. Growing frustrated that the cola machine could not sort out his Susan B. Anthony quarter-sized coin from other 25-cent pieces and give him his expected can of soda, the former congressperson fumed: "That damned Susan Anthony quarter was my second-worst vote in Congress!" Being a trained political scientist, this author naturally felt obliged to inquire what the Congress member considered to be his *worst* single vote during his long tenure on the Hill. "Revenue sharing," he answered, without a moment's hesitation.

That Congressional hostility to RS, in this case years after the program had been axed by Congress, illustrates a strength of RS. RS gave funds to local officials who were free to choose spending paths—liberal, conservative, and in-between, unsupervised or mandated by Washington, D.C. While it is true that many jurisdictions used the funds for existing programs and not for charting new and innovative policy and programmatic waters, it is also true that—as was the case later with the block grant programs following RS—local decision-makers acted in this fashion, in part, because of the mixed signals that Washington, D.C., sent out concerning the short lifespan that RS was likely to experience. As Ross and Levine note, "Local governments were especially fearful that Congress would terminate the program, leaving them responsible for the new social services and cost" (1996: 419). Indeed, in *The Contested City*, John Mollenkopf (1983) shows that cities were right to fear such a result. Cities that spent RS and subsequent funding for senior and neighborhood programs, and then experienced the loss of such federal funds later, ended up not with revitalized cities so much as highly politicized and *contested* cities. "Rational" behavior in such circumstances, from the viewpoint of local politicians, is likely to be a distinct preference for existing and known political programs, interest groups, and expenditures. Blaming cities for "safe" and non-innovative expenditures under RS is hardly a definitive criticism of RS: Cities acted rationally in what proved to be a short-term augmentation environment. Whether cities *might* have behaved differently if the program had been longer-term and fiscally secure, and whether the RS program would have been more effective if counter-cyclical, needs-based elements favoring areas with, for example, high unemployment and poverty populations, had been included with the per-capita formula grant allocation method chosen by Congress is difficult to determine. What is worth determining, and what we shall raise as a viable policy option in Chapter 6, is reconsidering a second round of RS this time a program designed for the needs of both the late 1990s and for the next century. The RS plan discussed in Chapter 6 proposes putting in place a round of *New Revenue Sharing* that includes both sound (and revenue-neutral) multi-year funding and counter-cyclical, needs-based eligibility criteria. RS as designed in the Nixon administration and eliminated by the Regan administration had program design deficiencies but, and this is worth emphasizing, *only during the RS years did cities in the United States receive a percentage of the federal domestic budget that approximates the rough percentage of Americans living in metropolitan areas.* Without RS, this percentage of assistance to cities once again began to decline, and has remained below the mid-to-late RS years ever since. RS, in the opinion of this author, is the only programmatically neutral, bipartisan mechanism for increasing aid to America's metropolitan areas that is acceptable to an American public and president largely suburban in their outlook, and an American Senate that is distinctly rural in a majority of its voting makeup.[6]

Life After Revenue Sharing: The Block Grant Approach

Congress modified the earlier RS approach by creating two *block grant* programs—the 1973 Comprehensive Employment and Training Act (CETA) and the 1974 Housing and Community Development Act (CDBG). CETA consolidated several existing Great Society job training and work experience programs into one large "block" program, loosening the "strings" associated with the earlier programs and placing local elected and administrative officials in charge of local program decisions. In a departure from grants-in-aid programs, local jurisdictions were not required to provide local "matching funds" for CETA or CDBG block-grant activities. Herson & Bolland (1990: 307) have argued that cities used CETA funds to subsidize traditional citywide services rather than concentrate on low-income projects and programs, and that cities using CETA funds tended, with increased local discretion, to shift employment programs away from job training to public works projects, maintenance work, and clerical assistance in city hall and city departments.

The 1974 CDBG program "blocked" seven preexisting categorical grants-in-aid programs, including Urban Renewal, Model Cities, Water and Sewer, Open Space, rehabilitation grant programs, and programs for aiding in the construction of public facilities (Marshall & Waste, 1977: Herson & Bolland, 1990: 307). The CDBG program, dubbed "Special Revenue Sharing" by some at the time, consolidated all of the foregoing programs into one block grant that, in a New Federalism victory for the Nixon White House, was distributed automatically to all cities with populations over 50,000 that completed a CDBG application demonstrating that "plans for using the funds were consistent with city needs" (Herson & Bolland, 1990: 306). Cities with populations below 50,000 were not automatically entitled to CDBG funds but, instead, were required to compete for 20 percent of the funds set aside as "discretionary" funding.

CDBG was a mixed policy victory for the Nixon White House (Nenno, 1974; Lovell & Korey, 1975; Frej & Specht, 1976; DeLeon & LeGates, 1976; Marshall & Waste, 1977). The new Act did "block" seven of the earlier categorical grants-in-aid programs administered separately up until 1974 by HUD. Second, by changing such funding from competitive grants-in-aid to automatic formula entitlement grants, the White House had altered the political equation of which jurisdictions would receive the lion's share of the earlier categorical grant funding.

This reconfiguration of federal grants-in-aid versus block-grant winners and losers was literally phased-in by members in Congress representing cities then-receiving large amounts of grants-in-aid monies with a "hold harmless" provision. This provision insured that during the first three program years of CDBG, cities that were receiving more HUD grants-in-aid totals than the dollar figures they would be scheduled to receive under the new CDBG formula would "receive a grant equal to the annual average of their prior HUD grants; but in the fourth year this hold harmless payment (the difference between the annual average of prior HUD grants and the grant formula) will be reduced by one-third, and in the fifth year it will be reduced by two-thirds" (Marshall & Waste, 1977: 4).

Block grants allowed local jurisdictions more freedom in determining how funds were spent than in earlier categorical grants-in-aid programs, but Congress still attached "strings," including a requirement that CDBG monies be spent on low- and moderate-income communities, and that neighborhood residents in affected communities participate in and be consulted on CDBG planning and spending (Keating, 1976). Thus, CDBG and CETA were, as is often the case with the legislative process, mixed legislative victories. Nixon and the congressional Republicans had secured a New Federalism blocking of several earlier Great Society programs, and redistributed the community development "pie," sending far more, if in many cases far smaller, "pieces" out to local jurisdictions in the United States (Hudson, 1980). For their part, congressional Democrats and advocates of larger urban constituencies had managed to "phase-in" CDBG, to keep some programs out of the block-grant approach altogether, and to attach "strings" requiring citizen participation and expenditures in low-income areas.

Current Status of CDBG and Nixon's New Federalism Approach

Compared to the earlier General Revenue Sharing programs, CDBG (Special Revenue Sharing) proved more popular and durable. CDBG has emerged over time as the "number one urban aid program" in the United States (Ross & Levine, 1996: 420). Popularity and funding levels of CDBG increased from 1974 until 1996, when the program faced its first major challenge from a budget-conscious Congress that, in one possible scenario, had threatened to cut CDBG funding levels in half, from $4.6 billion to $2.3 billion.

CDBG was a mixed policy victory for the Nixon White House (Nenno, 1974; Frieden & Kaplan, 1976; Frej & Specht, 1976; DeLeon & LeGates, 1976; Marshall & Waste, 1977; Nathan & Domel, 1978). The new Act chipped away at Great Society programs by "blocking" seven of the earlier grants-in-aid; freed-up local officials in the use of federal urban aid funds; reduced the oversight role of HUD professionals managing the heretofore grants-in-aid programs; and democratized the distribution of HUD urban aid monies by changing categorical and competitive grants-in-aid to automatic formula grants. In this sense, CDBG, or Special Revenue Sharing, decentralized federal spending for cities and local jurisdictions and gave a vote of confidence to local elected and appointed officials in allowing them to determine how such funds were to be spent. In this sense, New Federalism I, of the Nixon years, is very different from New Federalism II, of the Reagan years, in which General Revenue Sharing was dismantled, and in which federal aid to local jurisdictions was reduced to a level unprecedented in the period from World War II to the present day. The Nixon administration opposed the programmatically liberal Great Society programs enacted by Congress in the Lyndon Johnson years and administered primarily by federal officials at HUD in Washington, D.C., and it attempted to return both aid and discretion to local elected officials. The Reagan administration held an implacable ideological hostility to most federal government spending in general, *even when such spending clearly was popular with local elected officials, and even when control over the direction of such spending had been returned to local officials via the block-grant process.*

Indirect Aid to Cities during the Nixon Years

In Nixon's major direct urban aid program, RS, cities were the indirect recipient of assistance due to the passage of environmental programs. The Nixon administration and the chief environmental aide to President Nixon, John Erlichman, the head of Nixon's Domestic Council, were key players in securing the passage of Clean Air and Clean Water Acts. While both the Clean Air and Clean Water Acts were modest legislative compromises requiring reconfiguration and legislative amendment as recently as FY 1995 to 1996, American cities owe the Nixon administration a real debt for placing the issues of clean air and clean drinking water on the front burner of national policymakers. That more was not accomplished for cities in those years, and that even more progress has not been made on important environmental issues of the day, has much to do with the rapid fall from power of the Nixon administration in the wake of the Watergate Crisis (ca. 1972–74), and the tentative use of the new Domestic Council policy instrument by the Nixon administration.

The Nixon/Ford Years–Policy Paths Not Taken: Increased Use of the Domestic Council and the National Urban Policy Report

However different the New Federalisms of Presidents Nixon and Reagan, both administrations favored decentralization and devolution of federal-local programs and aid. In between the Nixon and Reagan administrations was a brief effort to recentralize block grants, and to articulate, in broad-brush terms, one coherent "urban national policy." The mechanism for creating a unified urban national policy had actually been laid earlier in the Nixon administration, when Nixon created the Domestic Council—headed by White House Advisor, former Seattle-area environmentalist and, later, convicted Watergate felon, John Erlichman.

The role of the Domestic Council was, in Nixon's view, to place the topics of cities and domestic issues, generally, on the same plane as foreign policy. Meant to be analogous to the National Security Council and the role of the National Security Advisor (who daily briefs the President on national security and foreign-policy issues), the Domestic Council, it was hoped, would raise the visibility of domestic and urban issues to the fore of the Nixon presidency. With the advent of the Watergate Crisis and the subsequent resignation of President Nixon in 1974, the Domestic Council approach fell from favor, and the potential of the council was never realized. Had it been utilized to the height of its potential, the Domestic Council could have proved an effective instrument in coordinating federal-local aid and intervention strategies.

A second Nixon/Ford era missed chance to coordinate and articulate urban policy arises from the Housing and Urban Development Act of 1970. The 1970 HUD Act required that each administration compile a "National Urban Policy Report" that spells out the state of American cities, and the plans and programs that the administration plans to put in place to address the concerns of America's urban areas. The urban-policy reporting was largely ignored by the Nixon/Ford administrations (Kaplan & James, 1990), but President Carter was elected in 1976, having "promised the nation's mayors that he would be the first president ever to formulate an explicit national urban policy" (Ross & Levine, 1996: 422). It was a promise that Carter would prove unable to keep.

CARTER, NATIONAL URBAN POLICY, AND THE NEW PARTNERSHIP (1976–80)

President Carter entered office with three urban goals. First, he wanted to shift urban-aid funds from the universal automatic funding available under CDBG to targeted spending for economic development and increased employment. Second, the Carter administration was committed to the creation of a coherent and unified urban national policy. Third, Carter wanted to reverse the New Federalism decentralization of HUD's overseeing responsibilities, granting HUD officials the authority to supervise and refuse the spending plans of local jurisdictions that sought to avoid spending CDBG funds on low- and moderate-income programs and neighborhoods.

To fulfill his campaign promise to create the nation's first-ever national urban policy, Carter moved quickly to create a working group, the intergovernmental Urban and Regional Policy Group (URPG), that was to produce "A New Partnership to Preserve America's Communities" (The President's National Urban Policy Report Washington, D.C.: GAO - August 1978). The Carter Urban National Policy proposed several big-ticket urban programs, including: (1) a $400-million grant to states to encourage the development of state-level urban strategies and intervention programs; (2) a proposed National Development Bank, a government agency aimed at redeveloping economically distressed urban areas with grants, loans, and financial assistance to firms expanding or relocating in distressed areas (Ross & Levine, 1996: 423); (3) a $1-billion Labor-Intensive Public Works Program aimed at job creation and infrastructure repair in America's cities; (4) a Targeted

Employment Tax Credit program allowing employers a $2,000 deduction for hiring economically at-risk persons aged 18 to 24; and, finally, (5) an additional $2 billion in Supplemental Fiscal Assistance was targeted for a two-year assistance program for economically distressed, high-unemployment cities (Ross & Levine, 1996: 423; Ames et al., 1992: 207).

The Short Life of the Carter National Urban Policy

The Carter attempt at a coherent national urban policy was short-lived. With the exception of the Targeted Employment Tax Credit, the Carter Urban Aid package was rejected by Congress, and, facing a difficult—and ultimately unsuccessful—reelection campaign, the Carter administration began a strategic retreat from direct programs to aid cities generally, and from a unified national urban policy specifically. Faced with a hostile Congress and a strain within the administration itself that was "ambivalent toward urban areas," the Carter administration shifted ground away from an urban policy toward a "national economic policy in which all cities would presumably benefit" (Ames et al., 1992: 423). As noted earlier in this chapter, Congress has since World War II to the present seen increased growth and influence from Sunbelt states—states *south* of an imaginary line drawn from Richmond, Virginia to San Jose, California—and increasing influence in the last four presidential elections from suburban rather than urban areas.

Given the strength of suburban and Sunbelt interests in Congress, the Carter administration programs were defeated, except for a modest program supervised by the Economic Development Administration (EDA). Even this program—originally aimed at "distressed" urban areas by the Carter urban policy architects—was expanded by Congressional bargaining "to the point that approximately 90 percent of the nation's population lived in areas defined as 'distressed' and hence eligible to apply for assistance under the legislation" (Ross & Levine, 1996: 424).

Recentralization and UDAGs: Carter Urban Policy Successes

President Carter was more successful with the Washington bureaucracy than with Congress in achieving control of the flow of money and aid to urban areas. Using the considerable powers of the presidency, Carter ordered the Department of Housing and Urban development (HUD) to monitor the use of CDBG funds, insuring that 75 percent of such funds during his administration went to low-income areas. Second, Carter thwarted Sunbelt and Southern interests in Congress by, again, using a presidential directive to HUD, shifting increased amounts of block-grant funds to cities in the Northeast and Midwest (Ames et al., 1992: 207).

The Carter administration did succeed in enacting a targeted and "high strings" urban aid program called the Urban Development Action Grant (UDAG). UDAG, enacted in 1977 and eliminated in the Reagan administration, targeted federal urban aid funds with an "only if" proviso (Derthick,

1978), requiring that local jurisdictions prove that (1) the area to be aided was economically distressed; (2) the local government was engaged in a public-private partnership to alleviate conditions in the affected area that was deemed likely to succeed; and (3) the locally designed intervention project(s) in question could succeed "only if" federal UDAG funds were given to the project(s) in question. Thus, the program epitomized the New Partnership recentralized approach to aid that characterized the brief Carter administration. Funds could only go to distressed areas, only in cases where Carter administration goals would be met—in this case distressed area intervention *and* the encouragement of public-private partnerships in cities. Even then, funds would be limited or highly targeted via UDAG rather than widely dispersed—in the case of the congressionally modified EDA grant programs— or distributed on an automatic entitlement basis—in the Nixon/Ford era CDBG programs (Rich, 1992).

The Late Carter Administration Retreat from the Cities: Paving the Way for Reagan/Bush Era Attacks on Urban Programs

The recentralization under HUD and CDBG in the Carter administration, and the increased funds available to cities in the highly targeted UDAG approach, represent urban policy "wins" for the Carter administration. Though limited in his success, Carter was able to deliver on his New Partnership efforts to combine elements of a effort to revive Johnson's Great Society Creative Federalism approach with that of Nixon's more decentralized New Federalism (Ross & Levine, 1996: 422). The New Federalism II of the Reagan administration following that of Carter sought not to integrate and synthesize earlier approaches to urban aid but, rather, to dramatically decrease federal spending and programmatic assistance to America's cities.

The retreat from aiding America's cities that reached a historic low-tide level in the Reagan administration was anticipated in part by two developments late in the Carter administration. First, as noted earlier, the Carter administration gradually adopted a stance that aiding cities *per se* was less important than aiding the national economy; a theme that would be echoed and enlarged upon in the subsequent Reagan years. Second, President Carter's own Commission for a National Agenda for the Eighties (1980) concluded that "urban issues were best forgotten" (Wood, 1995: 137). Reminiscent of language that would find its way into an early draft of Ronald Reagan's 1982 *National Urban Policy Report*, the Commission concluded: "Contrary to conventional wisdom, cities are not permanent . . . an oft-noted 'urban renaissance' within cities, while enriching and laudable, seems not to be taking place on anything like the scale suggested in popular commentary . . . we forget that cities, like all living things, change" (Wood, 1995: 137). This late–Carter administration conclusion that people, not places—and national economies rather than local economies—were the proper focus of national social policy paved the way for a similar, if more enthusiastic, set of diminished national-local aid polices in the Reagan and Bush administrations.

REAGAN AND NEW FEDERALISM (NEW FEDERALISM II)

Although President Reagan labeled his domestic program of budget cuts and new programs for local governments as *New Federalism*, we will refer to the Reagan federal-local aid variant as *New Federalism II* or *Reaganomics* to avoid confusion with the earlier Nixon administration philosophy and approach. The Reagan New Federalism II federal-local approach had five elements that had an impact on cities and local jurisdictions. (1) a basic attempt to lower the scale of government expenditures across the board; (2) an ill-fated federal-local "swap," in which the federal government would have assumed responsibility for Medicaid while yielding to the states the responsibility for the primary federal welfare program—Aid to Families with Dependent Children (AFDC)—as well as a proposal to "turnback" to the states over "forty federal education, transportation, community development, and social service programs, which would be financed by a trust fund of $28 billion for three years, and then federal support would be phased out by 1991" (Cole & Caputo, 1981: 61); (3) a combination of new urban programs and initiatives, including the Job Training Partnership Act (JTPA), support for the Kemp-Garcia Urban Enterprise Zones legislation, and a call for increased "privatization" of public functions and tasks with private contractors and service deliverers (Savas, 1982); (4) the combining or blocking of several federal-local programs and the elimination of several urban programs, including the Comprehensive Employment Training Act (CETA), several other Special Revenue Sharing (SRS) programs, and an additional measure conceived by the Reagan administration as part of the Reaganomics package; (5) the enactment in 1986 of the Gramm-Rudman Hollings Act, a measure that attempted to eliminate the federal deficit by 1991 by requiring cuts in the federal budget ranging from $38–50 billion per year beginning in federal fiscal year 1986.[7]

BUDGET CUTS, DEFICITS, AND BLOCK GRANTS: THE REAGAN/BUSH RETREAT FROM THE CITIES

With the exception of the ill-fated "swap" of federal–state/local responsibilities on Medicaid and AFDC, the Reagan administration was remarkably successful in achieving the key administration goal of a reduction in levels of spending for social services in general, and city aid and grants-in-aid programs in particular. Indeed, the Reagan and Bush administrations were so successful that one critic charged that Washington "abandoned cities" in this period (Caraley, 1992). Caraley's charge, although harsh, may, in fact, be accurate. Consider three telling examples of such "abandonment." First, in the 1982 *President's National Urban Policy Report*, the Reagan administration announced a retreat from urban aid and economic development programs in favor of encouraging cities to adjust to the changed realities of the then-downturning American economy. (Consider, for example, that in 1982 unemployment was at the highest level in the United States since the Great Depression.) As Ross and Levine note, an even earlier June 1882 draft of the Reagan administration *National Urban Policy Report* indicated the animosity toward urban aid programs clearly in a line omitted from the final draft of the report, which read: "Cities are not guaranteed eternal life" (1996: 426).

Second, consider that the Reagan administration moved quickly to reduce aid to cities and local governments, cutting federal grants to state and local governments by 14 percent in Reagan's first year in office alone. In subsequent years, he was less successful in achieving across-the-board reductions in federal-local aid but still managed to greatly reduce the flow of money from Washington, D.C., to local jurisdictions. Demetrios Caraley and Robert Wood have documented the scale of these reductions. Over a ten-year period (1980–90), the Reagan/Bush Administrations: (1) refused to spend $6 billion in public housing modernization money authorized by Congress; (2) reduced overall federal aid to cities by over 46 percent, an amount exceeding $26 billion dollars in federal-local aid; (3) trimmed the budget of HUD by 57 percent from annual expenditures in the range of $36 billion in the early 1980s to $18 billion in 1987—plunging HUD's 7-percent share of the federal budget at the start of the Reagan years to 1 percent by 1989; and (4) mounted a cynical campaign to provide thousands of low-income families with housing vouchers (during which period 62 percent of the applicants reported being unable to find available housing) while simultaneously cutting the number of units of public housing from 129,000 to 19,000 and while also decreasing the authorization for assisted-housing funding levels from $27 billion annually in 1980 to $7.5 billion annually (a 75-percent budget cut) in the final Reagan budget years (Wood, 1991: 230–31; Caraley, 1992; Ross & Levine, 1996: 426–29). One experienced urban critic, himself a former Secretary of HUD, has described the net effect of these Reagan era cuts as "plundering HUD" and "savaging the housing and neighborhood programs designed to help cities and their people" (Wood, 1991: 230).

A third element of the Reagan administration's abandonment of people programs in cities—more specifically, in the words of Anthony Downs, of creating "money-driven markets instead of demand-driven ones" (1985: 14) in center cities—was Reagan-administration support for the Banking Deregulation Act of 1983. The Deregulation Act created a tax incentive for creating a massive infusion of new office space in traditional central-city business districts, reaching a crescendo of new and largely vacant (but tax-code-encouraged) new office space in 1986 when a billion square feet of new commercial office space became available in one year in twenty-two large American cities (Leinbergen & Lockwood, 1986: 11). This Reagan administration–inspired creation of "the entrepreneurial city" to replace the older central-city business district, and the encouragement of *urban villages* and *edge villages* of concentrated office, retail, or entertainment centers—in Andres Duany's phrase, single purpose "pod developments"—quickly created a vacancy crisis, since the rapid development was, in large part due to the 1983 Banking Deregulation Act, tax-driven rather than occupant needs–driven.

Vacancy rates in the new developments quickly reflected the folly in the artificially induced Reagan office building boom. Vacancy rates of over 20 percent were average for each of the twenty-two major cities with office building booms, with some cities such as Hartford (Connecticut) experiencing highs of 28.1 percent and Dallas averaging 26.9 percent in September of 1990 (Coldwell and Banker, 1990: 29). As Robert Wood noted, as the taxpayer bill for the Reagan-era savings and loan fiasco reached upwards of a half-trillion dollars: "One metropolitan area after another was pockmarked by abandoned shopping centers and vacant upscale condominium developments that only months ago were designed as an antidote for dreary suburban lives" (Wood, 1992: 139).[8]

The 1986 Tax Reform Act modified some of the worst aspects of the earlier Banking Deregulation Act, decreasing the incentive to develop unneeded office space by eliminating tax breaks for state and local bond issues and also eliminating development-boom encouraging tax breaks for real estate equity and tax write-offs. This 1986 remedy to the 1983 legislation offered only partial relief for the worst aspects of the 1983-inspired empty-office development boom, since the 1983 Act had previously allowed for accelerated depreciation on new buildings and a short, five-year amortization rate. Robert Wood (1991: 230) has estimated that accelerated depreciation and five-year amortization alone fueled $13 billion in construction spending, while an additional $6 billion was invested in the same time period in tax-exempt state and local industrial development and housing bonds.

Reagan Administration Block Grant Successes

The Reagan era retreat from cities and federal-local aid to cities continued with the elimination of RS and UDAGs; the reduction in the number of grants-in-aid available to local jurisdictions by 21 percent, from 534 in 1981 to 422 in 1989 (Levine, 1996: 428); and the consolidation of several categorical and employment programs into the JTPA. Reagan attempted but failed to "zero out" several popular urban aid programs, including CDBG, the Economic Development Administration (EDA), and, more paradoxically given the conservative philosophy of the Reagan Administration, the Small Business Administration (SBA) but, overall, achieved significant budget reductions and consolidation of existing block grants and grants-in-aid (Perlman, 1988).

The Congressional Urban Policy Legacy in the Late Reagan Years: McKinney (1987), Moynihan (1988), and Gramm-Rudman (1985, 1987)

If the package of assistance programs to urban areas is slight in the Reagan years—and it is difficult *not* to describe the Reagan-era budget cuts as anything but a slight nod to the pressing problems in America's cities—that does not mean that Congress was inactive in the urban policy arena during the late Reagan administration. Indeed, the main urban programs during the Reagan years were congressional initiatives in the late 1980s, including the McKinney Act of 1987 and the Moynihan Welfare Reform act of 1988.

One year after New York State courts held—in a precedent-setting case, *McCain v. Koch*—that New York City had a legal obligation to house the homeless in a "timely and humane fashion," Congress enacted the Stewart B. McKinney Homeless Assistance Act of 1987, authorizing funds to assist cities and homeless services providers in funding services for the growing homeless populations in America's cities—populations estimated in the late 1980s to have ranged from 600,000 persons on any given night (Burt & Cohen, 1989) to "the startling finding that about seven million Americans experienced being homeless at least once in the latter half of the 1980s" (HUD, 1994: 17. See also Link et al., 1993; Culhane et al., 1993).[9]

From fiscal years 1987 to 1993, Congress authorized $5.6 billion (but only appropriated $4.2 billion) in coordinated homeless assistance funds under the McKinney Act. The McKinney Act was reauthorized in subsequent years by Congress, but at far lower levels. For example, McKinney-fund appropriation levels in 1992 were $1.1 billion, and in 1993, $.9 billion.

Additional attention to the plight of homeless persons and those at risk of homelessness was provided by the requirement in Title I of the National Affordable Housing Act of 1990, which required that states and local governments file an approved CHAS (Comprehensive Housing Affordability Strategy) document with HUD in order to be eligible for several HUD grant and funding programs. Briefly, the CHAS documents must address fourteen concerns grouped into three areas: (1) a *community profile* (facilities and services for the needs of the homeless population); (2) a *strategy* (investment and intervention plans of the community in question); and (3) a *one-year plan* (resources, timetable, implementation plans, and goals) for assisting homeless persons in a given jurisdiction.

The McKinney Act directed HUD to use the CDBG formula to determine which states and local jurisdictions were eligible to receive McKinney funds, and how much funding would be allocated to each jurisdiction. In addition, in fiscal year 1991, Congress earmarked a McKinney fund to be set aside for Indian tribes and Alaskan Native Villages. As a recent U.S. Government General Accounting Office (cited hereafter as GAO, June 1994: 25) noted:

> The CDBG formula is really two formulas. State and local jurisdictions are entitled to an allotment on the basis of the formula that yields the larger amount of money. Both formulas assign weights to and consider certain factors: the first includes the jurisdictions population and population below poverty level, as well as the number of housing units with one or more persons per room. The second includes the jurisdiction's population in poverty, number of housing units built before 1940, and decline in the population rate. (1994: 25)

McKinney funds go directly to either states or local jurisdictions in each state. Cities and counties not qualifying under CDBG formulae for McKinney Emergency Shelter Grant (ESG) funds may obtain sub-grants from McKinney funds provided to the state government. Each jurisdiction receiving McKinney funds must submit a CHAS document (approved by HUD) explaining the homeless needs of the jurisdiction, strategies to be used, and the one-year plan to be implemented with McKinney funds, if appropriated. Congress modified the McKinney funding process once more, in the Housing and Community Development Act of 1992, by amending the ESG program element to allow grantees (including the local shelter providers) to spend up to 10 percent of their McKinney grant monies on staffing and operations costs.

The Moynihan Welfare Reform Act of 1988

At about the same time that Congress enacted the McKinney Act, years of debate over welfare reform resulted in the passage of the Moynihan Welfare Reform Act of 1988. The centerpiece of the workfare-oriented reform was a welfare-to-work element requiring that each state put in place demonstration projects that moved a fixed percentage of their AFDC population into job training, counseling, and work requirement programs in exchange for receiving monthly AFDC monetary assistance. Despite the demonstrated failure of earlier workfare demonstration projects (in which workfare recipients rarely received more than 7 percent more job placements than did control groups simply required to search for employment on their own as a condition of receiving AFDC) (Gueron, 1986; Waste, 1987; 1989b; 1995b; Friedlander & Burtless, 1996),[10] such as the nationally recognized ET-CHOICES program in Massachusetts, the statewide "GAIN" program in California (Gueron, 1986; Gueron, Wallace, & Long, 1987; Waste, 1987; 1995b), and those in other states such as Arkansas and California as well as in local jurisdictions ranging from Baltimore to San Diego (Goldman et al., 1985), Congress mandated a workfare/work requirement in the Welfare Reform Act. The Act did contain several child care, health care, and mandatory child support benefits, which proved to be significant incremental aids to the urban poor. However, the centerpiece workfare approach merely served to fuel a later controversy resulting in the 1996 Welfare Reform Act, and subsequent controversy, during the Clinton administration.

Gramm-Rudman I and II—"Jaws I and II"

The Reagan administration retreat from the cities and the related reduction in federal-local assistance program was assisted by a mood in Congress to address the growing national deficit, and two legislative victories of congressional "deficit hawks." The Gramm-Rudman-Hollings Deficit Acts of 1985 and 1987—popularly referred to in journalistic and inside-the-beltway accounts as Gramm-Rudman, or "Jaws I" and "Jaws II"—were ultimately unsuccessful attempts by Congress to eliminate the federal budget deficit by fiscal year 1991, a schedule requiring annual reductions in the federal budget ranging from $38 to $50 billion beginning in fiscal year 1986. Gramm-Rudman–inspired budget reductions cut heavily into several domestic and urban-related programs in the 1986 to 1989 period. Efforts such as Gramm-Rudman I and II were helpful to a Reagan administration that made consistent efforts from 1981 to 1988 to "zero out" or dramatically reduce the size and scale of federal-local assistance flowing outward from Washington, D.C., to America's cities. Reagan's successor, former vice president George Bush, while less philosophi-cally opposed to federal-local assistance programs than was President Reagan, was also influenced by deficit hawks in Congress.

BUSH ADMINISTRATION URBAN POLICY (1989–92)

George Bush inherited a troubled urban and budgetary ship of state from his predecessor, Ronald Reagan. By 1989, the Savings and Loan Crisis had run up a bill approaching $500 billion. A Ford Foundation Report in the same year, *The Common Good: Social Welfare and the American Future* (1989), argued that the country was also running up what the report labeled a "social deficit"—the costs associated with ignoring or neglecting basic human needs, especially the needs of the poorest Americans. The Ford Foundation report listed several important priority areas that Congress and the Bush administration would need to address to resolve what in their view was a progressively deepening social deficit, including:

- 30 million Americans living below the poverty line;
- 31 to 37 million Americans without health insurance;
- 25 percent of American children under age six living below the poverty line;
- 25 percent of America's youth dropping out of high school before graduation;
- 2 million children victims of child abuse annually.

The Ford Foundation report estimated that it would cost "a minimum of $30 billion" (Wood, 1991: 231) annually—much of this invested in con-centrated center-city poverty neighborhoods—to address the growing social deficit in America's cities in the later 1980s.[11] Regrettably, the Bush admin-istration proved unable to successfully address even the tip of this growing iceberg.

George Bush assumed the office of the Presidency in January 1989, having made one key commitment in the course of his campaign—"*Read my lips: No new taxes.*" This presidential commitment was reinforced at the congressional level by adoption of the 1990 Budget Accord—technically known as the Budget Enforcement Act (BEA) of 1990. The BEA required that all new programs or grants would need to be "revenue-neutral," meaning that new programs needed to be paid for with new taxes, budgetary cuts in existing programs, or both. Given these budgetary constraints, and the growing pessimism generally from the late Cater administration through the Reagan years to launching new urban programs generally,[12] it is hardly surprising that the Bush urban agenda was meager, and only modestly funded.

The Bush Administration HOPE Program

The Bush administration launched three major urban initiatives: the Home Ownership and Opportunity for People Everywhere (HOPE) program, support for urban enterprise zones (UEZs), and an urban aid package passed in 1992 in response to the 1992 South-Central Los Angeles riots following the controversial Rodney King jury verdict. Unlike the Reagan administration, the Bush administration launched a major urban initiative in the HOPE program. The centerpiece of the HOPE approach, as with the unsuccessful companion-program UEZ program, was an "empowerment" approach, seeking to empower individuals and communities by assisting lower-income public-housing residents to purchase their current public housing units or to form tenant management groups, presumably decentralizing control of such public housing from the federal or local government to tenants themselves (Ross & Levine, 1996: 430).

The HOPE program failed to achieve tenant-owner empowerment for a number of reasons. First, funding was inadequate to fulfill the stated goals of the program (Ross & Levine, 1996: 430). Second, simply transferring ownership to a former tenant or control to tenant organizations without buttressing the new home owner or tenant management status with extensive training, and adequate—often expensive—transitional assistance measures proved to be problematic, at best (Stegman, 1991; Stegman & Luger, 1993). Third, many of the public housing units were in need of extensive, and expensive, repairs requiring expenditures far in excess of the funding allocated for the HOPE program (Stegman, 1991; Stegman & Luger, 1993; Walker, 1993).

A more recent study has suggested that the approach of HOPE and other low-income assistance programs stressing home ownership as an empowerment strategy to rebuild neighborhoods and support low income families may be fatally flawed; arguing instead that "low income families may benefit more from stable, long-term housing, whether owned or leased, that is situated within an active and supportive community network" (Balfour & Smith, 1996: 173. See also Meyer, Yaeger, & Burayidi, 1994). Without such supportive community networks—such as the nationally prominent Cleveland Housing Network (CHN), which serves as a financial and management clearinghouse for fourteen community development corporations in the Cleveland area, and which has rehabilitated more than 1,200 units for eventual purchase by low-income tenants—empowerment, and home ownership or tenant management, are simply not enough to provide successful ownership and management experiences for low-income public-housing tenants (Balfour & Smith, 1996: 174–75).

The Kemp-Roth Urban Enterprise Zone Legacy

Jack Kemp, the Bush administration Secretary of Housing and Urban Development and vice presidential candidate in the unsuccessful 1996 Dole/Kemp Republican presidential campaign, is a political figure long associated with the *empowerment* approach to urban aid and economic development. As a member of Congress in the 1980s, Kemp made repeated unsuccessful efforts to secure passage of the Kemp-Roth Urban Enterprise Zones legislation, a package of tax incentives and governmental support provided to employers who would remain in or relocate to distressed low-income areas in America's cities, first proposed at the presidential level by Ronald Reagan in 1980.

Secretary Kemp remained optimistic that a UEZ program—first introduced in the British Parliament during a June 1978 speech by Sir Geoffrey Howe—would transplant successfully on the American side of the Atlantic ocean despite a sizeable body of scholarly literature (Goldsmith, 1982; Hall, 1981; 1989; 1991; Massey, 1982; Morrison, 1987) as well as consulting reports and government reports (Tym, Partners, & Weeks, 1984; Great Britain Department of the Environment, 1987) documenting the repeated failures of enterprise zone efforts in the United Kingdom.

The Bush administration continued to attempt to sell the American public on UEZs despite Harris Poll data (Waste, 1989b: 22) showing that empowerment approaches such as the enterprise zones were supported by only 42 percent of the American public as opposed to far stronger support for programs to assist the homeless (71 percent) or a child-care tax plan then also under discussion. Congress, willing to encourage states to experiment with UEZs, was unwilling to adopt a national UEZ urban package or program.

In contrast to congressional opposition to the Kemp-Roth UEZ program, thirty-four states enacted UEZ legislation, resulting in over 350 locally or state-identified enterprise zones. The success of these zones has been hotly debated (Green, 1991; Green & Brintnall, 1991; Hansen, 1991), but the political durability of the UEZ approach, billed this time as *empowerment zones*, proved to have a life beyond the Reagan/Bush years, making a successful comeback in Congress during the first term of the Clinton administration.

Regionalism Makes a Comeback—Congress Enacts the Intermodal Surface Transportation Efficiency Act of 1991

In enacting the Intermodal Surface Transportation Efficiency Act (ISTEA)—popularly referred to as "Ice Tea"— of 1991, Congress took a large step toward facilitating the role of Councils of Government (COGs) and regional approaches to metropolitan issues. ISTEA mandated regional planning for transportation and decentralized (albeit, centralized in one agency at the local level) transportation planning for states and local governments. The Act required that local governments in urban or metropolitan areas develop an integrated transportation plan, provide for environmental protection in their plan, and designate a Metropolitan Planning Organization (MPO) to serve as a clearinghouse for federal transportation funding in the region, and to accomplish mass transit and highway goals specified in the Act. As Ross and Levine have noted (1996: 375), ISTEA and the Clean Air Act are "notable exceptions" to most federal-local aid programs that have generally served to discourage rather than encourage regional planning and metropolitan area-wide coordination and cooperation.

By mandating the use of MPOs, ISTEA put in place a distribution mechanism for almost all federal transportation funds that flow to state and local governments. Since its creation, ISTEA has provided $155 billion in federal funds to MPOs in support of highways, bridges, and transit systems. ISTEA is due for Congressional renewal, modification, or elimination in 1997. Several interests are seeking changes in the 1997 ISTEA reauthorization debate in Congress. As Bell (1996: A3) noted, powerful interest groups such as highway construction and the public transit industry are currently lobbying Congress to preserve their share of ISTEA funding, while local jurisdictions are lobbying to replace ISTEA with a program that local governments view as more flexible and more responsive to local needs.

The Post–South Central Riot Urban Aid Package

In June 1992, following in the wake of the South Central Los Angeles riot—the largest and most costly episode of urban violence in American history—Congress passed a $1 billion urban aid package. That measure fell far short of the $35 billion post-riot urban aid package requested by the U.S. Conference of Mayors meeting in Houston in June 1992. Large-city mayors and congressional supporters argued, first, in favor of the $35 billion urban aid package, and—later—in favor of a package reduced in Congress to $2 billion in aid. The $2 billion figure was, in turn, cut in half (to $994.65 million) by congressional negotiators in response to a threatened veto of the bill by President Bush.

Despite claims by supporters in Congress that the $2 billion requested for the aid package "was slight in comparison to the billions in aid sought by the Administration for the former Soviet Union," (Welch, 1992b: A4), and an early insistence (later abandoned) by the Bush administration itself on a "weed and seed" program increasing law enforcement and some social programs in poorer inner cities, the administration later eliminated both its own "weed and seed" component as well as summer Head Start and disadvantaged summer school programs that the Senate had attempted to add to the legislation. In the end, the post-riot urban aid package was pared down to (1) doubling federal summer jobs for at-risk youth (360,000 summer jobs for the summer of 1992) and (2) disaster relief loans to businesses and individuals attempting to rebuild

riot-torn Los Angeles neighborhoods. As William Welch has noted, even the
$1 billion urban aid figure was not all that it appeared, since "although the
stated intention was to help inner-city youths, some of the money would flow
to rural and suburban areas," while another portion of the funds was set aside
by Congress to assist neighborhoods in Chicago that had recently been the
site of a flood (Welch, 1992b: A4).

URBAN POLICY IN THE CLINTON ADMINISTRATION, PART I: A BAKER'S DOZEN "BIG TICKET" DIRECT AND INDIRECT URBAN AID INITIATIVES

Remarkably, despite the built-in difficulties, noted in Chapter 3, in raising the
problems associated with urban politics in national policymaking circles, the
Clinton administration has advanced thirteen major urban policy initiatives.
In their totality, the Clinton urban aid package is the most significant set of
urban intervention initiatives since the Lyndon Johnson War on Poverty and
Great Society years (1963–68).

The Clinton urban assistance package was a welcome relief from the
1980-to-1992 Reagan/Bush years in which *virtually no explicit urban policy
existed*. If cities gained at all in terms of national policy and programs in the
Reagan/Bush years, it was as an afterthought and the consequence of other
more important, and more pressing, Reagan/Bush national economic and
foreign policy priorities (Wolman & Agius, 1996).

The Clinton administration initiatives illustrate serious but ultimately
ineffective efforts by policymakers *trapped within a functionally suburban and
rural national policymaking system*—many of whom are genuinely concerned
about raising the problems faced by urban dwellers, and crafting policies
and programs to make cities more liveable—who are destined, at best, to
strike only glancing blows at the "acute problems facing America's cities"
(Swanstrom, 1993: 57). In a celebrated treatise entitled *City Limits*, Harvard
political scientist Paul Peterson (1981) discussed that fundamental concept
from a political economy sense, arguing that there are limits to how much
cities can tax themselves, how much cities can compete with other cities and
other governmental jurisdictions, and limits to how much conflict local city
politicians can process and accept (Waste, 1993a).

There is another aspect to city limits, in this case, the limits beyond
which actors in the national policymaking arena are not prepared to go to
benefit city residents, resulting in what Myron Levine and Bernard Ross have
labeled "stealth urban policies" (Ross & Levine: 1996: 432–33); meaning that
city residents will be assisted not by programs designed to *directly* intervene
in assisting city residents but, instead, to provide *indirect benefits*, as in the
case of increases in the minimum wage, health care reforms, or educational
reform initiatives. The present Clinton administration is illustrative of an
administration closely attuned to recognizing the limits of national urban

policy, and to putting forward proposals that seek to operate at the politically acceptable margins, the "edge of the envelope" of politically acceptable urban national policy initiatives.[13]

The Clinton administration effort has been at least partially successful. Cities will get some or much in terms of benefits in the thirteen items set forth by the administration. Thus, cities may well benefit from the Clinton urban policy blueprint for cities, but precisely because it is partial or "stealth" in scope, because it accepts the existing edge of the national urban policy envelope instead of seeking to push out the edge of the envelope, the Clinton blueprint will inevitably fall short of the fundamental assistance desperately needed by modern American cities. In order to meet these more fundamental needs, U.S. cities need, not a Clinton administration urban blueprint but, instead, a blueprint for literally reinventing cities in the United States. Perhaps in its second term, an administration that has shown the courage to raise the issue of fundamentally "reinventing government" (Osborne & Gaebler, 1992; Gore, 1993) may ultimately prove to have the courage to reinvent cities and reinvent national urban policy in America. A blueprint short of such reinvention will surely fail America's cities, whereas a blueprint that succeeds might well constitute the *Third American Revolution*,[14] a revolution in which the American political system creates a level playing field for America's cities. Without such a revolution, American national urban policies will necessarily continue to be partial, remedial, reactionary, and inadequate. An examination of the Clinton administration blueprint for cities, a blueprint which in many ways is strongly supportive of urban concerns, supports the contention that a national policymaking arena comprised of a suburban presidency and a rural Senate cannot advance the coherent urban policy desperately needed by the vast majority of Americans living in metropolitan areas (Wolman, 1986).

The Clinton administration has put together a thirteen stage blueprint—a baker's dozen of intervention and assistance proposals—for aiding America's cities. Given the structural constraints imposed by a suburban presidenctial constituency and a rural U.S. Senate, and given the increasing political invisibility of America's cities, the Clinton urban package is a substantial urban policy achievement. In his first term, Clinton launched the following initiatives:

1. Expansion of the Earned Income Tax Credit (EITC) program for the nation's poor—a program of sliding benefits for low-to-moderate-income earners ($27,000) in which a working mother with two children, at the bottom end of the income scale, could receive up to $3,370 a year in EITC assistance (Ross & Levine, 1996: 434).

2. Permanent extension of the mortgage revenue-bond authority for state and local governments, which HUD Secretary Cisneros predicted will "create tens of thousands of units of affordable housing

. . . [and inject] $400 million for credit unions and development banks that work in and for poor neighborhoods" (Peirce, 1993b).

3. Beefed-up enforcement of the Community Reinvestment Act (CRA), making mortgage loans easier to secure for lower-income and minority residents.

4. Full funding for Head Start immunization programs for children.[15]

5. Failure to move ahead on large-scale health-care reform (with the exception of achieving incremental gains on health insurance "portability" for workers changing jobs), in which the stake for cities is large since, as Secretary Cisneros noted: "a vast majority of the 37 million Americans without health-care insurance are urban residents" (Peirce, 1993b).

6. Creation of six *empowerment zones* (Atlanta, Baltimore, Chicago, Detroit, New York City, and Philadelphia), two supplemental zones (Cleveland and Los Angeles), three rural zones, and sixty-five *enterprise communities.*

7. Encouragement of the work of the Community Empowerment Board and the Gore National Policy Review Board for "reinventing" the federal government, coordinating urban-related programs of the federal government from Labor to HUD to Education to Transportation and Justice. The Empowerment Board is also expected to lift several mandates and federal regulations affecting local communities, and allow local governments to combine monies from several federal sources and programs into one revenue stream to be used for locally determined projects.[16]

8. Signing the summer 1996 Welfare Reform Act aimed at eliminating AFDC benefits for recipients after two years, and food stamp and supplemental security assistance for *legal immigrants* immediately—a program that David Ellwood, former Kennedy School policy modeler and policy analyst, and former Clinton administration Assistant Secretary of Health and Human Services (one of a small number of key administration officials who resigned when Clinton signed the Welfare Reform Act), estimated may involve a federal jobs program for 2.3 million former aid recipients not placed in the private sector at the end of two years of traditional welfare assistance (DeParle, 1994: 1).

9. Reorganization of the main spending program for America's estimated 3,000,000 plus homeless people, the $1.1 billion annual expenditure funded by annual reauthorizations of the McKinney Act of 1987, a cabinet-level task force on the homeless buttressed by increased spending for the homeless. During the Christmas season of 1993 $400 million was allocated to homeless advocacy groups, $148 million disbursed by HUD in February 1994 in rental

assistance for specially targeted funds for the disabled homeless population, an additional $15 million for homeless groups and advocacy groups to develop homeless programs, and a record amount of $400 million HUD–SuperNOFA (Notification of Funding Availability) funds awarded to homeless programs and housing efforts in April of 1995.

10. The Clinton administration backed successful efforts in Congress to enact the 1994 Crime Bill, a measure also supported by the U.S. Conference of Mayors, to place 100,000 more police on the streets. Some commentators have estimated that the Crime Bill may cost in the neighborhood of $22 billion, funds that, like many of the other explicit and implicit "urban" proposals must, because of the Budget Compromise of 1990 (BEA), be paid for by spending cuts, tax increases, or savings from the Clinton-Gore "reinventing government" program.

11. "Reinvention" of the HUD Agency, which announced in August 1996 the Targeted Urban Homeownership Initiative (TUHI) designed to generate over $1 billion in annual mortgage loans for approximately 15,000 families in 72 inner-city communities across the nation (Walker, 1996). The loan program is part of a larger multi-year Clinton administration plan, the national Homeownership Strategy, credited in part with helping to increase home ownership in the United States to 65.4 percent—the highest rate since 1981. The TUHI was placed under the overall supervision of the Government National Mortgage Association, commonly known as "Ginnie Mae." In a modest reversal of post–World War II home mortgage FHA and VA programs, Ginnie Mae will cut in half the fees charged to lenders for guaranteeing loans to home buyers in the center cities, and hopefully "mitigate" still-present "vestiges of red-lining . . . still apparent in minority and lower income communities" (Walker, 1996).

12. Worked with Congress to cut the federal deficit in half. The Congressional Budget Office projected that the 1996 deficit will be $109 billion, the smallest federal deficit since 1981, a steep decline from the $164 billion deficit of 1994, and the fourth consecutive annual decline in the overall federal deficit figure.

13. Legislation enacted by Congress and signed by the President increasing the minimum wage by ninety cents an hour, from $4.25 to $4.75 on October 1, 1996, and from $4.75 to $5.15 on September 1, 1997.[17]

This thirteen-part urban package is unquestionably the strongest set of urban intervention programs introduced at the presidential level since the

War on Poverty and the Great Society era of LBJ. Three of these programs—reinventing government and reinventing HUD; the Crime Bill; and empowerment zones—deserve more extensive analysis.

"Reinventing" Government and "Reinventing" HUD

It is hardly surprising that President Clinton should launch a Commission to reform the federal government. Indeed, eleven of the seventeen presidents from 1904 to 1996 have established such reform efforts (Wilson, 1994; Downs & Larkey, 1986). The latest round of government reform follows the *Reinventing Government* argument raised in the popular book of the same name by Osborne and Gaebler (1992). In a recent account of the origins of the contemporary meaning of *reinventing government*, Richard Nathan (1995: 213) went directly to the source, asking David Osborne, coauthor of *Reinventing Government*, how the word "reinventing" came to appear in the title of their book. Gaebler's answer was both amusing and instructive. As Nathan relates it:

> His answer did not surprise me. It was momentary impulse. He and Gaebler were sitting in Osborne's living room. They had a working title, *In Search of Excellence in Government*, but they did not feel that it had enough punch. Osborne saw a book on his shelf, *Reinventing the Corporation*, by John Naisbitt. Although he had not read the book (and he said he still has not), he felt the first word of the title gave a sense of dramatic change, not just tinkering, and was a fresh way of making their point. The rest, as they say, is history. (1995: 213)

The Osborne/Gaebler view of reinventing government is, in short, the argument that it would well serve the public-sector management to adopt ten reforms that were thought by the authors to have improved managerial entrepreneurialism, flexibility, and cost-effectiveness in various locales—including such diverse venues as Visalia (California), East Harlem, and the United States Department of Defense, each identified by Osborne and Gaebler as successful innovation incubators. These ten reforms (and thirty-six specific strategies to accomplish them, depicted in Table 4.1) are (1) catalytic government inclined, in the words of E. S. Savas, toward "more steering, less rowing" (1987; Osborne & Gaebler, 1992: 25–48); (2) community-owned government aimed at "empowering rather than serving" (49–76); (3) competitive government capable of "injecting competition into service delivery" (49–75); (4) mission-driven government rather than ossified "rule-driven government" (108–38); (5) results-oriented government oriented to "funding outcomes, not inputs (138–65); (6) customer-driven government (1166–94); (7) enterprising government capable of earning as well as spending (195–218); (8) anticipatory government (219–49); (9) decentralized government facilitating teamwork over hierarchy (250–79); and (10) market-oriented government capable of "leveraging change through the market"

(280–310). Collectively, Osborne and Gaebler hoped that these ten directions, in company with the thirty-six strategies, would produce "many arrows
in the quiver" (1992: 30) to help show, as the subtitle of their book suggests,
"how the entrepreneurial spirit is transforming the public sector." It should
be noted that for some critics of reinventing, the current debate involves a
discussion too narrowly focused on the *means* of government—the techniques
or tools of government (both national-federal and local government) and not
enough on the *ends* of government, meaning what is or ought to be the
goal of government—what it *ought to be doing*, as opposed to how cheaply it
can do it, or with what new and innovative tools, strategies, and techniques
(Wilson, 1994).

Triumph of Technique over Purpose

Herbert Kaufman (1996: 131) recalled that Wallace Sayre once labeled an
earlier iteration of such thinking in American government and public administration as a "triumph of technique over purpose." Indeed, this strain of

TABLE 4.1
The Osborne/Gaebler Service Delivery Typology

Traditional	Innovative	Avant-Garde
1. Creating legal rules and sanctions	11. Franchising	29. Seed money
2. Regulation or deregulation	12. Public-private partnerships	30. Equity investments
3. Monitoring and investigation	13. Public-public partnerships	31. Voluntary associations
4. Licensing	14. Quasi-public corporation	32. Coproduction or self-help
5. Tax policy	15. Public enterprise	33. Quid pro quos
6. Grants	16. Procurement	34. Demand management
7. Subsidies	17. Insurance	35. Sale, exchange or use of property
8. Loans	18. Rewards	36. Restructuring the market
9. Loan guarantees	19. Changing public investment policy	
10. Contracting	20. Technical assistance	
	21. Information	
	22. Referral	
	23. Volunteers	
	24. Vouchers	
	25. Impact fees	
	26. Catalyzing	
	27. Convening nongovernmental leaders	
	28. Jawboning	

Source: This table is a reconfiguration of "Many Arrows in the Quiver," presented in David Osborne and Ted
Gaebler (1992), *Reinventing Government: How the Entrepreneurial Spirit Is Transforming the Public Sector*
(New York: Penguin Books, p. 30).

thinking in American public administration is not new, dating back at the least to the efforts of the Hoover Commission in the 1950s, although the current reinvention approach and its attendant emphasis on public entrepreneurialism represent new variations on this approach. Terry (1990, 1993) criticized this approach as one seeking to reconcile differences between entrepreneurialism and democracy in favor of entrepreneurialism instead of the reverse, although admitting that mere democracy cannot account for equity. H. George Frederickson (1994, 1996) criticized the new approach as a reductionist inquiry into managerial techniques, employed in lieu of deeper normative questions. For Frederickson, the effort to cloak deeper policy and equity questions with an easier and less substantive inquiry into process rather than normative ends rang true with Sayre's admonition to avoid the rather Pyrrhic victory represented by elevating "technique over purpose."

It should be acknowledged that a narrow view of managerial "efficiency" is not new to either American public administration or American local governments. In some respects, the reinvention efforts of the 1990s are a continuation of the privatization efforts of the Reagan administration–era Grace Commission—formally known as the Private Sector Survey on Cost Control—in the 1980s. Indeed, many of the emphases are similar: customer service, down-sizing or "right-sizing" agencies and programs, and eliminating unnecessary government regulations and red tape. The ends of privatization in the Reagan administration and reinvention in the Clinton administration are, however, profoundly different; as the former administration used privatization to shrink the public sector and the public sector mission, while the Clinton administration has sought both to down-size the federal workforce and to extend federal services and the federal mission. As Johns Hopkins University political scientist Ezra Paul has noted: "Unlike the Grace Commission, the rhetoric of the NPR has been redolent with phrases emphasizing the positive uses of government as well as its capacity to reinvent and rejuvenate itself" (1996: 27).

Reinventing Government Achievements in the Clinton Administration

Vice-President Al Gore has chaired the National Performance Review (NPR), charged with "right-sizing" the federal workforce and producing a more customer-driven federal government. Besides cost-cutting measures, the Gore NPR effort has sought to

> improve government efficiency by "stream-lining" the bureaucracy, and to narrow the government's scope by enhancing the autonomy of field offices and regional government bureaus, merging agencies and eliminating duplicative programs and decisions, and relaxing civil service rules and procurement regulations. (Paul, 1996: 2; see also Clinton, 1993)

Following two years of NPR task force *reinvention teams*, involving over 200 top-level administration officials in which three task force teams were used to analyze recommended changes in the federal government,

Vice President Gore met with Cabinet officers reviewing changes suggested in the 1993 NPR report, *Creating a Government That Works Better and Costs Less* (NPR, 1993; Barr, 1994). The next year, a 1994 NPR status report analyzed the progress toward goals set out by the Gore Commission a year earlier. Several of the proposals were urban-oriented. The 1993 report recommended: (1) restricting the use of unfunded governmental mandates; (2) consolidating several categorical grants into fewer, more flexible block grants; (3) decentralizing management of public housing projects in cases where local housing authorities had "a demonstrated record of managerial excellence" (Ross & Levine, 1996: 443); and (4) waivers for states and local jurisdictions attempting innovative approaches to health and welfare programs (NPR 1993).[18]

There are several indications of early success (U.S. House of Representatives, Ways and Means, *Hearings*, Oct. 1993). The Unfunded Mandates Reform Act of 1995 authorized the Advisory Commission on Intergovernmental Relations (ACIR) to investigate mandates impacting states and local jurisdictions, and to recommend to both the President and Congress changes that the ACIR believed appropriate. As recently as February 1996, the ACIR reviewed 200 federal mandates affecting local government, and recommended modifying seven major laws such as the Clean Air and Water Acts, and the Occupational Safety and Health Act to lighten the burden on local jurisdictions attempting to comply with regulations in each of the Acts.

Additionally, the savings achieved by NPR reforms range from one-half billion dollars from the elimination of superfluous wool and mohair subsidy programs (Wilson, 1994: 671) to estimates of several billion dollars contained in the 1993 NPR Report (1993). In fairness, it should be noted that, as James Q. Wilson has noted, not everyone in Washington, D.C., "least of all in the General Accounting Office and the Congressional Budget Office, takes these numbers seriously" (Wilson, 1994: 668. See also Moe, 1994: 114, 120). It should be emphasized, however, that even the 500-million-dollar wool and mohair subsidy savings is not an inconsiderable sum, especially when contrasted with the fact that the earlier Grace Commission produced less than 15 percent of the savings recommended in the Grace Report (testimony before the House Ways and Means Committee, 1993 by Representative Amory Houghton, R-NY). One element of the 1993 Report calls for a 12-percent reduction (an amount equivalent to over a quarter million federal employees) in the federal workforce,[19] a savings that, in turn, the Clinton administration has argued can be used to finance the 100,000 police officers presumably placed on America's streets as a result of the August 1994 passage of the Crime Bill.

Reinventing HUD

During his tenure as Secretary of the Department of Housing and Urban Development (HUD), Henry Cisneros worked with Vice-President Al Gore and the NPR Commission to fashion a "reinvented HUD." Under fire from a legacy of corruption associated with a number of scandals at HUD during the Reagan years, associated with the tenure of HUD Secretary of Samuel Pierce, and under fire from "Contract with America" budget hawks in the 103rd Congress who had vowed to eliminate HUD, the Department of Education, and the Department of Energy if possible (they proved unsuccessful in all three cases), Secretary Cisneros was put on notice early in the Clinton administration that dramatic changes were needed at HUD—changes needed not only to stave off an assault from Contract Republicans in Congress, but also to secure support from President Clinton, who was advised by some insiders after the Democratic electoral debacle of 1994 that, perhaps, HUD, Education, Energy, and other federal departments should be either consolidated or eliminated.

Following the November 1994 election, HUD began to take action to prevent its dismantling or elimination, either by a hostile Congress or the yet-to-be convinced "New Democrat" President Clinton. Secretary Cisneros admitted at a December 1994 press conference that he had received a "direct order" from the President to reinvent HUD or supervise its elimination. As Cisneros was to remark (in an apt paraphrase of a famous quotation by Winston Churchill) at the now-celebrated December 1994 press conference: "There is something about the prospect of elimination that focuses your attention" (cited in Ross & Levine, 1996: 438).[20]

Changes at HUD were put in place quickly, and ranged from the small to the large. HUD developed a customer-friendly culture, almost overnight installing a web page on the Internet providing a number of services and information to users, and making available toll-free telephone lines to people requesting information and publications. An earlier set of HUD reforms reorganizing the department and giving priority to six key goals—including revitalizing dangerous and dilapidated public housing projects, decreasing homelessness, providing open housing, "move to opportunity" housing programs, providing freer and less red-lined housing markets, redesigning UEZ proposals dubbed *Empowerment Zones* and *Empowerment Communities*, and reforming management of HUD itself (HUD, 1994)—was placed on the back burner. While such changes would have constituted genuine reform of the HUD agency, in the wake of the defeat of Democrats in the off-year 1994 congressional elections by the "Contract with America" Republicans, the Cisneros reform package was viewed at the White House as too little, too late.[21]

The new reforms ambitiously called for by the reinvented HUD included: (1) consolidating over sixty categorical grants into three broad and more flexible performance-based grants; and, (2) attacking the appalling conditions in public housing projects by granting more local management authority to tenants, encouraging tenant ownership, and providing vouchers (in a transition program designed to last only three-to-five years) for tenants desiring to relocate outside of the traditional housing project settings. Ultimately, the new HUD approach envisioned a newly reinvigorated public housing scenario in America's cities in which tenants either owned their housing units outright and managed housing units financially assisted by local governments in a plan that called for the elimination of subsidies for public housing over a five-year transition period, or former housing project tenants now dispersed throughout metropolitan regions—the MTO/Move to Opportunity approach—paid for rental housing with housing vouchers.

It is impossible to forecast with any accuracy, at this early juncture, the progress (or lack thereof) of the sweeping changes attempted in the Clinton-era reinvented HUD. HUD has defended the approach and pointed to early examples of what appear to be clear successes, such as a celebrated inclusionary housing program in Montgomery County, Maryland, requiring housing developments with fifty or more units to set aside 15 percent of the units for low- and moderate-income home buyers or tenants (Cisneros, 1995b:18; HUD, 1996). Housing activists, on the other hand, as Ross and Levine have noted, have taken issue with the reinvention efforts at HUD, most notably with the housing proposals, and have branded the HUD proposals "breathtakingly irresponsible" (Ross & Levine, 1996: 439). Whether the HUD defenders or HUD detractors are correct about its most recent changes in form and policy remains to be seen.

The Clinton Empowerment Zone Gamble

During the 1992 presidential campaign, candidate Bill Clinton endorsed the enterprise zone concept. The UEZ idea of reducing taxes and governmental regulations in order to attract businesses, economic development, and revitalization to America's urban inner-cities had, as noted earlier, proved a programmatic failure in England and, despite a decade of lobbying Congress—first as an Upstate New York Congressman, and later as President Bush's Secretary of Housing and Urban Development—by Jack Kemp, as well as by Presidents Reagan and Bush, failed to persuade Congress to enact UEZs as national urban policy. Given President Clinton's deserved reputation as a "policy wonk" well acquainted with numerous social programs and intervention strategies, along with the badly checkered track record of UEZs and the increasing confidence, by much of the urban scholarly and practitioner community, that the real action in terms of neighborhood revitalization was increasingly to be viewed in the community development corporation (CDC) idea—first introduced in the late 1960s but begun in earnest in large numbers of American cities only in the mid-to-late 1980s (Vidal, 1992; Lemann, 1994; Keating, Krumholz, & Starr, 1996)—it is ironic that President Clinton decided to endorse a modestly retooled version of UEZs as his centerpiece urban development strategy. The Clinton Empowerment Zone plan is, in effect, a gamble that a relatively modest package of tax incentives and $2 billion—roughly $1 billion for six key Empowerment Zones, and an $1 additional billion to be divided among 100 Enterprise Communities, Supplemental Zones, and Enhanced Enterprise Communities—will achieve substantial economic development and neighborhood revitalization gains.

In an interview with the staff of the *Atlantic Monthly* shortly before the 1992 Democratic National Convention, Clinton said:

> I agree with Kemp about Enterprise Zones but . . . I think it's a very narrow idea of what needs to be done to . . . recreate that sort of economy here . . . I think that they will be of limited impact unless you have . . . the national initiatives I've called for on education, health care and the economy." (Lemann, 1994)

Clinton's New Democrat version of enterprise zones evolved into the current empowerment zone program. Employers moving into these communities and hiring local workers could save $3,000 a year in payroll taxes for each employee; however, after Senate-House conferees finished with the legislation, such employees *no longer needed to be residents of poverty neighborhoods.* Thus, businesses were to be brought to poverty neighborhoods, but poverty neighborhood residents were not necessarily required by the legislation to be brought to the businesses. In the end, the Empowerment Zone legislation established $2.5 billion in tax breaks, and $1 billion in financing for economic development to be provided to six cities selected as empowerment sites. By 1995, HUD had announced the six cities selected as Empowerment Zones: Atlanta, Baltimore, Camden/Philadelphia, Chicago, Detroit, and New York. Two additional cities were selected as Supplemental Zones: Los Angeles and Cleveland, which, despite its deserved reputation as an economic renaissance "comeback city," is an impoverished city with some of the most glaring examples of concentrated inner-city urban poverty in America (and also home to Louis Stokes, a distinguished senior Democratic member of Congress and then-Chairman of the House Ways and Means Subcommittee on VA, HUD, and Independent Agencies). As Supplemental Zones, Los Angeles received $125 million and Cleveland $90 million in federal aid.

Boston, Houston, Kansas City, and Oakland each were awarded $25 million, and were designated as Enhanced Enterprise Communities. In addition, rural areas in Kentucky, Mississippi and Texas were designated as Rural Empowerment Zones, as were a number of additional rural sites, each designated as Rural Enterprise Communities. Importantly, only the six main Empowerment Zones received the full benefit of the federal tax breaks and new financing established in the Empowerment Zone legislation.

Problems with the Empowerment Zone Approach

It is early in the lifespan of the Empowerment Zone (EZ) program to accurately gauge whether the program will achieve notable successes. The early indications, however, are not good. There are five major problems inherent in design of the EZ urban aid intervention strategy.

First, the total funding package of $3 billion is insufficient to match the magnitude of the urban development challenges. Compare, for example, this amount with the $35 billion in annual urban aid funding requested in the 1990s by the U.S. Conference of Mayors following the South Central Los Angeles riot, or the annual multi-year Marshall Plan–style $30 billion urban aid program advocated by the Eisenhower Foundation. Three billion dollars in urban aid, while perhaps likely to produce some visible results in the EZ communities, is unlikely to turn the tide of the *permanent crisis* in American cities.

Second, states have actively pursued the tax-break, business-magnet UEZ strategy over the past ten years, with over 200 UEZs currently located in thirty states *prior* to the enactment of the EZ program (Green, 1991), many of which have resulted in only minimal economic development and neighborhood revitalization gains (Green & Brintnall, 1991; Erickson & Friedman, 1991). This suggests that many of the gains that can be achieved from a UEZ approach have already been available at the state and local level to most businesses in most states prior to the enactment of the Clinton EZ program. The addition of $3 billion to this equation is likely, regrettably, to produce little movement that was not visible in such locales before the program was enacted at the federal level.

Third, state and local jurisdictions are the primary architects of tax policy at the local level and the distribution of incentives and services in order to attract new firms. It is difficult to imagine significant tax relief being added by federal tax breaks to firms relocating to the limited number of zones envisioned by the Clinton EZ program. A $3,000 payroll tax deduction may attract some firms—firms that, by definition, would already be economically marginal if responding to such limited incentives, unless, in the rare case, a large corporate player actually decides to relocate out of a sense of civic or corporate social responsibility. It is precisely such marginal firms that economic development experts would want to deter rather than attract to inner-city urban neighborhoods, if only because—again, by definition—marginal firms would need to relocate outside the empowerment zone when federal assistance (both direct assistance and indirect tax relief) ceased to flow at the end of the EZ program.

Fourth, there is the thorny issue of worker mobility. Assuming that workers within zones were required to be hired by EZ firms—a feature conspicuously absent from the final language of the EZ Act—are such employees to be fired if, as a result of the new earning level, they elect to move *outside* the EZ area? In this respect, EZ strategy flies in the face of "one of the most obvious phenomena of this century—people do not *want* to live near their work" (Lemann, 1994: 54).

Finally, as Nicholas Lemann has noted in a trenchant review of the EZ's likelihood of success, even those instrumental in the design of the new approach admit that it is unlikely that any big-ticket employers are going to relocate to the new zones because tax incentives are far less telling to contemporary employers than are issues of safety, transportation, and service.

Lemann quotes one knowledgeable administration insider as predicting that, at most, one of the six EZ sites might produce a "visible economic success, while the rest can only hope to be somewhat safer and less deteriorated looking" (1994: 54). While, as we have noted, it is still early in the lifespan of the EZ program, it is probable that it is fatally flawed. Even if, in a best case scenario, it were successful in all six major sites, the program would still constitute, in the words of urban analyst Dennis Keating, less of a coherent and unified national urban policy or program than a Clinton-Cisneros version of the Great Society's troubled Model Cities program. It too promises to be a "demonstration of the ability of the federal government to gild the ghetto (at least six) so as to make a demonstrable impact on social problems" (Keating, 1994a: 4).

The 1994 Crime Bill

With strong backing from President Clinton, Congress enacted the Crime Bill in the summer of 1994. The administration noted that the estimated $22-billion price tag of the new legislation could be paid for as a result of savings achieved in Vice-President Gore's NPR effort to reinvent the federal government. The centerpiece of the program was an effort to add 100,000 police to the streets of American cities. Under the legislation, cities could apply for additional police officers under the Crime Bill if the jurisdiction in question: (1) submitted an application demonstrating the ability to put in place at least 25 percent in matching money; (2) demonstrated that the police officer would be retained after the federal money ran out; (3) demonstrated a local commitment to implementing a *community policing* approach to local law enforcement. Ironically—and we shall return to this point in a moment—*crime rates are not presently considered in determining whether or not a local jurisdiction should be awarded additional police officers under the Crime Bill.*

The additional police that communities were to receive under the Crime Bill were buttressed with a small number of social programs added by congressional negotiators, including a controversial *midnight basketball league*, restrictions on some assault weapons, and support for research and implementation of community policing approaches to attacking crime in metropolitan areas. Opposed by the National Rifle Association (NRA), and congressional Republicans who did not want President Clinton to preempt the traditional GOP near-monopoly of law enforcement and law and order policy advocacy, President Clinton narrowly secured passage of the Crime Bill in the summer of 1994.

Policing the Crime Bill

Problems with the Crime Bill surfaced almost immediately after its passage by Congress. "Contract" Republicans in the 103rd Congress, dominated by a Republican majority and led by activist Republican Speaker Newt Gingrich, sought unsuccessfully to repeal the assault weapon ban provisions, and to change the allocation formula into a block grant format to be used at the discretion of state and local jurisdictions rather than to specifically earmark the money to fund the promised 100,000 additional police officers. Although largely successful in the House of Representatives, the GOP effort to modify the Crime Bill and assault weapons ban stalled in the Senate.

The defeat of efforts to eliminate or modify the Crime Bill did not, however, spell the end of the controversy it caused. The Crime Bill remains a controversial approach for several reasons. First, less than one-third of the promised officers have been forthcoming to America's streets and cities. As of the Fall of 1996, only 43,028 police officers have been hired, and less than $2.24 billion has been granted, to local jurisdictions in what, under the legislation, is forecast as a six-year program to phase in the additional 100,000 officers. Second, as an Associated Press computer analysis (Meckler, 1996: A6) shows, one-third of the new "officers" are not police patrol officers at all but, rather, civilian employees tasked with office work or, in a number of additional cases, the funds were used to help pay departmental overtime pay costs or office equipment (Meckler, 1996). It should be added that several of these latter expenditures can be reasonably justified. Sworn officers freed of the obligation of office tasks are more readily available for street and community patrol duties. One noteworthy example is Crime Bill grant money spent for a new computer system for the City of Los Angeles. The City estimates that the newly installed system will save each officer from thirty minutes to one hour of paperwork daily; a figure that the Los Angeles police department suggests, perhaps over-optimistically, translates into 680 new officers (Meckler, 1996: A6).

Third, as the Associated Press computer analysis documents, the 43,028 police officers that have resulted from the Crime Bill are not targeted for cities with large urban centers and/or demonstrated high crime rates but, instead, are "as likely to end up in quiet small towns as in dense city neighborhoods devastated by violence" (Meckler, 1996: A6). Of the over 43,000 police officers funded by August 1996, more than half went to cities with either *below-average crime rates* or to cities so small that they do not even report their crime data to the Uniform Crime Reporting Program coordinated annually by the FBI. Thus, the Crime Bill is, itself, in need of serious policing. Few police officers have actually been added to city streets, and of those who have, about half have gone to communities with below average numbers of violent crime or communities that do not even report crime statistics.

Aside from the obvious fact that the Crime Bill needs to actually place more police on the streets of communities genuinely experiencing a need for increased law enforcement to be successful, it should also be noted that the number of police officers targeted and implemented in the Crime Bill is, unfortunately, somewhat deceptive. Assuming that the Crime Bill had deployed 100,000 additional officers immediately, and that the officers had been deployed in jurisdictions experiencing crime threats at or above the national average for violent crime in recent years, the image of 100,000 extra officers hitting the streets is inherently misleading. In fact, 100,000 new police officers—assuming that every officer was deployed for community policing on the streets of America's cities—would actually mean the deployment of 33,333 officers on America's streets over a typical 24-hour period, with three full shifts of officers. Viewed in this light, 100,000 police officers becomes 33,000—factually and politically, a far less compelling "war on crime" than the image psychologically associated with the 100,000 figure. Indeed, the estimate of 100,000 new officers translating into 33,333 officers actually patrolling beats may be far too optimistic. Some police staffing formulae call for a ratio of five to one, meaning that a congressional plan allocating sufficient funds to hire additional police officers would actually yield only 20,000 additional officers deployed *nationwide* in a typical 24-hour period.

Applying these staffing considerations to the 43,028 police officers allocated at present, we regrettably must conclude that $2.24 billion in Crime Bill funds has produced approximately 14,343 additional police officers, over half of whom are more than likely patrolling the streets of small towns experiencing either below average crime or no reported crime at all. Little wonder, then, that the Crime Bill, in the assessment of the author, is in major need of policing.

The Crime Bill was a significant political victory for Clinton, and a significant political asset in his 1996 reelection campaign. Given the problems that we have identified in this section, it should be clear that the Crime Bill needs serious rethinking about eligibility criteria, retargeting to line up with real crime in communities facing above-average crime threats, and reconfiguring the allocation pattern so that far more officers are placed on America's streets far more quickly than accomplished by the Crime Bill at present. We will discuss such a redesigned Crime Bill approach in Chapter 6.

"Eliminating Welfare as We Know It": The 1996 Welfare Reform Act

In his first presidential campaign, then-governor Clinton pledged to "eliminate welfare as we know it," replacing traditional Aid to Families with Dependent Children (AFDC) entitlement grants with a time-limited (two-year) assistance and transition-to-work (workfare) approach. The cornerstone of the Welfare Reform Act was the two-year cutoff point for assistance, and the historic shift from AFDC as an entitlement program to a program providing roughly comparable amounts of money to the states in "low strings" welfare/workfare block grants. Importantly, since the entitlement approach was terminated in the new plan, eligible welfare recipients were no longer guaranteed federal assistance if and when the state block grant funds ran out. The Republican-dominated, "Contract with America" 103rd Congress handed the President such a bill in August of 1996, a bill that the President signed and pledged that its flaws would be remedied after the November 1996 elections.

The 1996 Welfare Reform Act eliminated the sixty-one-year-old AFDC welfare entitlement program, replacing it with a lump sum block grant program to the states, Temporary Assistance to Needy Families (TANF). The Act sets a two-year limit on heads-of-family receiving TANF assistance, and sets a five-year lifetime limit on welfare assistance. The Act also prohibits parents of children older than five years from asserting that child care needs prevent them from working or participating in workfare programs. The new Act also continues Medicaid coverage for families on welfare and provides a one-year transitional period when Medicaid will still be provided to client families after the head of the family obtains a job. Finally, the Act prohibits future immigrants, including legal immigrants, from receiving federal benefits during the first five years in the country, and bars immigrants already in the United States from receiving supplemental security payments or food stamps. Critics, including a report from the administration's own Department of Health and Human Services, have argued that these newly narrowed eligibility restrictions will "push more than 1 million children into poverty" (Bane, 1996).

Most policy analysts are unsure how the significant design problems in the new approach to welfare will be resolved. For example, are recipients who cannot find employment after the two-year cutoff period implicitly guaranteed a government job, funded by the state or federal government, if after a "good faith" effort, they fail to find employment in the private sector? One knowledgeable analyst, a key architect of the administration's plan, has estimated that the two-year welfare/workfare program would—in the event that jobs are not found in the private sector by former AFDC recipients—involve either no federal assistance of any kind to former AFDC recipients or the federal government creating "between 500,000 and a million jobs, an undertaking that is itself virtually unparalleled in the last half-century"[22] (DeParle, 1994. See also DeParle, 1993).

Former HEW Under-secretary and policy scholar Richard Nathan (1994: A11) has speculated that Congress may eventually enact a more limited program, building on the JOBS component of the Family Support Act of 1988 and aimed at employing only the highest risk group—16-to-20-year-old heads of welfare families that have one child (a key vulnerable group that stays on welfare the longest of any subgroup of the welfare population)—which may only involve 213,000 jobs (Nathan, 1994; See also Nathan, 1993). Other suggested modifications have included a call by Senator Daniel Patrick Moynihan (D-NY) for a return to an approach represented by the 1988 Moynihan Welfare Reform Act that emphasized child care and education, and which required a limited number of AFDC participants to enter a workfare program as a condition of receiving continued assistance (Moynihan, 1996). Yet other proponents of modification have endorsed New Deal WPA–style large-scale job programs built on the work-ethic assumptions of the FDR New Deal era, but modified to meet current national and local needs (Kaus, 1996a). Yet another proposal, advanced by former Clinton administration Assistant Secretary for Children and Families in the Department of Health and Human Services, Mary Jo Bane, is an incremental voucher program to cover the basic needs of children whose parents lose benefits under the new Welfare Reform Act. Other incremental reforms suggested by Bane include additional funds to states provided by Congress to be used in the event of a recession or other economic downturn. Bane's final criticism is a telling one. The new Welfare Reform Act promotes fifty different levels of support and regulation in each of different states, a patchwork quilt new welfare approach to replace the uniform national AFDC entitlement program in place since its inclusion in the Social Security Act of 1935. Bane argues that children in poverty would be better served, and better protected, under a program "offering more or less uniform protection across the nation" (Bane, 1996).

Mickey Kaus, an editor for *The New Republic* and author of a recent book on anti-poverty efforts, *The End of Equality* (1995), has reported that there are two additional problems with the new Welfare Reform Act. First, it will probably not result in saving the federal government any money, since $55 billion is saved over six years—primarily on food stamps and cuts in aid to legal immigrants—but the basic welfare/child care grant package includes $3 billion more than the AFDC traditional expenditures that would have taken place during the six-year period. Second, if states, rather than the federal government, are to be the laboratories of welfare innovation and the creators of immense numbers of jobs for former TANF clients after the two-year cutoff period, state governors are likely to demand, and receive, considerable more money from Congress than is currently allocated for such efforts in the present legislation (Kaus, 1996).

At the heart of the controversy over the new Welfare Reform Act is an old argument, typified by the position of Senator Moynihan that welfare reform is less about poverty than it is, or should be, about attacking dependency (Moynihan, 1996). On the other end of the policy continuum is the argument by Mary Jo Bane, the Children's Defense Fund, and others that confronting and considering poverty is crucial in welfare reform, especially when such "reforms" carry with them the very real possibility that more than one million children will be "pushed into poverty" by the new legislation (Bane, 1996). At least to the present author, the dependency/poverty dichotomy is a false distinction. Welfare reform that fails to strike at both dependency *and* poverty is not welfare reform at all; at best, such an approach can only be modestly described as welfare reconfiguration. The Clinton welfare reconfiguration plan of 1996 will almost certainly result in significant modification in the near future.

CLINTON URBAN POLICY, PART II—"SMALL CHANGES" AS URBAN POLICY: THE REFRIGERATOR LIST PRESIDENCY, OR THE PRESIDENT AS MAYOR/ POLICE CHIEF/SCHOOL BOARD PRESIDENT

In sharp contrast to the thirteen "big ticket" legislative proposals of the Clinton administration is a second set of eight issues and actions—"small issues"—many of which were suggested to the president by his controversial former political advisor, Dick Morris. These small issues were purposely set in play by the administration after what, for the Democrats, was the debacle of the 1994 Congressional elections, which produced a floodtide of newly minted GOP "Contract With America" congress members, and a low tide for the president in terms of approval ratings and popularity. In an environment unusually hostile to bipartisan cooperation—and unusually hostile even by prevailing Washington, D.C., standards for such cooperation—the president began to fashion a number of seemingly small changes and small proposals that (1) sought to show that he was capable of innovative leadership in a time in which Congress could not even agree to enact a budget for weeks at a time, and (2) help shore up support by female voters: the legendary "soccer moms" who proved to be the difference for the president in his 1996 reelection, in which the "gender gap" widened to such an extent that women and men had a seventeen-point gap between their voting preferences, with women giving the president 54 percent of their vote, a majority of white males voting in favor of Bob Dole, and voters of color choosing Clinton by large percentages.[23]

Interestingly, not only was the use of *small issues* politically sound for the president, it may have resulted in substantive policy in the urban arena as well. On the heels of the floodtide Republican victory in the November 1994 elections, beginning as early as the January 1995 State of the Union Address, Clinton began to reach out for small issues and programs that were fundable, doable, required little or no cooperation from a hostile Congress, and would resonate well with female voters concerned with issues of family, safety, education, and health care (Alter, 1996). The president launched a number of small-change boomlets, appearing in so doing to look less presidential than as a candidate running for mayor or school board president, or, perhaps, running for local sheriff.

Between January 1995 and November 1996, the president: launched a crusade against tobacco marketing aimed at teen-agers; advocated the use of "V Chips" to counter violence on television; pressured Congress to enact an election-eve measure guaranteeing mothers the right to stay in hospitals more than forty-eight hours after the birth of a baby; urged employers to let working spouses convert overtime to "flex-time" to be used helping with the arrival of new children, or for family emergencies. In another initiative, Clinton persuaded private industry to provide 50,000 cell phones for use by neighborhood crime watch groups—a move that, given the problems with the 1994 Crime Bill, may prove of more immediate help in decreasing crime in dangerous American neighborhoods than the Crime Bill to date.

In three education-related proposals, the president endorsed school uniforms in some local schools, advocated a get-tough-on-truants policy; and along with the vice president participated in "Net Day," hooking up K-12 schools to the Internet and advocating an Internet hook-up for every school in America. Finally, in a measure that spans the difference between the other small-issues and big-ticket initiatives discussed earlier, the President called, while on an August 1996 pre-convention train trip to the Democratic Convention in Chicago, for an "America Reads" literacy program, encouraging a million volunteers to ensure that every American can read by third grade. (Forty percent of all eight-year-olds in America presently *cannot read* a book on their own, Associated Press, 1996c.) Clinton later expanded on the "America Reads" initiative when, campaigning in Georgia in November 1996, he called for 100,000 college students receiving federal work-study money to teach young children to read. George Sperling, an economic advisor to the president, estimated that the College Tutor program would not require additional funds, assuming that Congress proves willing to designate 100,000 work-study positions for tutors, and (since employers traditionally pay 25 percent of the cost of work-study salaries), the additional cost to the Clinton administration would be approximately $25 million, an amount they proposed to finance by rearranging funding priorities from funds already allocated for the work-study program.

Small issues proved useful for the president at the ballot box, notably with female voters, but also—as in the case of 50,000 cell phones provided to neighborhood crime watch groups, or the "Net Day" campaign—were small but substantive direct and indirect urban policy success for the administration. The ambitious America Reads Literacy Corps proposal of 100,00 to 1,000,000 volunteers helping American learn to read is, in many respects, a large and exceedingly *presidential* action to propose; in the words of one analyst: "This is a big goal—almost a JFK, let's-go-to-the-moon goal. Its ripple effects would transform education" (Alter, 1996: 38). If sustained, the Literacy Corp proposal has the potential to be one of the most far-reaching urban-related achievements of the Clinton presidency. It also has the potential, as yet unrealized, to translate the "small—issues" Clinton second term agenda—an agenda satirized, with some justice, in *Newsweek* as "modest proposals that reads like a 'to do' list taped to the national refrigerator" (Alter, 1996: 38)—and with it, many of the urban policy aspects of the Clinton presidency, from an issues du jour or flavor of the month, refrigerator checklist approach suitable for the administration of someone running for mayor, school board president, or county sheriff, to the larger palette of a national Chief of State willing and able to stand up for, and if necessary to, his largely urbanized electoral constituency.

SUMMING UP THE CLINTON URBAN AID POLICIES

While never articulating a clear urban national policy agenda or goal, the Clinton presidency has launched thirteen major and eight minor initiatives aimed directly or indirectly at improving the lives of Americans living in metropolitan areas. Many of these initiatives have shortcomings, which we have noted in our analysis. Despite these shortcomings, the Clinton administration effort is the strongest urban aid package advanced since the LBJ-era War on Poverty, but—like the War on Poverty—it will almost certainly founder and run out of political will and financial resources, for five reasons. In the status quo environment, major urban initiatives and programs will founder because (1) all new programs—urban or otherwise—must be revenue-neutral after the Budget Accord (BEA) of 1990; (2) the United States is now demographically more suburban than urban; (3) the American presidency has now become firmly suburban in political outlook; (4) the Senate is structurally biased toward a rural outlook; and (5) the American city is largely invisible in an increasingly suburban nation except for occasional urban mega-crises such as riots, earthquakes, or media-spotlighted criminal events (e.g., the videotaped police beating of Rodney King or the December 1993 rampage on a Long Island commuter train in which a deranged individual shot twenty-three people, six of them fatally). Even then the national media and policy/political spotlight shines only momentarily on the problems of cities and urban residents. Even riots produce only momentary national policy interest in (and a woefully inadequate $1 billion allocation to help fight) the problems of cities. In the words of one knowledgeable congressional observer, Representative Charles E. Schumer of Brooklyn: "If Los Angeles were to erupt again, there's usually a paroxysm throughout the nation that lasts about a month and that says we have to do something about the cities . . . [It's a] strange world we live in" (Roberts, 1993).

Schumer is correct, as is Senator Moynihan. Mega—and invariably negative—urban news events will momentarily bring back the appearance of what Senator Moynihan has described as "our old friend, the urban crisis," but inevitably the "urban crisis" fades quickly from the flickering and fickle screen of national media coverage and national policymakers' attention. Because of this built-in semi-permanent invisibility of urban areas, urban dwellers—the vast majority of the American population—have become politically invisible, a modern-day equivalent of the impoverished *other America* that Michael Harrington wrote about so eloquently in the 1960s (Harrington, 1962). Because of this political invisibility, urban issues and urban spending will continue to be ignored in American national politics unless successful efforts are made, at changing the political outlines of the "strange world we live in" (Roberts, 1993).

For this reason, the Clinton urban blueprint, like all modern American attempts at federally financed urban revitalization, will *necessarily founder* unless (1) the current American political conception of "urban" programs, problems, and policies is changed, (2) the current rules of the game of "urban politics" in the American national political arena is changed, or (3) both. Chapter 6 presents an argument for altering both ends of the urban politics equation. We have examined in this chapter how *Washington's cities*—cities that, since World War II, have become increasingly micro-managed by and financially dependent on Washington, D.C.—have emerged and evolved from the 1940s through the 1990s. We will turn in Chapter 6 to a discussion of progressive policy reforms that suggest a way of breaking the dependency and failed centralized federal management cities have experienced since 1940. Before doing so, however, it is useful to consider the virtues of independence and self-sufficiency, long praised in American history, perhaps most ably by the image of the independent yeoman farmer in the writings of Thomas Jefferson. Chapter 5 describes how *Jefferson's cities*—the subnational community of local jurisdictions, foundations, think tanks, and individual scholars, as well as local public-private partnerships working independently and in unison—have attempted to address (in many cases, successfully) urban ills approaching the solution not from the vantage point of Washington, D.C., and the national urban policymaking apparatus, but from the vantage point of local actors and local efforts, aided often by local and national philanthropic organizations.

Thus, we turn next, in Chapter 5, to a consideration of Jefferson's Cities— in many respects these represent the best of status quo approaches to urban aid and urban intervention strategies. In Chapter 6 we will suggest a non– status quo approach—a progressive set of policies and programs that are, in keeping with the BEA of 1990, revenue-neutral; they would not require the federal government to spend one dime on American cities, but, if adopted, would help create vital, healthy urban areas—cities increasingly *independent* of direction and micro-management from the nation's capital.

5

Jefferson's Cities
Status Quo Subnational Policies for American Cities

Responsibility is a tremendous engine in a free government.

THOMAS JEFFERSON (letter to A. Stuart, 1791)

When all government, domestic and foreign, in little as in great things, shall be drawn to Washington as the center of all power, it will render powerless the checks provided of one government on another, and will become as venal and oppressive as the government from which we separated.

THOMAS JEFFERSON (letter to C. Hammond, 1821)

WASHINGTON'S CITIES: A SUMMARY OF FAILED NATIONAL URBAN POLICIES

Chapter 4 argued two key points: first, that in the long, fifty-year history of American national urban policy from 1946 to 1996, Washington, D.C., has constructed a number of urban aid and urban intervention programs. Second, that with the noteworthy exception of Head Start (Phillips & Cabrera, 1996; Senate Subcommittee on Children, Families, Drugs, and Alcoholism Report, 1995) and Revenue Sharing, many—perhaps *most*—of the federal programs—such as Urban Renewal, FHA and VHA home-loan programs, highway funding, CAP programs, Model Cities, Urban Development Action Grants, Urban Empowerment Zones, and the Crime Bill—have tended to backfire on, and injure, the very metro populations they were meant to aid, often producing a disastrous set of unintended (sometimes *intended*) consequences for American cities.

As we have noted earlier, these consequences have included: (1) the "federal bulldozer" (Anderson, 1964); (2) the eradication of low-cost housing in America's center cities (Greer, 1965); (3) "Negro removal" (Jacobs, 1961; Gans, 1962; Anderson, 1964; Lowi, 1966; Listokin & Casey, 1979;

Hirsh, 1983; Lemann, 1994; Ross & Levine, 1996); (4) white flight (Banfield, 1974) (labeled "Caucasian removal" in the present text); (5) ghettoization and the abandonment of America's center cities (Gans, 1962; Keating, 1994; Lemann, 1994; Jargowsky, 1996; Ross & Levine, 1996); (6) doughnut cities and sandbox cities (Sternlieb); (7) "maximum feasible misunderstanding" (Moynihan, 1969) and "contested cities" (Mollenkopf, 1983); (8) failed attempts at enterprise zones in Britain transmogrified into failed attempts at empowerment zones in the United States, zones almost certainly destined to fail yet again or, in a best-case-scenario, to be a Clinton administration version of "the Great Society's ill-fated Model Cities program . . . [that] promises to be a 'demonstration' of the ability of the federal government to gild the ghetto [or] (at least six)" (Keating, 1994a: 4); and, finally (9) a Crime Bill that, to date, has produced slightly more than 43,000 additional police—one-third of whom are not new "officers" at all but, rather, overtime expenses, office equipment, or civilian employees performing desk work; half of the remaining additional officers have been assigned to communities with *below average* crime rates, or to cities so small that they do not even report their crime data to the Uniform Crime Reporting Program coordinated annually by the FBI.

Washington's cities, it would seem, have surely been recipients of funding and programs from 1946 to 1996 that have been designed and micro-managed from Washington, D.C.; programs it seems safe to assume were meant to aid cities, empower city citizens, economically develop cities, make them safer, and make their neighborhoods stronger and more vital. Equally certain, however, is that American cities—in terms of national urban policy, *Washington's cities*—have also been *Washington's victims*. With the striking exception of Head Start[1] and the brief experiment under Presidents Nixon, Ford, Carter, and Reagan with revenue sharing, which provided largely unrestricted "low strings" federal money for local planning and efforts, Washington's cities have found over fifty years of heavy- handed federal-local interventions and aid to be, at best, a very mixed blessing.

JEFFERSON'S CITIES: CITY REVITALIZATION THAT *WORKS*

To say that many of the urban policies and programs designed by the national policy apparatus in Washington, D.C., have actually backfired on the very cities they were designed to aid is not the same thing as saying that successful urban policy and metropolitan revitalization programs *are not taking place every day*. In fact, they are—although most of these (with the noteworthy exception of Head Start[2] and other federal indirect metro aid programs such as food stamps, the School Lunch programs, and, perhaps, Medicare, Medicaid, Social Security, and minimum wage legislation, as well as more direct metro aid programs typified by some of the recent HUD "reinventions" involving tenant ownership and Move to Opportunity Programs [MTOs]) are *local interventions* and locally designed program and policies. The overall pattern that accompanies successful metro aid programs is emerging after fifty years of such attempts with an indisputable clarity: *most* federally driven and managed federal-local urban interventions have failed—or worse, have actually exacerbated urban problems and the permanent crisis in American cities, while *many* locally designed and managed metro interventions succeed. The logic of this policy lesson is unequivocally clear. The two levels of government, the national level primarily centered in Washington, D.C., and the numerous local jurisdictions in the United States, have unique and distinctly different metro intervention competencies. The federal government is uniquely suited to provide material assistance in the form of broad gauge entitlement programs (e.g., Medicare, Medicaid, Social Security, food stamps, veterans' benefits [Skocpol, 1990a, 1990b, 1994, 1996; Wilson, 1990, 1992]).[3] Financial assistance to local metro jurisdictions is inherently different since local jurisdictions are uniquely situated to best determine local policy design, implementation, and goals. Programs that ignore these two separate competencies and confound them are almost certainly destined to not only fail to aid America's cities, but actually make life in such cities worse.

In order to distinguish highly successful locally generated and locally supervised programs from the more problematic national urban policy programs designed and, in many cases, micro-managed from the nation's capital, I will refer to the former local or sub-national group of programs/policies as those taking place in *Jefferson's cities*, while the latter, in keeping with Chapter 4, I have denoted as involving *Washington's cities*. Local jurisdictions—Jefferson's cities—have been remarkably successful in a number of metro revitalization efforts. This chapter is a brief account of these successes. The validity of these locally designed interventions is, at present, not in dispute. The successes have been documented by what now constitutes a small cottage industry of chroniclers of urban metro success stories, led notably and ably by Neal Peirce and David Rusk (Peirce, 1993a, 1993b, 1993c, 1995; Peirce, Johnson, & Hall, 1993; Rusk, 1993, 1994a, 1994b, 1995, 1996; Rusk & Mosley, 1994).

REALLY REINVENTING HUD: NOT AS THE *TREE* BUT AS THE *ACORN*

Since these locally driven, designed, and managed metro intervention programs have been capably described elsewhere, this chapter is designed to briefly catalog and update the leading successful locally driven metro interventions, and by contrasting this success with the lengthy experience of federal-level metro intervention failures, to suggest that future national urban policymaking should be driven by the largely local logic of policy and programmatic success, rather than the largely national logic of policy and programmatic failure. Meaning, in plain language, that if the federal government has succeeded in providing funds but failed at designing successful metro interventions, while local jurisdictions have—more often than not—failed to possess the financial resources to expand locally driven metro interventions but succeeded at many of the programs that they designed locally, isn't it about time to admit the internal logic of the current national urban policy dilemma?

National and local funding combined with locally driven solutions tends to succeed, while nationally driven mandated "solutions" imposed on local neighborhoods and elected leadership tends to fail. The logical course of action in such a case would appear to be to extend a reliable—but revenue-neutral—federal revenue stream to local jurisdictions, and for the federal government and HUD to serve *primarily* as a pass-through agency, a clearinghouse serving as an inventory of locally successful intervention strategies and programs, perhaps as a training center/facilitator helping to send funds and ideas successful in the rest of the country out to local jurisdictions. This would be the *real reinvention of HUD*; a reinvention that would simultaneously reduce the scope and increase its effectiveness. HUD would be reconfigured along the lines of a latter-day equivalent of Saul Alinsky's 1970s era ACORN (Association of Community Organizations for Reform) Institute in Chicago, in which successful innovations were inventoried, neighborhood and local elected officials were provided "good offices" for information, coordination, cooperation, and training in new intervention strategies, energized, and sent back to their local jurisdictions to engage in locally driven solutions to metro problems. The primary task of a *genuinely reinvented HUD*[4] should be to serve as an "honest broker," as a physical and electronic web page clearinghouse helping locals to become familiar with intervention strategies that are proving successful in various metro areas throughout the country. In such cases HUD would be inventorying and helping to inform and assist metro neighborhood residents and elected leaders to become familiar with programs such as those described below.

Mail Ballot Elections: "Kitchen Table Democracy" that Increases Turnout and Decreases Expenses

As noted in Chapter 3, several cities as well as the states of California and Oregon have been successful in fighting the decrease in voter turnout and increase in civic apathy that Harvard's Robert Putnam has labeled the *bowling alone* syndrome (Putnam, 1993, 1995a, 1995b, 1995c, 1995d, 1996). Cities as geographically and politically diverse as Rochester (New York), Berkeley, and San Diego have all experimented with mail ballot elections, in each case cutting traditional precinct election costs in half and nearly doubling voter turnout (Waste & Sparrow, 1985). In a 1996 statewide election for the U.S. Senate, the state of Oregon increased state-wide turnout from 40 percent to 66 percent. Stanislaus County and other smaller California jurisdictions have used mail balloting with similar results in legislative elections throughout the 1990s, in each case with no discernible voter fraud issues, and with increased levels of voter turnout and cost savings to the local administering jurisdiction (Endicott, 1993).

Local jurisdictions have discovered and put in place one effective and inexpensive antidote to Putnam's observed decline in the "social capital," the "bowling alone" syndrome, and "the strange disappearance of civic America" (Putnam, 1993, 1995a, 1995c). Civic—and metro—America has resurfaced strongly in the use of mail ballot elections in local and state jurisdictions. The mail ballot election technique, described by the *New York Times* as "kitchen-table" democracy (Feb. 2, 1996: A20), has helped solve and, if adopted on a larger scale, will continue to aid in solving some of the civic apathy and voter alienation that are such prominent features of the contemporary *permanent crisis* in American cities. Finally, as we shall argue in Chapter 6, the continued success of mail balloting suggests that Congress erred with the "Motor Voter" approach, which simply increases *voter registration* but does little to insure increased *voter turnout*. Increasing voter turnout is crucial if, at some point in the future, center cities and their suburbs are to join hands and cease "bowling alone."

The Community Policing Approach: High Touch/High Cooperation

While violent crime is still at an epidemic level in American cities, crime did decrease 8 percent in 1995 (the last reporting period available, as of this writing). According to Alfred Blumstein of Carnegie-Mellon University, this decrease has less to do with federal assistance such as the Crime Bill or state assistance as in state "three strikes" legislation and increased expenditures for prison construction than with the results of "local policing, local culture and factors in the community rather than national policy" (Associated Press, 1996b).

Second, it has to do with the transition to *community policing*[5] strategies of several key police departments. Community policing is a recent approach to community public safety that emphasizes *high touch/high cooperation* approaches by local police departments (Trojanowicz & Carter, 1988; Trojanowicz & Moore, 1988; Trojanowicz & Bucqueroux, 1990; Rosenbaum, 1994);[6] meaning that as long as a police department is viewed as an external force coming into a neighborhood from outside, and primarily responsible for the safety of neighborhood residents, it will almost certainly fail. Turning this proposition on its head, however, in which community residents assume *ownership*—high cooperation—in public safety tasks such as Neighborhood Watch, block associations, ride-along patrols, Court Watch activities,[7] as well as participation in phone-tip and gun buy-back programs, have been highly effective. For their part, police officers engage in "high touch" activities such as sidewalk beat patrols, bike patrols, DARE programs in schools, handing out police trading cards to area residents, or sponsoring Police Athletic League sports activities.

While many of these activities are traditional policing strategies, the combination of high touch/high cooperation strategies into a unified approach is the cornerstone of the new community policing approach (Rosenbaum, 1994). While community policing will, and must, differ from jurisdiction to jurisdiction, its implementation has, in recent times, resulted in dramatic reductions in crime in a number of metropolitan areas, including Boston, Chicago, New York City, Sacramento, and San Jose. New York City, for example, under the leadership of former Police Commissioner William Bratton and Mayor Rudolf Giuliani, has cut violent crime 50 percent since 1993. In fact, this dramatic decrease in New York City's violent crime accounts for over one-third of the post-1993 decline in violent crime nationally.

Thus, what appears to be a decrease in violent crime nationally is more accurately described as a number of local innovations that, taken as a whole, have statistically combined to lower the national crime rate. Several of these local community policing strategies are noteworthy (as is the mayoral support for them, without which genuine community policing is impossible):

1. Albuquerque's mayor Martin Chavez advocated in favor of a curfew for teens, and before-and-after school activities for at-risk middle-school children.

2. Atlanta's mayor Bill Campbell advertised reward money drawn from his own campaign funds after the commission of a major felony in Atlanta.

3. Mayor Scott King of Gary Indiana brought FBI and ATF agents to Gary to aid in the fight against gangs and drugs.

4. Under Mayor Guiliani and former Police Chief Bratton in New York City, as we noted earlier, *crime was reduced by 50 percent* from 1993 to 1995 with a combination of increased police visibility and citizen cooperation strategies, an effort that has plateaued more recently with the removal of the innovative Bratton by Mayor Guiliani (*Newsweek*, 1996: 29–35).

5. Fort Worth, Texas, under Police Chief Thomas Windham, has put in place a Citizens on Patrol (COP) program, with 3,000 volunteers trained at the Fort Worth Police Academy and equipped with police radios. The four-year program has reduced the city's overall crime rate by 44 percent, auto theft is down 60 percent, aggravated assaults by 56 percent, burglaries by 51 percent, and robberies by 30 percent. In Fort Worth, the COP program is part of a larger "Code Blue" approach to public safety that emphasizes the city's priority on reclaiming city streets and neighborhoods for ordinary law-abiding citizens, and beyond that, it is a philosophy emphasizing that community policing seeks to replace conventional law enforcement with *crime prevention* (Loh, 1995).

6. East Palo Alto, California has parlayed an increase in police presence and extensive use of community groups into a remarkable decline in murders, down from forty-two in 1995 to one in 1996, a dramatic decline in drug-related murders and violence that has inspired big-ticket business like CompUSA to anchor a large shopping center in the community, a project that promises to create hundreds of jobs and generate more than $1.4 million in sales taxes into a city with a 1996 unemployment rate of 12 percent (Wilson, 1996).

Policies Supported by Local Chiefs of Police

Forth Worth, Texas, and East Palo Alto, California, are excellent examples of recent successes with innovative community policing approaches. A recent survey of police chiefs conducted by the National League of Cities suggests that innovations such as those pursued in the cities described above, and neighborhood-based community policing approaches in cities in general, are, in the opinion of police professionals, the "public safety measures that are most likely to reduce crime" in American cities. Asked by the National League of Cities to indicate which of a lengthy list of policy options are "most likely to reduce crime," the chiefs responded with the following preferences: (1) strengthening and supporting family stability, 63.6 percent; (2) jobs and targeted economic development, 48.4 percent; (3) more police officers, 39.8 percent; (4) after-school programs, 33 percent; (5) Neighborhood Watch, 33 percent; (6) more foot patrols, 32.2 percent; (7) school-to-work programs, 31.2 percent; (8) more recreational programs, 30.4 percent; (9) early childhood education (e.g., Head Start), 29.8 percent; (10) reintroducing punishment into schools, 18.1 percent; (11) mandatory sentencing, 17.8 percent; (12) conflict resolution programs, 17 percent; (13) court/bail reform, 16.8 percent; (14) funding of drug treatment, 14.9 percent; (15) boot camps, 13.1 percent; (16) citizens reporting crime, 12 percent; (17) gun control, 11.8 percent; (18) elimination of parole, 9.9 percent; (19) building more prisons, 8.4 percent; and (20) more death penalties, 8.1 percent (National League of Cities, 1995: 5).

City-County Consolidation: Charlotte-Mecklenburg and Unigov

Charlotte, North Carolina—the third largest banking center in the United States—was forced by court order to consolidate city public schools with the surrounding Mecklenburg County public schools in 1973 in order to achieve area-wide racial integration in public schools. Since that time, the City has annexed 204 square miles of the County, increasing the city population by 300 percent and increasing overall city incomes to the point where they are currently 22 percent *above* suburban income levels (Cisneros, 1995c: 6–7).

The City and County formally scheduled the issue of consolidation on the November 1995 ballot as a referendum but, at the last moment, the motion to place the measure on the ballot failed by one vote on the County Board of Commissioners. In all likelihood, the consolidation measure will be placed before Charlotte-Mecklenburg voters in the near future. The November 1995 proposal called for leaving in place five, smaller communities (as was the case with similar consolidations in Indianapolis, Jacksonville, and Nashville), retaining their legal and political identities as separate cities within the larger consolidated framework. Even prior to the contemplated November 1995 referendum on city-county consolidation, Charlotte-Mecklenburg had achieved many of the gains of consolidated metropolitan governance by basing their operations in a shared government center, and by combining the city/county planning staffs and planning commissions, merging parks and recreations staffs, and achieving a partial merger of the city police department and county sheriff's office and functions (HUD, 1995b: 6–7).

Indianapolis, as David Rusk has chronicled (1995: 96–97), combined earlier, in 1970, under mayor and later U.S. Senator Richard Lugar, into "Unigov," a consolidation of the City of Indianapolis with Marion County achieved by an Act of the state legislature. The Unigov format encourages less racial and economic integration than does Charlotte-Mecklenburg because, like Charlotte-Mecklenburg, it leaves three smaller cities as distinct separate political jurisdictions within the larger Unigov framework, but unlike Charlotte-Mecklenburg, it also leaves over twenty separate school districts, creating a balkanized and stratified system of educational opportunities throughout the otherwise increasingly politically and economically integrated Unigov jurisdiction (Rusk, 1995: 97). Nevertheless, it should be emphasized that: "All progress in racial integration has occurred totally within Unigov's jurisdiction" (Rusk, 1996: 41–44).

Earlier city-county consolidations in Nashville-Davidson County (Tennessee, 1962) and Jacksonville-Duval County (Florida, 1967) had exhibited similar success for increasing political, ethnic, economic, and planning cooperation and coordination for American metropolitan areas. City-county consolidation is a demonstrated advantage in managing metropolitan planning and the political administration of metro areas. The problem with consolidation is not that it doesn't work—clearly *it does*: the social, political, administrative, and economic integration achieved by areas such as Charlotte-Mecklenburg, Indianapolis, Jacksonville, and Nashville are nationally recognized (Waste, 1989b, 22–23; Cisneros, 1995c; Rusk, 1993, 1995, 1996). But, the number of jurisdictions willing to set aside parochial localism in favor of the economic, social, political, and administrative gains of consolidated metropolitan governance is relatively small. Since the end of World War II to the present only twenty successful city-county consolidations have been approved, while over 100 have been rejected between 1947 and 1996—a success ratio of only one in five (ACIR, 1993). Since 1980, the most promising opportunity for city-county consolidation, Charlotte-Mecklenburg, has failed to reach the ballot.[8]

Despite the fact that such consolidations have demonstrated administrative and planning advantages, the political advantages of not entering into such metro-wide political compacts appears, as least for the moment, to be carrying the day (Wallis, 1994). The New Regionalists (Ledebur & Barnes, 1997; Swanstrom, 1994; Peirce, 1995; Peirce, Johnson, & Hall, 1993; Drier, 1995; Hill, Wolman, & Ford, 1995; Savitch, 1995; Savitch et al., 1993; Voith, 1992) described in Chapter 3, appear, in the case of selling metro-area consolidated government to a reluctant and balkanized body politic, to have their work cut out for them.

University of California policy scholar Nelson Polsby once argued (1984) that policy innovations vary in terms of their political attractiveness or ripeness, with some *Type A* innovations viewed as *acute* responses to a pressing social need (community policing, for example, in response to a public perception of increased violent crime, *even* when one can demonstrate that such violent crime is, in fact, *decreasing*), while other equally pressing innovations, are *incubatory*, or *Type B*, requiring a lengthy gestation period before being adopted and implemented. Despite the best efforts of the New Regionalists and the prominent national activism in favor of "elastic cities" and annexation by the prominent urban consultant David Rusk and *Washington Post* columnist Neal Peirce, city-county consolidation remains, in the late 1990s, decidedly Type B in character.

Successful Examples of Regionalism: Minneapolis and Portland (Oregon)

The most innovative examples of successful regional cooperation in American metropolitan areas are the Minneapolis/Twin Cities region and Portland, Oregon. The Minneapolis-St. Paul, Minnesota Twin Cities area is, as a HUD Secretary once observed: "the Nation's most far-reaching regional revenue sharing mechanism" (Cisneros, 1995c: 15). Under legislation created by the Minnesota State Legislature in 1971, the 7-county, 189-municipality Twin Cities area has a Metropolitan Council (the Met Council) and an inner-city suburban tax sharing mechanism entitled the Fiscal Disparities Plan (FDP). Minnesota state legislator Myron Orfield, a prominent spokesperson for the FDP approach, has argued persuasively that the FDP can, and should, serve nationally as a regional model for area-wide metropolitan stability (Orfield, 1994).

Under the Fiscal Disparities Plan, 40 percent of all increases in commercial and industrial property taxes are placed in an area-wide FDP financial fund. The annual fund is then allocated to each of the 189 municipalities based on population and the ratio between the per-capita valuation of property within each jurisdiction and the per-capita valuation of property in the Twin Cities area as a whole. In 1991, for example, the FDP fund represented $290.5 million, over 30 percent of the region's assessed property valuation, and resulted in tax transfers to 157 jurisdictions, and net contributions from 31 communities in the Twin Cities area (Rusk, 1995: 106–7; 1993: 103). Interestingly, the City of Minneapolis, which was the largest net recipient of FDP funds in earlier years, now shares more with the suburbs than it receives, since they have now become net recipients rather than net contributors. Thus, the FDP plan was structured with sufficient flexibility so that a decade that called for inner-city tax transfers recognizes the current need to spend area-wide funds to address contemporary problems in suburban areas of the Twin Cities. The economic and political benefits of such an area-wide tax sharing mechanism are dramatic. As Rusk noted (1995: 107), the gap between rich and poor communities in the Twin Cities area has been narrowed in terms of per-capita valuation of commercial and industrial property from 17-to-1, to 4-to-1, since the program began in 1971. FDP has also helped to forge a political coalition between urban and suburban members of the state legislature that in recent years has

> passed a metro wide "fair share" housing bill twice [twice vetoed by the state's governor] . . . restricted the use of tax increment financing to only depressed communities, changed State tax laws to remove incentives to subdivide farm-land, and placed three regional agencies controlling transportation planning, transit services, and sewer services under the Met Council. The coalition failed by a narrow margin to add high-end residential property to the 23-year-old tax sharing plan, and its attempt to convert the Met Council from gubernatorial appointment to direct election was defeated by a single vote. (HUD, 1995: 16)

Portland Metro: More Regionalism that Works

In 1970, the state legislature of Oregon created the Portland area Metro-politan Services District (MSD), a metro–area-wide governmental unit that has been given increased responsibilities by area voters of the three-county, twenty-four-municipality metro area MSD jurisdiction. Initially funded with an area-wide tax on automobile tires to fund planning for regional solid waste disposal needs, MSD responsibilities have expanded to include a regional zoo, planning and construction of a convention center, air and water quality programs, and, more recently, area-wide planning and "home rule" status for the MSD regional governmental unit.

MSD has responded with Portland 2040, a fifty-year planning vision that calls for incorporating a million additional Oregonians into regional suburban communities with state-of-the-art mass transit and vast areas of preserved green space. The fifty-year "Future Vision" and still-unfolding 1997 "Regional Framework Plan" are widely regarded as among the pre-eminent participatory and comprehensive metro-wide planning documents in the United States. The twelve-member, directly elected nonpartisan MSD Commission operates with a chief executive, an annual budget exceeding $200 million, 1,200 employees and taxing authority; and MSD has the primary planning responsibility for the Portland regional area, a responsibility carried out in recent years with arguably the most participatory series of community meetings, hearings, and citizen surveys of any metropolitan area in the United States.[9] Despite the national leadership provided by the Twin Cities and Portland regional COGS, it is also important to emphasize that innovative and successful examples of metro revitalization are taking place at lower sub-jurisdictional levels such as county and city government. Montgomery County, Maryland, and Albuquerque, New Mexico, are excellent examples of such successful innovation.

Inclusionary Housing in Montgomery County, Maryland, and Albuquerque

David Rusk (1993, 1995) has argued that Montgomery County, Maryland, has "the Nation's most comprehensive and balanced local housing program" (cited in HUD, 1995: 18). It is hard to disagree with Rusk's conclusion. The Washington, D.C., area upper-income suburban Montgomery County, with over 750,000 residents in 1990—a figure that would place the county in the top fifty-five metropolitan areas in the country—adopted the Moderately Priced Dwelling Unit (MPDU) policy in 1972, making it the first mandatory inclusionary zoning ordinance in the country at the time. MPDU requires developers building fifty or more housing units to set aside 15 percent of the units for low-to-moderate home buyers or tenants. In exchange, developers are granted a MPDU bonus allowing 22 percent more units than would be allowed under conventional county zoning and general plan ordinances.

Additionally, the County Housing Opportunity Commission (HOC) is allowed by law to purchase up to 40 percent of the additional MPDU units, and to operate them as "deep subsidy" HOC rental units (HUD, 1995: 18–19; Rusk, 1993, 1995). By the mid 1990s, MPDU policy has resulted in over 8,800 low- and moderate-priced housing units—one-third sale units, two-thirds rentals—and has purchased over 1,100 scattered-site public housing units, 5,554-unit elderly apartment complexes, and 328 family or family/elderly mixed 7-unit apartment complexes. HOC also administers the county's federally subsidized low-income rental housing (Section 8) program, which assists over 3,100 Montgomery County families annually to locate low-income rental housing (HUD, 1995: 18–19).

Bottom-Line Assessment: With MPDU and HOC, Montgomery County has helped transform a prototypical upper-income "white flight" suburban bedroom county that was 92 percent white in 1972 to a metropolitan "rainbow" suburb that, in the 1990 Census, listed a population that is 12 percent African American, 8 percent Asian, and 7 percent Hispanic.

Albuquerque Succeeds at Economic Integration in Housing

Rusk, a former New Mexico state legislator and former mayor of Albuquerque, is justifiably proud of the progress that Albuquerque has made in achieving *economic integration* in public housing by building scattered public housing sites, housing projects bitterly opposed in many American cities. As Rusk tells it (1993: 116), cities can emulate Albuquerque's threefold formula by (1) building small projects for sixty families or less (remember that Montgomery County, Maryland, found wide public acceptance by limiting projects to four- or seven-unit developments); (2) scattering these sites widely throughout the city—in the case of Albuquerque eight of the ten high school attendance areas have such scattered sites; and (3) using rent subsidy programs to insure that economically mixed housing, both high and low income, are promoted in all areas of the metropolitan area. In the case of Albuquerque, which used zip codes as a point of demarcation, no Albuquerque zip code area has less than 3 percent of assisted families within its boundary, while the most affected zip code has only 20 percent of resident families receiving scattered site housing assistance from the City (Rusk, 1993: 116). Thus, as the examples of Montgomery County, Maryland, and Albuquerque, New Mexico illustrate, it doesn't take a COG or regional government to promote ethnic and economic integration in American communities; it takes political leadership such as evidenced in the examples above.

The Chicago Gautreaux MTO Experiment

Sometimes, in the absence of local political leadership willing to bite the bullet and exhibit the moral and political courage necessary to link America's center cities up with America's suburbs, it takes court action. This was exactly what happened in the case of public housing in the celebrated Chicago *Gautreaux* case in 1976. Since 1976, Gautreaux has served as the leading example of Move to Opportunity (MTO) programs by proving that when a metro area assists families to move from dangerous neighborhoods to safer, more economically stable neighborhoods, in the words of the most celebrated "equity planner" in the United States, Norman Krumholz, "it works."[10] Here's how it works.

As several scholars have shown (Massey & Denton, 1994; Goldsmith & Blakeley, 1992), Chicago is one of the most racially segregated cities in America.[11] Circa 1960, Mayor Richard Daley, Sr., endorsed the creation of several high-rise public housing projects, which had the net effect of increasing the concentration of poor, primarily African-American families in a city already justifiably noted for its highly segregated housing and residential patterns. In 1976, public housing activist Dorothy Gautreaux won a federal court appeal, holding that the Chicago Housing Authority (CHA) was, in fact, guilty of racial discrimination. The federal court ordered the CHA to begin a program moving CHA tenants, dispersing them throughout not only the city of Chicago but throughout the entire six-county suburban greater Chicago metropolitan area.

Administered by a nonprofit organization created by court action, the Leadership Council for Open Metropolitan Communities, the Gautreax Experiment, has resulted in subsidizing over 5,600 families since 1976 to shift to alternate rental housing. Two-thirds left Chicago for suburban jurisdictions, one-third remained in the Windy City (Rusk, 1995: 121). A celebrated study of the socioeconomic histories of the "black pioneers" or "suburban movers" versus "city movers" by James Rosenbaum of Northwestern

University (Rosenbaum, 1995), documented that, as Krumholz argues, "Gautreax works": suburban movers had significantly higher subsequent rates of continued education, graduation, employment, and lower rates of welfare assistance than did city movers who, in turn, had more successful experiences on each of those indexes than did families remaining in the massive and dangerous public-housing projects administered by the CHA.[12] Not only does Gautreaux work, it shows that successful metro interventions to combat the permanent crisis in America's cities can take place—and *succeed*—at levels below COGS and regional governments, levels below county government, in fact, even when either passively or actively opposed by county or city government. The next set of successful status quo metro interventions in Jefferson's cities takes place at the urban equivalent of the cellular level—neighborhoods, and individual citizens within those neighborhoods.

CDCs: Neighborhood Corporations Producing Change

As Chapter 4 illustrates, the nonprofit community development corporation has been in existence since the mid 1960s but did not "take off" in terms of public acceptance or numbers of CDCs actively engaged in American cities until relatively recently (Vidal, 1992; Rubin, 1993; Keating, 1994a; Lemann, 1994; Keating, Krumholz, & Starr, 1996; Glaser, Soskin, & Smith, 1996). Chapter 4, for example, details the example of Newark's New Community Corporation, which has provided 2,500 housing units to over 6,000 low-income Newark residents while also managing to produce a supermarket, day-care center, nursing home facility, job counseling services, a restaurant, and, even a newspaper.

The Community Reinvestment Act (CRA) of 1977 attempted to deter bank home loan "redlining" practices by requiring that institutions engaged in home purchase and mortgage transactions be required to disclose the locations of all home loans. As Ross and Levine noted (1996: 44), community groups could then use this information to pressure banks and savings-and-loans to make "loans in inner-city neighborhoods." While the effects of the required disclosure have been shown to have been quite modest, the CRA Act (under fire and narrowly escaping modification or termination by Congress in 1996) has acted to encourage lending institutions to lend for center-city home buying, and to view CDCs as reliable and profitable markets for home-loan credit. The union of banks and CDCs is, in this case, extremely symbiotic, as lending institutions regain the high ground in terms of avoiding the appearance of bank redlining, while the relative stability of CDCs, and their nonprofit status, allow the lending institutions to engage in modest inner-city loan programs with an increasingly high level of assurance that the loans will not result in default or insolvency.

More recently, in 1995 and 1996, lending institutions lobbied Congress heavily in favor of a relaxation of CRA requirements, seeking reductions in the costs and requirements of CRA reporting. Narrowly unsuccessful in 1995–96 in persuading the Republican majority in Congress to enact diminished CRA requirements that would have exempted over 85 percent of the banks in the country (Ross & Levine, 1996: 45), the issue of recalibrating the CRA is likely to remain on the congressional docket for the foreseeable future.

At present, with increased home and development loans from banks available to CDCs in inner-city neighborhoods, the CDC approach holds considerable promise for successful neighborhood revitalization (Vidal, 1992; Rubin, 1993; Keating, 1994a; Lemann, 1994; Keating, Krumholz, & Starr, 1996). In the meantime, CDCs will continue to offer an attractive linkage between lending institutions and neighborhood activists seeking renovation, rehabilitation, and increased stable quality home-building. Lemann (1994) and Keating (1994; Keating, Krumholz, & Starr, 1996) argue that Newark's New Community Corporation is the leading CDC effort in the United States. Larger-scale efforts, linking the CDC approach with larger volunteerism, private foundation, and private contribution effort, are also underway in Atlanta and Baltimore. The Atlanta Project (TAP) begun in 1991, in part as a result of the support of former President Jimmy Carter, is an effort to assist neighborhoods in a city that Orfield and Ashkinaze has documented has one of the highest concentrations of urban poverty in the United States (Orfield & Ashkinaze, 1991). Aimed at twenty neighborhoods, "cluster communities," TAP seeks to leverage existing programs and CDC efforts, raising to date over $30 million for assistance to the Atlanta neighborhoods, between 1991 and 1994.

Baltimore, with the support of the James Rouse Foundation—founded to provide private-sector support for low-income housing[13]—as well as a coalition of local churches and residents of the impoverished, primarily African-American Sandtown-Winchester neighborhood, formed the Community Building in Partnership (CPB) organization in 1990. Funded in part by the Ford Foundation and other private philanthropic organizations, CBP put in place a comprehensive plan adopted in 1993 seeking ambitiously to both empower neighborhood residents and to "totally transform the neighborhood within a decade" (Keating, 1994: 9). While the CPB effort has not been without its critics, it has earned the confidence and renewed funding from large foundations such as Ford and Rouse, and could well serve as a national model for such efforts in the future.

What Can One Person Do? Muhammad Nassaradeen Rebuilds LA

Post-riot South Central Los Angeles suffered before the riots from conditions the combined Human Relations Commission for the City and County of Los Angeles once described in a report written in 1985—well before the 1992 Los Angeles riot—as worse than those leading to the Watts riot of 1964. The 1985 report found that "the overall conclusion of those testifying was that conditions are as bad or worse today [1985] as they were 19 years ago [at the time of the Watts riot] . . . We should not have to wait for a second

Los Angeles riot to erupt to bring these problems to serious public attention" (Joint Report of the Human Relations Commissions, City and County of Los Angeles, January 1985). Regrettably, Los Angelenos—and the residents of all the other metro areas in the United States facing the pressures that produced the present permanent crisis in American cities—did have to wait, and did have to live through yet-another destructive Los Angeles urban riot.

After the 1992 riot, the Bush administration approved little more than $1 billion in assistance, a figure hopelessly inadequate to effect even remedial repairs from the most expensive urban riot in the history of the United States. A state and local effort, Rebuild LA (RLA), was formed under the leadership of Peter Uberroth, the successful entrepreneur who helped Los Angeles manage and profit from the recent Los Angeles Summer Olympics. Despite some early success at attracting large supermarket chains and banks to relocate and reinvest in the riot-torn South Central neighborhood, ultimately Uberroth moved out of the leadership at the RLA effort, which subsequently foundered.

Into this vacuum stepped Muhammad Nassardeen, founder of Recycling Black Dollars (RBD), who became, in effect, a one-man effort to rebuild (South Central) LA. Formed prior to the South Central 1992 riots, in 1988, RBD has successfully enlisted corporate giants such as Arco, AT&T, IBM, Pacific Bell, and Sony Pictures to invest in programs and businesses in the South Central area. Probably the most innovative project in which RBD has succeeded is in attracting contributions and investments from African Americans who have long lived outside South Central or who have recently moved outside South Central to "recycle" their savings and checking dollars into black-owned neighborhood banks.

Nassardeen, seeking to link success for neighborhood ex-patriates with the need for assistance and self-sufficiency of the South Central neighborhood and South Central residents, noted that:

> I am not going to fault someone for moving for better schools, or to get away from police helicopters flying overhead at night. But don't just come back on Sunday. . . . You've got to give back by going back. We can't afford to have that anonymity that others can choose when they are successful."
> (Langie, 1996)

RBD has been remarkably successful. Deposits at one bank alone, the Founders Bank of Los Angeles, were increased by $600,000 in a single day after a recent RBD "change bank day" appeal in February 1996 (Langie, 1996). In 1996 alone, RBD has been responsible for over 1,400 new accounts and new deposits, totaling over $7,000,000 to the four black-owned lending institutions in the City. This initial amount may be dwarfed in the future, if RBD succeeds in persuading larger numbers of the African-American community in metropolitan Los Angeles—a group with an estimated $9 billion in bank deposits—to "change banks," since recent estimates indicate that only 3 percent of these deposits are currently invested in neighborhood-oriented black-owned lending institutions.

Epilogue: Monticello and Blade Runner—The Mixed Legacy of Jefferson's Cities

This chapter has summarized what *Jefferson's Cities*—sub-national governmental units, foundations, Community Development Corporations, and individuals from police chiefs to neighborhood activists—are doing, and how they are succeeding in combatting the permanent crisis in American cities. Despite the great disparities in terms of resources and political muscle available to Jefferson's Cities versus the national urban policymaking apparatus implied by the term *Washington's Cities*, there have been a number of remarkable status quo approaches and programs at the sub-national level that, when taken as a group, have tended to be far more successful in combating the permanent crisis than has the fifty years of urban national policy described in Chapter 4. *Every cellular level of the metropolitan area has exhibited success.* We have recounted successes with state programs, regional programs, county programs and policies, as well as successes involving citywide coalitions, center-city–suburban coalitions, neighborhood-based groups such as Community Development Corporations, and individuals ranging from former New York City Police Commissioner William Bratton to the African-American community activism of South Central Los Angeles resident Muhammad Nassaradeen.

Nassaradeen's RBD project illustrates what one skilled and visionary neighborhood activist can accomplish in attempting to revitalize American cities. Nassardeen's success and that of the RBD organization is, given the scale of the problems it is responding to, and the magnitude of success achieved even at this relatively early point as of this writing, admirable in the extreme. However, since its very success is premised on ethnic nationalism, and racial separation, it is also troubling.

RBD illustrates the two-edged sword that sometimes accompanies such actions when, perhaps, such actions lead not only to unprecedented opportunities for the South Central neighborhood to leverage resources in pursuit of bettering center-city neighborhoods, but also, to increased racial and ethnic balkanization by encouraging a "buy only, invest only" ethnic nationalism among the Los Angeles African-American community.[14] As the videotaped police beating of Rodney King, the subsequent trial, the South Central riot, and the sharply divided opinions of Americans over the results of the O. J. Simpson murder trial illustrate so tragically, ethnic hostilities in American cities are at an all-time high. Los Angeles, as the South Central riots illustrated with the beating of white trucker Reginald Denny and the torching of large numbers of Asian grocery markets, liquor stores,[15] and small businesses during the South Central riot illustrate, is closer to what University of California, San Diego urban politics professor Steve Erie has labeled the "rainbow's end" (Erie, 1988)[16] than Jesse Jackson's much-touted, multiracial "Rainbow Coalition."

Regrettably, the economic nationalism and ethnic balkanization that lies at the root of the success of RBD in Los Angeles mirrors an economic balkanization that is taking place *more virulently in Los Angeles than in any other metro area in the United States.* Recent studies by the United Nations, the Economic Policy Institute in Washington, D.C., and the Public Policy Institute of California in San Francisco underline three grim socioeconomic realities of the late 1990s (Stein, 1996). First, the United States is one of the most economically stratified countries in the industrialized world, exhibiting a greater divide between rich and poor incomes than most industrialized nations in the world. Second, due in part to a massive influx of immigrants competing for low-wage jobs, three border states—California, New Mexico, and Texas— have the greatest income inequality in the United States.[17]

Of these three states, California has the greatest income inequality. In California, for example, between 1976 and 1994, inflation-adjusted incomes for the poorest 10 percent of the state's population fell by 30 percent, compared with a decline of 8 percent for such households nationally over the same time-period. This leads us to our third point, namely, that, as California is the unfortunate leader in income disparities and income inequality in the United States, recent studies by the Public Policy Institute of California (Stein, 1996) demonstrate that Los Angeles County has the largest gap between rich and poor in the state of California—thereby making Los Angeles County the site of the greatest income disparities in the United States.

The story of who bears the greatest burden of this income gap between the rich and poor in Los Angeles County will come as no surprise to students of urban politics in America. African Americans and Hispanics bear the brunt of much of the poverty in Los Angeles. Overall, Los Angeles experienced high levels of poverty in the late 1980s to the 1990s; 18.9 percent in 1989 citywide as opposed to a national poverty rate of 12.8 percent. The African-American community fared far worse. South Central registered, in the most recently available year, 1993, a 32.9 percent poverty level. The picture is only marginally better, if at all, for the Los Angeles Latino community, whose one million working poor constitute a majority of the county's working poor, working usually in poorly paid labor-intensive agricultural and manufacturing jobs.

The City of Angels and the Blade Runner Scenario

As this chapter has attempted to make clear, Jefferson's Cities are making significant progress toward combating the permanent crisis and revitalizing American cities and their neighborhoods. Readers should be cautioned not to read this finding over-optimistically. It should also be clear from the economic data reported in the preceding paragraphs, that Jefferson's Cities are not without their problems—their share of the permanent crisis in American cities. As the data makes clear, Los Angeles is leading the nation in a metropolitan scenario seemingly destined to act out the hard-edged, dangerous, impoverished bipolar city of affluent high-tech whites and low-tech, low-skill, impoverished people of color depicted in the movie *Blade Runner.*[18]

More than two centuries after Jefferson's remarkable leadership helped craft the Declaration of Independence, American cities—like Jefferson's majestic Monticello—continue to exhibit a distinctly plantation demography, divided, as in Los Angeles, into ethnically and economically "separate societies" (Goldsmith & Blakely, 1992): an "American Apartheid" (Massey & Denton, 1994) containing "urban reservations" (Waste, 1995a) for whose population, very definitely, "race matters" (West, 1994).[19] Half of Jefferson's legacy—the depiction of independent yeoman farmers, decentralized, well educated by a rigorous and free system of public education, and, thus, well prepared to act in their own interests and in the interest of the larger body politic—is depicted in the present chapter as a significant component in helping to eliminate the permanent crisis in American cities.

The second half of Jefferson's legacy—the separation of society into those who inhabit Monticello and those who, due to the dictates of law and society's practices, are denied the opportunity to do so—is less helpful in addressing the permanent crisis in America's cities; indeed, it is the root cause of that crisis. Metropolitan areas divided into semi-permanent separate societies of rich and poor, separated by gender, by race, and by profoundly different life opportunities for each of these subgroups, is a *Jeffersonian problem*[20] beyond the scope of the Jeffersonian (or Washingtonian) solutions analyzed in the present or preceding chapters. Fortunately, as we shall argue in the next chapter, it is *not* beyond the scope of progressive politics and the American tradition of progressive policy solutions; a tradition that, perhaps ironically, can arguably also be traced back to the gentleman farmer from Virginia, and third president of the United States.

Chapter 6 sets out a set of progressive policies that joins issue with both halves of the Jeffersonian legacy and outlines a revenue-neutral proposal to revitalize American cities and to end the seemingly permanent crisis facing America's cities. To do so, it is only necessary for national urban policymakers to do three things. First, put in place a long-term and reliable round of New Revenue Sharing from the federal government to American cities. Second, greatly expand the Head Start program to a "Jump Start" program providing education support and assistance from kindergarten to grade twelve. Third, and not least since this renders financially possible the Revenue Sharing and Head Start expansion programs, to put in place a reliable and *revenue-neutral* stream of financial assistance from the federal government to sub-national jurisdictions. We turn now to a discussion of the progressive agenda for America's cities.

6

MetroBall, Safe Cities, and the Letter Voter Bill
Progressive Policies for American Cities

I believe in a government that promotes opportunity and
demands responsibility, that deals with middle class economics
and mainstream values; a government that is different radically
from the one we have known here over the last 30 to 40 years, but
that still understands it has a role to play in order for us to build
strong communities that are the bedrock of this Nation.

> PRESIDENT BILL CLINTON—March 13, 1995
> Cited in President Clinton's National Urban
> Policy Report (July 1995)

Japan spends 5 percent of its gross national product on urban
infrastructure needs, the U.S. spends less than .05 percent. . . .
We are a nation of cities. Eighty percent of Americans live on
2 percent of America's land surface. If we don't save America's
cities, we won't save America's children.

> FORMER ATLANTA MAYOR MAYNARD JACKSON—July 15, 1992
> Interview on National Public Radio, "Morning Edition"

American society can never achieve the outer reaches of its promise
as a society as long as it tolerates the despair in its inner cities. We
must address the problem of the inner cities.

> FORMER HUD SECRETARY AND VICE PRESIDENTIAL
> CANDIDATE, JACK KEMP, addressing the 1996
> Republican National Convention (August)

We must make sure that reduced government spending does not single out just the poor and the middle class. Corporate welfare, and welfare for the wealthy, must be first in line for elimination.

> FORMER CHAIRMAN OF THE JOINT CHIEFS OF
> STAFF, GENERAL COLIN POWELL, addressing the
> 1996 Republican National Convention (August)

What Can the Feds Do?

Enact broad programs, and leave cities alone. Make cities independent, not *Washington's cities*; in some respects not even *Jefferson's cities*. I lay out a broad set of anti-crime, Head Start, and Revenue Sharing programs funded with "free" money from a national MetroBall lottery; cuts in corporate welfare; and/or modest tax equity adjustments. A national Letter Voter Bill is proposed to mobilize millions of newly registered voters, to shorten the presidential primary election process, and to shift the focus in presidential primary elections away from Iowa and New Hampshire to the other forty-eight states, and to metropolitan areas.

What Can the States Do?

Enact Letter Voter Laws immediately. Many jurisdictions can go ahead with the Letter Voter plan and mail ballot elections without state enabling legislation.

What Can Local Jurisdictions Do?

Adopt Letter Voter measures and implement mail ballot elections. Use the money generated from a national lottery, tax adjustments, or cuts in corporate welfare shifted to the "Safe Streets, Safe Cities" Revenue Sharing money, to fund local programs. Choose from the several programs that are listed in Chapter 5—from Gautreaux to Montgomery County, Maryland to Portland (Oregon), to Unigov in Indianapolis to regional tax-base sharing in Minneapolis, to emulating New York City's experience with community policing, *and make it work.*

Here's the Plan:

REVITALIZING CITIES: A PROGRESSIVE PLAN TO CREATE GENUINELY *INDEPENDENT CITIES*

This chapter explores a set of innovative policy options for America's cities, policies that are bipartisan, and progressive. By *progressive*, I mean fiscally conservative, fair-minded, and reform-oriented—aimed at creating a *level playing field* for America's cities and *all* American citizens by attacking un-justified financial and political privileges of those holding disproportionate concentrations of individual or corporate wealth and political power (and in *increasing the inclusion and the political voice of underrepresented groups,* including the American working class; the rural, suburban, and urban poor;

women; ethnic minorities; and ordinary American voters of all political persuasions). This is not a partisan view of Progressive policies since both major political parties can honestly claim Progressive roots, with the Democrat's progressive lineage going back, in the long view, to Presidents Jefferson, Madison, and Andrew Jackson. The GOP claim to a Progressive tradition is firmly rooted in the presidency of Theodore Roosevelt, and in Roosevelt's later heroic, if failed, attempt to resurrect Republican Progressivism with the Bull Moose Progressive Party presidential election ticket.

This chapter outlines a *Safe Streets, Safe Cities* anti-crime package, which includes a desperately needed expansion of the Head Start program; the initiation of a Jump Start preschool early-childhood education program; a revision of the 1994 Crime Bill to more effectively place greater numbers of police in troubled American communities, as well as providing funding for the Police Corps; anti-hunger efforts; and the initiation of a national Teacher's Credential Corps.

While all of these proposals are crucial to a Progressive plan for aiding America's metropolitan areas, none would be possible unless a revenue-neutral source of funding for all or part of the Safe Streets, Safe Cities Progressive program is identified. We turn now to exactly such a task, the identification of a revenue-neutral source of funding for aiding America's cities, and—by extension—America's children.

WHAT WASHINGTON CAN DO: PROVIDE $14 BILLION IN "FREE" MONEY

Any plan to address the permanent crisis in American cities will need to put in place a separate and reliable revenue stream for American cities. Importantly, this will need to be a revenue-neutral funding stream—or, like many of the social spending proposals of recent years, proposed city programs will continue to be held hostage to the 1990 budget accord, the Budget Enforcement Act (BEA). At present, any new metro programs must be matched by cuts in existing programs or new tax revenues, or both. That places any ambitious metro initiative on the same footing as welfare reform, forced to live off the projected savings from the Gore reinventing government program. It is unlikely that any existing urban or metro program will be able to survive on such savings alone, and it is a virtual certainty that additional programs—metro or otherwise—cannot be supported by such savings, however necessary or visionary in scope (Berke, 1994: 33–34; Wilson, 1994: 668).

THREE POSSIBLE FUNDING SOURCES: SAVINGS, TAXES, OR UNANTICIPATED REVENUES

Given the BEA and the reasonable concern of the president, Congress, and the general public to address the issues of the budget deficit, there are three possibilities for funding new metro programs. These are: (1) *cuts* in current programs combined with savings from the Gore reinventing government program; (2) *increased funds* produced by a round of urban-metro oriented *new taxes or tax increases*; or (3) an entirely *new source of unanticipated federal revenue*, successfully implemented, and successfully earmarked to address the permanent crisis in American cities. Given the current climate in Washington, D.C., and in the nation generally, none of these three scenarios seems at all likely to secure support either inside or outside the Washington, D.C., beltway. The first of these three scenarios is, as I have noted above, self evidently implausible. The Gore reinventing savings have been designated by the Clinton administration to fund the troubled officer deployment and community policing efforts of the recent Crime Bill. Indeed, the reinventing government savings have exhibited great elasticity for the Clinton admin-istration, having been offered as the source of funding for a wide array of Clinton initiatives. Whatever the true magnitude of such savings, the amount involved is (a) previously allocated to the Crime Bill and elsewhere and (b) simply insufficient to a task that the Eisenhower Foundation has estimated would require expenditures in the range of $30 billion annually for programs addressing poverty neighborhoods and at-risk youth.

If new metro programs funded from government savings and cuts in existing programs seem unlikely, so, too, does any new metro program built on the unlikely foundation of new or increased taxes. As such, we will turn to the most innovative source of Safe Streets, Safe Cities funding—creating an entirely new (and, thus revenue-neutral) revenue stream for funding metropolitan policy initiatives at the national level; namely, the creation of a national lottery with earnings earmarked for allocation to the Progressive Plan to save America's cities.

THE METROBALL NATIONAL LOTTERY: A FUNDING IDEA WHOSE TIME HAS COME

The United States federal government should create a national lottery, not unlike the Irish National Lottery or the British or U.K. National Lottery, cre-ated in November 1994. While thirty-six states and the District of Columbia currently operate lotteries, there is, in principle, no reason that the United States government could not create a national lottery, dubbed MetroBall, with the net profits from such a venture specifically earmarked for aiding America's cities.[1] The state lotteries currently in existence, spent, using 1995 as a base year, a total of $372 million on advertising in the twelve-month 1995 lottery year, sold more than $32 billion in lottery tickets, and increased their 1995 combined net profits to $11 billion, up from $9 billion in 1985 (Sterngold, 1996).

The cost of running such lotteries varies, with American state lotteries typically earning roughly 30 percent of all sales revenues, spending 20 percent on advertising and administrative costs, and spending another 50 percent on jackpot payouts. The U.K. National Lottery, for example, appears to have a higher level of profitability and lower level of advertising and administrative costs. The U.K. Lottery pays only 5 percent of earned revenues to a private consortium, the Camelot Group, for administration and advertising. American state lotteries typically pay out 50-to-60 percent of their ticket sales income for jackpots, while the figure is 50 percent and 45 percent, respectively, for the Irish National Lottery, and the U.K. National Lottery.[2] Assuming that a U.S. national lottery would produce annual net profits of, at least, $22 billion,—a figure equal to twice the total of state lotteries per annum, or three times the annual sales figures for the U.K. National Lottery (an assumption that would seem to be borne out by the differences in the size of the population base eligible for purchasing the proposed U.S. national MetroBall lottery tickets, and assuming that administration of such a lottery can be privatized under a competitive bidding contract such as the U.K. National Lottery, which pays no more than 5 percent to local sales outlets and 5 percent to the managing consortium, or assuming that a national lottery utilizes the same mechanism nationwide now used by the various state lottery commissions, each of which averages a revenue stream equal to 30 percent of total sales)— the net profit for MetroBall would be in the range of or at least $25-to-30 billion dollars generated for cities and city programs annually. Let's err on the side of conservative financial projections and argue, for the purposes of discussion, that a national lottery such as the one outlined above would net proceeds of only $14 billion a year, after expenses.

How would, or should, such MetroBall revenue—an amount estimated to be in the neighborhood of $14 billion annually—be spent? The answer, if one reviews the rise and fall of federal-local urban aid and intervention programs analyzed in Chapter 4, carefully, is obvious. Two national urban programs have stood out as clear programmatic successes. The first is the Head Start Program created under the Lyndon Johnson presidency, the second is Revenue Sharing, created under Richard Nixon's administration. I would add a third element to such considerations, and that is the compelling necessity and political popularity of a reconfigured Police Bill—a bill that itself needs to be *policed* in order to provide significant numbers of new officers for the streets of America's most dangerous cities.

SPENDING METROBALL MONEY

The *Safe Streets, Safe Cities* Aid Package, Head Start and Jump Start Early Childhood Education Programs

The *Safe Streets, Safe Cities* policy package advocated here calls for congressional action to enact enabling legislation for the creation of a national MetroBall lottery, with one-third of the revenues generated to be earmarked for a Special Revenue Sharing round of assistance to Head Start programs; the second third to be set aside for funding additional police officers for America's cities, anti-hunger, and teacher certification programs; and the remaining third to be returned to metropolitan jurisdictions in a round of unrestricted New Revenue Sharing. Let's turn to an examination of each of these three programmatic elements of the Safe Streets, Safe Cities policy package.

One-third of the MetroBall lottery annual earnings would be roughly $4 billion, an amount that would double the current $4 billion annual allocation for Head Start to $8 billion. While such an amount falls far short of European levels of spending for child care and education—if, for example, the United States were to match the French level of spending for child-care and early childhood education and associated health services, the comparable figure for the United States would be "approximately $23 billion per year" (Harris, 1996: 77)—$8 billion would create a funding base sufficient to fund a *nearly universal entitlement* for all American children to participate in Head Start programs.[3] At present, less than 63 percent of four-year-olds, and less than 29 percent of three-year-olds who were eligible for the Head Start program actually received spaces in the Head Start classrooms (Harris, 1996: 75). The needs for an expanded Head Start are, thus, painfully obvious. Over 60 percent of the impoverished three-year-olds currently eligible for Head Start never find a space in the program. The social costs of this hole in our national education safety net are disastrous, both for the children and the larger society. Studies have repeatedly demonstrated that every dollar spent for early childhood education saves from three to ten dollars that would later have been needed in expenditures on juvenile medical care, juvenile crime and probation costs, and juvenile court and prosecution expenses (Harris, 1996: 75).

The Social Costs of Excluding Head Start Participants   The Carnegie Foundation for the Advancement of Learning found in their 1991 report, *Ready to Learn: A Mandate for the Nation*, that 35 percent of the five-year-olds in U.S. kindergarten classes *were not ready for school when they entered kindergarten* (Carnegie Foundation Report, 1991). Second, a 1991 report by educational and public health researchers at Brown and Harvard Universities found that fully 12 percent of all U.S. schoolchildren are learning impaired *before reaching kindergarten due to preventable conditions*, including alcohol and drug abuse, lead poisoning, low birth weight, and malnutrition (Harris, 1996: 75).

Early-childhood learning years are irreplaceably important to the development of children, and by extrapolation, to the continued development of the health and welfare of the United States. Noted Harvard pediatrician T. Berry Brazelton and University of Chicago scholar Benjamin Bloom have stressed the crucial nature of early childhood (birth to four years old) development in the subsequent educational success of children. Bloom has documented that: "General intelligence appears to develop *as much from conception to age four as it does during the 14 years from age 4 to age 18"* (emphasis added, cited in Harris, 1996: 75).

The Family Development Research Program in Syracuse, New York, found over a multiyear period that not only did early childhood programs aid the success of children later graduating from the program, but that such children were three times less likely to engage in criminal behaviors requiring supervision by local juvenile probation departments, and that those children cost society ten times less than children in the control group in terms of probation, supervision, and court costs—a figure of $186 per child versus $1,985 per child for the control group (Harris, 1996: 76).

The bottom line for the current approach of inadequately funding Head Start, child care, and related preventive health costs in the United States—not to mention the short-lived attempt to cut Head Start by an additional $100 million in fiscal year 1996 that was eventually rescinded by members of Congress facing reelection campaigns in the Fall of 1996—is that children are placed at risk by the current American reluctance to adequately invest in pre–school-age children. At the present we spend only $4 billion annually on Head Start, and more than 90 percent of that amount is spent on children three to five years old. Congress should allocate an additional $4 billion from the MetroBall new revenue sharing funds to create a *Jump Start* program, aimed at assisting at-risk children from birth to three years old, concentrating on educational skills, child care, health care screening, and treatment and intervention programs for children at risk due to low birth-weight, poverty, malnutrition, alcohol or drug abuse, or physical or sexual abuse.

A Jump Start program covering children from birth to three years coupled with the current funding level for Head Start, is a minimal effort to mend the current gaping tear in the education and health safety-net for America's at-risk and impoverished youngest children. A far more adequate approach would be the establishment of Jump Start/Head Start support as a national entitlement for all children in the United States, but the funding for such a proposal would far outstrip the meager funds made available by the institutionalization of the MetroBall national lottery. MetroBall would provide $4 billion annually for Head Start, an amount that would achieve the maximum impact by being allocated primarily for both Jump Start and Head Start programs.

The Safe Streets, Safe Cities Anti-Crime Program

Two things follow from our discussion of the 1994 Crime Bill in Chapter 4. First, the Crime Bill has serious—perhaps fatal—flaws in its formula for distributing new police officers to American communities. The Crime Bill, itself, stands in need of serious policing. Second, although a repaired Crime Bill would contribute a great deal to increased safety in American communities, the Crime Bill alone is not enough to stem the tide of rising violence in American cities. The solution needs to be two-fold. First, the Crime Bill needs to be policed, rewritten to provide real officers and real assistance to cities and metro areas facing serious threats of violent crime. Second, the most innovative section of the original Omnibus Crime Bill (circa 1992), the Police Corps, needs to revitalized and refunded—via the use of $1.6 billion annually from MetroBall. These two elements, a better functioning Crime Bill, and a newly implemented Police Corps, are the key anti-crime elements in a much-needed Safe Streets, Safe Cities Progressive policy package advocated in this book.

Policing the Crime Bill: Real Cops for Real Crime   Beginning rather modestly and creatively as the $3.3 billion Omnibus Crime Bill of 1992, a poorly funded and eventually hopelessly underfunded and compromised but originally quite promising collegiate cop corps program entitled the *Police Corps*, the current crime legislation eventually emerged as the 1994 Crime Bill, at a total price tag of $30.4 billion, covering everything from prisons to midnight basketball leagues, authorizing multi-year spending of $8.8 billion in funding for 100,000 new police officers. Had the Crime Bill police officer distribution formula proved optimal, it would have increased the police/citizen ratio nationally from 2.4 to 2.7 officers per 1,000 citizens. The 1994 Crime Bill as we currently know it, and subsequent annual reauthorizations, has fallen far short of this ambitious goal.

Let me make myself clear. I am not against expenditures of this magnitude of public funds for increased police protection. Quite the reverse is true. The annual ratio of police officers to crime has fallen precipitously from 3.3 officers per violent felony in 1960 to 3.5 such incidents per police officer in 1993 (Walinsky, 1995: 39). Crime costs Americans $425 billion a year, $14 billion a year alone is spent on the annual costs of firearm injuries. Money to stem the tide of crime is well spent, or should be. Under the 1994 Crime Bill legislation, the allocation of the proposed 100,000 new officers is well intentioned but poorly planned. The new police officers are widely dispersed throughout the United States, with at least half currently going to communities experiencing below-average crime levels or to jurisdictions so small that they do not even report crime data to the FBI on an annual basis. The 1994 Crime Bill simply fails the test of sending the medicine—in this case, additional police officers—where it really belongs. The small number of police actually added to the streets due to the Crime Bill, and their counter-productive deployment pattern (inherent in the design of the Bill itself) is, at best, an inadequate response to the realities of modern crime and violence in America.

Violent crime, as we have noted earlier, is concentrated in narrow vectors, whirlpools of violence, zones not of empowerment but of personal danger and disproportionate risk. For example, using 1992 as a base year, according to the 1992 FBI *Uniform Crime Report*, 88 percent of all murders occur in metropolitan statistical areas (MSAs), and only a handful of MSAs (forty-six accounted for 64.3 percent of all homicides in 1992. Of these, less than half twenty-five MSAs) account for 56 percent of all murders in the United States in 1992, and 86 percent of all homicides in MSAs in 1992.

Let's try again on the Crime Bill in subsequent years in which the 1994 Bill comes up for budgetary reauthorization. This time, let's target 50,000 police officers for where the crime is actually taking place—the top twenty-five MSAs in the country, "top" in terms of highest numbers of homicides in the United States. For a modest cost, between $4 to $4.4 billion (funding that would be revenue-neutral and "free" because it would be drawn at the rate of $1.1 billion annually over a four-year period from the proceeds of the annual MetroBall lottery), Americans can assign an *additional 50,000 police officers*— 500 officers annually over a four-year period to *each* of the twenty-five MSA's with the largest numbers of homicides. Further, let's require that cities match a share of the federal grant with a locally raised public safety sales tax or levy targeted for improving the essential community policing strategies such as creating after-school teen centers on school campuses, truant enforcement capabilities, aid to local community development corporations, and other strategies to be locally determined as a condition of receiving the additional officers. Any community that failed to pass such a levy would lose its share of police officers to the next qualified MSA, or to the remaining MSAs on that year's list of twenty-five jurisdictions.

In this way, the federal government would be helping to turn whirlpool cities and neighborhoods into independent cities, cities and neighborhoods capable of taking back their share of the responsibility for the middle of the doughnut of poverty and crime in American urban areas. The public safety tax levies required by the new legislation as a condition of receiving additional police officers would be added to the overall community policing, public-safety budget of the local jurisdiction to complement the new officers made available to the city by the Safe Streets, Safe Cities anti-crime bill. At the end of an eight-year waiting period, jurisdictions that were funded in the first four-year round of funding could apply for a second round of 2,000 additional officers funded by the Safe Streets, Safe Cities legislation.

Police troops funded by a reformulated Safe Streets, Safe Cities crime bill, and even increased local efforts to raise the funds necessary for adequately funding police, is hardly a magic formula for building safe cities, but it's a bold start and a genuine—and dramatically cost-effective—step toward safer American streets. We need to rethink, reinvent, and redesign the 1994 Crime Bill so that it effectively fights crime and violence on America's streets. A reconceptualized crime bill could provide 50,000 officers—*2,000 police officers per city for each of America's most troubled MSAs for half the cost of the current legislation*—with cities receiving such assistance eligible to reapply for further assistance after an eight-year waiting period. With a reconfigured crime bill, President Clinton and Congress have a chance to show that they mean business about deficit reduction and fighting crime; with MetroBall funding at the level of $1.1 billion annually, the President and Congress have the opportunity to fight crime in a fashion that is both significant and revenue-neutral. The same is true of the long-discussed, promising, but never fully-implemented Police Corps program.

The Police Corps: A Police/GI Bill in Reverse   Included in the 1994 Crime Bill but poorly funded—originally priced at one $1 billion and funded early in the legislation at the $350-million level, which in turn shrank to $100 million and is now for all intents and purposes an unfunded and shelved program—was the Police Corps, an idea long-championed by Adam Walinsky, lawyer and former advisor to former Attorney-General and U.S. Senator Robert Kennedy (D-NY). The Police Corps is an idea that deserves funding, and for which $2.72 billion of the MetroBall lottery funds annually could be set aside for a special revenue sharing Safe Streets, Safe Cities Police Corps program. The Police Corps program would function as originally proposed in the 1994 Crime Bill but in the current proposal as *an annual expenditure of $2.72 billion* rather than a poorly funded and inadequately staffed one-time, one-shot $1-billion-dollar program.

The Police Corps legislation would authorize $2.72 billion annually to support a series of scholarships, annually funding over 80,000 college students receiving $7,500 per academic year, and $250 per week for two summers of additional training over a four-year period.[4] The expenditure for each Police Corps graduate would be $34,000. Funding the Police Corps program at the full four-year scholarship level (80,000 cadets $\times$ $34,000 = $2.72 billion) in a *pay as you go* approach would speak volumes to American cities, and to the cadets in the Police Corps program. Basically, it says unequivocally: "Here is the money for your police programs, and your scholarships deposited in a four-year trust fund. You can count on support during your four years in college, and cities can count on receiving the predicted financial assistance and the predicted number of graduates." Unlike the Crime Bill, the numbers *will not be reduced* and budgets will not be cut. The commitment to college support and police augmentation is unequivocal. In exchange for the college assistance and training, Police Corps members must commit to serve a local or state police force at prevailing union wages.

For students accepted into the Police Corps, including currently serving police officers, who for the first five years, may elect to sign on as Police Corps recruits, the Police Corps stipend would amount to a nearly free college education. Using 1992 as a base year, for example, the College Board estimated the annual cost of one year of tuition, meals, and incidental costs for attending a public university at approximately $7,300 (Wilson, 1992).

What will the American public receive in return for funding Police Corps educational scholarships? First, this reverse G.I. Bill would require Police Corps Cadets to serve five years of police duty after graduation. Even if such officers would not choose to make law enforcement a career after the five-year obligatory period of service, it would provide any community in which former Police Corps Cadets lived with an increased measure of security, having additional members of the local citizenry well trained in community policing and crime prevention. Second, the approximately 20,000 annual Police Corps scholarship opportunities would provide a means of attending college, and an opportunity to serve in the metropolitan and state police forces never before available on such a scale to the average American citizen. As Police Corps founder Walinsky has argued, the benefits to the larger American society from such an approach are immeasurable, since Police Corps alumni would be:

> not just people who are doing a job, but people who are figures of respect . . . who are on their way somewhere . . . who are exercising the authority of the state today, and who may be lawyers or reporters or teachers or scientists or accountants . . . when their tour of duty is up. People who express the fundamental notions of what it is to be citizens of the United States. (Walinski, cited in Wilson, 1992: 6)

Using MetroBall lottery money, essentially free money for funding the most innovative part of the original 1994 Crime Bill, is a solid investment in public safety. Given that the funding is revenue-neutral, critics may still raise the argument that a program annually providing new scholarships to 80,000 Police Corps Cadets in a public safety version of the R.O.T.C. program is an overreaction, producing too many additional cops on the streets, too quickly to be of real assistance. Nothing could be further from the truth. The United States presently has approximately 600,000 police officers (Kolbert, 1994: 44). While, at first glance, this seems like an impressive number, bear in mind that with three shifts a day and assuming absolutely no sickness, transfers, or accidents, that means 200,000 officers are patrolling America's streets on any given day. In 1960, as we have noted, there were three officers per violent felony; currently there are *more than three such incidents per police officer*. The leading advocate of community policing and the Police Corps concept, Adam Walinsky, has estimated that reversing this trend will require a lot of additional police troops: "To do this we need forces. We need a very large number of additional police officers; at least half a million in the next five years, and perhaps more thereafter" (1995: 53).

Is Walinsky correct that addressing America's crime problem will require an additional 500,000 police officers? A society with limited resources and multiple demands for all available funding will probably never deploy enough officers to find out. Even the Police Corps element in the proposed, progressive Safe Streets, Safe Cities anti-crime package only anticipates providing 80,000 scholarships annually; a figure that, assuming that every Police Corps cadet eventually served—and remained for a permanent career (a dubious assumption, at best)—in the nation's police forces, would still require 6.25 years to produce the number of additional police whom Walinsky estimates are necessary to stem the tide of crime, and to return to 1960 levels of policing and public safety.

Walinsky is correct about the need for thousands of additional police officers, and the Police Corps idea is a modest down-payment on returning to a 1960s level of public safety and security on America's streets and in America's communities. Make no mistake about it: Walinsky is correct.

America's cities are at war, the toll is staggering, and as a nation we need to deploy considerably more troops in the field. The numbers for this case are frighteningly compelling. As Walinsky noted:

> In the past decade 200,000 of our citizens have been killed and millions wounded. If we assume, with the FBI, that 47 percent of them were killed by friends and family members, that leaves 106,000 dead at the hands of strangers. Ten years of war in Vietnam killed 58,000 Americans. Over an equal period we have had almost the exact equivalent of two Vietnam Wars right here at home. (1995: 53)

This is a war that we can no longer ignore, and cannot afford to continue trying to fight passively, and on the cheap. In this section we have presented a Safe Streets, Safe Cities, set of progressive programs—including a modified version of the Crime Bill, and a revitalized Police Corps—that can turn the tide of violent crime in America's cities, and do so in a meaningful and revenue-neutral way.[5]

Second Harvest and the Teacher Credential Corps Programs

The permanent crisis in American cities is about hunger and Kindergarten through Grade 12 education, as well as crime, jobs, early-childhood education, and community policing. The MetroBall lottery is capable of providing funding for two additional programs to address metro hunger and K–12 schooling issues directly, albeit at a modest level of financial assistance. Second Harvest, as noted earlier in Chapter 1, is the largest private anti-hunger agency in the United States, attempting to address the needs of the approximately 25 to 30 million people at risk of hunger in the United States. As the lead anti-hunger agency in a vast coordinated network involving over 3,000 local anti-hunger agencies throughout the United States, Second Harvest is uniquely situated to continue providing anti-hunger assistance to needy Americans. Rather than create a large and expensive governmental program to assist those at risk of hunger in America, $.2 billion in MetroBall funds should be earmarked for annual transfer to Second Harvest to use in their already successful but underfunded war against hunger. It would be left to Second Harvest to determine the appropriate allocation of these funds, including the local projects and agencies to whom it might be appropriate. Naturally, congressional oversight prior to subsequent annual funding reauthorization for Second Harvest would be appropriate.

A September 1996 Report by the National Commission on Teaching and America's Future sounded an alarming note for the nation's schools. America's schools have serious troubles. They are facing tremendous financial needs as a record enrollment of 51.7 million students fuels a need for 6,000 new schools in the next decade alone. Adding to this financial drain from the demands for new school construction are the pressing needs of existing school facilities documented by a 1995 General Accounting Office report, which found that $112 billion is needed for construction repairs to the nation's existing 80,000 schools (Applebome, 1996).

The report by the National Commission on Teaching and America's Future found that: "Many states pay more attention to the qualifications of veterinarians . . . than to those of the teachers educating the nation's children" (Bazar, 1996). The report documents that less than three-fourths (72.6 percent) of teachers in the United States are fully licensed. Further, nearly one-quarter of all American secondary-school teachers did not *major or minor* in their main teaching field during college. A U.S. Department of Education report, *Schools and Staffing Survey, 1990–91*, found that teachers are among the poorest paid professionals in the country, ranking dead last in a survey comparing teaching salaries to professionals employed as social workers, writers, sales persons, accountants, and registered nurses. K-12 teachers are making only half as much as engineers or managers, and only 30 percent of the salaries paid to lawyers, judges, or physicians. For example, teachers in California, a relatively high-wage state for K–12 teachers, are paid an average starting salary of $25,500, and the average annual salary for teachers in California was $40,636 in 1996 (Bazar, 1996). Most experts, such as the director of the California State University Institute for Education Reform, have urged school districts to establish incentives such as pay differentials to attract qualified teachers in difficult-to-staff areas such as math, science, special education, and bilingual education (Bazar, 1996).

One last indictment of American K–12 education, as if another were necessary, is the results in Fall 1996 of the Third International Mathematics and Science Study (TIMSS). The TIMSS results are not a good report card for American school children. United States seventh- and eighth-grade students fell below the median in math for the forty-one-country study—the largest such study ever taken—and slightly above the median in science.[6]

Fortunately, the ingredients of the K–12 problem—low numbers of trained scientists and mathematicians in the teaching field, low pay and a lack of teachers with a state license, adequate certification, and a major in their main teaching field—are also the ingredients of the solution. Decades ago, the Carnegie Foundation, in a successful attempt to attract ambitious and talented persons to choose teaching as a profession, created TIAA-CREF, a retirement annuity fund to provide America's teachers with a reliable pension upon retirement. The Carnegie action, which today stands in need of improvement to adjust teacher's pensions to the real-dollar retirement needs of the 1990s and beyond, was successful in increasing the supply and quality of America's teacher force. Using MetroBall lottery funds, a similar "supply side" remedy is available today.

While the logistics are complex, and require further refinement and amplification beyond the present discussion, it is enough for our present purposes to suggest that a Teachers Credential Corps Endowment Fund be created by the federal government, and endowed annually with $.98 billion in MetroBall money. The purpose of this fund would be to create a pool of money that would eventually finance a Teachers Credential Corps. Credential Corps members would (1) be duly credentialed by the state in which they teach; (2) have majored or minored in their main teaching areas; and (3) have successfully passed, and re-passed at state-determined intervals, all appropriate teacher certifications and examinations *required and recommended* by the state in which they teach. In exchange, Teacher Credential Corp members would be eligible for annual salary supplements from the endowment fund that would equal a 30 percent increase above the base-figure salary union wages for a teacher in their same district employed at a similar level and with the same number of years experience in their local teaching jurisdiction. Credential Corps members meeting the above requirement and having majored in math or science and teaching primarily in that field would earn a 50 percent increase in their salary base. Further, a qualified Credential Corps teacher securing a teaching position in an inner-city school where over 10 percent of the students fall below the federal poverty guidelines would be eligible for a 60 percent salary increase. Qualified Credential Corps teachers who majored in math or science, are teaching primarily in that field, and have secured a teaching position in a qualified poverty-area school would be eligible for a 100 percent annual salary increase, to be paid for from the Teacher Credential Corps Endowment Fund.

These two measures, the provision of financial assistance from MetroBall funds to Second Harvest, and to the Teacher Credential Corps Endowment Fund, would greatly aid American cities confronting the permanent crisis of metropolitan areas. There is one additional measure that would also greatly aid cities, the creation of new revenue sharing to help American cities as they attempt, in the words of President Clinton, "to build a bridge to the twenty-first century."

The New Revenue Sharing Program

MetroBall would raise approximately $14 billion in revenue-neutral funds annually. Of this amount, we have suggested a progressive policy package for combating the permanent crisis in America's cities, allocating annually: (1) $4 billion to the current Head Start and a new Jump Start early childhood education program; (2) $1.1 billion for a reconfigured crime bill that would produce 50,000 new police officers—2,000 new officers in each of the top crime cities in the United States over a four-year period; and (3) $2.72 billion for a revitalized Police Corps envisioned in the original Crime Bill but currently inoperative, which would provide 80,000 Police Corps scholarships annually to college students obligated in return to serve a fixed term in state of metropolitan police forces. In addition two further programs in the Safe Streets, Safe Cities policy package are: (4) a $.2-billion allocation to the Second Harvest hunger relief agency in an effort to help create the access to at least one decent meal a day as a basic American right; and (5) an annual investment of almost $1 billion a year ($.98 billion) to be paid into the national

Teacher Credential Corps Endowment Fund, to help create a fund of money that eventually will allow every certificated K–12 teacher in America to raise their pay above the level of the prevailing union wages in their teaching district, a "supply side" solution to the crisis of under-credentialed teachers working in America's classrooms.

These five program expenditures total $9 billion in MetroBall-generated funds annually. The remaining $5 billion should be allocated for a round of unrestricted New Revenue Sharing, annual funding to be awarded to local jurisdictions on the basis of population size and local needs. While the precise distribution formula for a round of New Revenue Sharing is best left in the legislative domain of Congress and the president, it is possible to suggest at present the rough outlines that such a distribution formula might take.

Allocational formulae that ignore differences in population or the poverty population should be assiduously avoided. For example, simply administering equal amounts of the $5 billion MetroBall Revenue Sharing funds to every MSA in the United States, while superficially equitable in that it would provide a formula awarding an annual amount of $69.4 million to each MSA in the country, ignores vast differences in the size and needs of the recipient jurisdictions. Alternately, limiting the New Revenue Sharing round to cities with populations of 200,000 or greater does implicitly acknowledge the plight of large cities in America but, again, an equal distribution among all seventy-seven of these cities would result in ignoring the differences in size and needs among them and would completely ignore the needs of smaller jurisdictions.

Better efforts should be made to fine-tune the Revenue Sharing (RS) allocation process. For example, as noted above, a good argument could be made to limit the RS program to cities with a population of 200,000 or more. As of 1995, there were seventy-seven such cities in the United States. To spread the majority of RS money more broadly would dilute its ability to fund meaningful programs and changes in large American cities; and it is in large American cities that the vast majority of the problems of concentrated crime and poverty exist. Second, lest the lessons of the past be forgotten, it is crucial to include a need-based element in the distribution formula.

Accordingly, I would argue for creating the creation five tiers of RS recipients as follows: *Type A cities* with a population of 1,000,000 residents or greater; *Type B cities* with a population range of 300,001 to 750,000; *Type C cities* with a population ranging in size from 196,001 to 300,000; and *Type D cities*, with populations between 25,000 and 196,000. *Type E jurisdictions* would include rural areas and Indian reservations.

Type A cities could be eligible for annual grants that divide equally the sum of $2 billion, and that also augmented a second share of the $2 billion amount to any city in the Type-A city set currently ranked in the top fifteen poverty cities in the United States (using the most recent Census Bureau data available). A city falls within the top fifteen cities ranked by poverty in the Census Bureau calculation by percent of persons living below the poverty level, or by percent of housing units built in 1939 or earlier. A single city "share" of the $2 billion RS money for a Type-A city is $142.8 million, an "augmented city" would earn two RS shares, for a total annual allocation of $285.6 million. Thus, as Table 6.1 illustrates, Chicago, Detroit, New York City, and Philadelphia each would receive augmented revenue sharing shares of $285.6 million annually, while Dallas, Houston, Los Angeles, Phoenix, San Antonio, and San Diego would receive $142.8 million annually under this formula.

Type B cities would use the same allocation process to distribute $2 billion among forty-one cities, fifteen of which earn augmented RS shares via the use of the needs-based Census Bureau poverty rating formula. Thus, there are fifty-six "shares"—forty-one cities plus fifteen city augmentation shares—divided into the $2 billion pool for Type-B cities. This produces a normal city share of $35.7 million annually, a share which, in fifteen cases, doubles to a needs-based augmentation for an annual revenue sharing allocation of $71.4 million. Type-B cities earning needs-based augmentations and funding at the $71.4 million level are: Atlanta, Baltimore, Boston, Buffalo, Cincinnati, Cleveland, El Paso, Fresno, Memphis, Miami, Minneapolis, New Orleans, Pittsburgh, San Francisco, and St. Louis. Type-B cities earning a normal RS share of $36.2 million include: Albuquerque, Austin, Charlotte, Columbus, Denver, Fort Worth, Honolulu, Indianapolis, Jacksonville, Kansas City, Long Beach, Milwaukee, Minneapolis, Nashville-Davidson (Tenn.), Oakland, Oklahoma City, Omaha, Portland, Sacramento, San Francisco, San Jose, Seattle, Toledo, Tucson, Tulsa, Virginia Beach, Washington, D.C., and Wichita.

The 26 Type C cities split a RS fund of $.5 billion among themselves, adding in six augmented shares for needs-based high poverty or cities with a high percentage of pre-World War II housing stock. This number results in a formula revenue sharing grant of $15.6 million for average Type-C cities, and augmented shares of $31.2 million for needs-based high poverty/high pre-War housing stock cities. Augmented Type-C cities receiving $31.2 million annually include: Birmingham, Baton Rouge, Jersey City, Newark (N.J.), Rochester (N.Y.), and St. Paul. Normal-share Type-C cities receiving $16.1 million annually would include: Akron, Anaheim, Anchorage, Arlington (Tex.), Aurora, Colorado Springs, Corpus Christi, Las Vegas, Lexington-Fayette (Ky.), Louisville, Mesa (Ariz.), Mobile, Norfolk, Raleigh, Richmond, Riverside, Santa Ana, St. Petersburg, Stockton, and Tampa.

There are approximately 900 U.S. cities with populations from 25,000 to 190,000. These Type D cities would each receive an equal 1/900th share of $.45 billion, netting each of the cities with populations of between 25,000 and 190,000 an annual RS grant of $500,000. Finally, $50 million in RS funds are set aside for Type E jurisdictions—Indian reservations and rural areas—in a formula pattern to be determined either by Congressional action, or by the administering agency, the U.S. Department of Housing and Urban Development.

Importantly, as the discussion below demonstrates, the New Revenue Sharing proposal discussed in this chapter does not require the adoption by

Congress of the MetroBall lottery idea. Several other funding sources are available, any one of which would produce more than sufficient funds to enact the entire Safe Streets, Safe Cities policy package, including a $5 billion New Revenue Sharing program.

PAYING THE PIPER: NON-LOTTERY SOURCES FOR *SAFE STREETS, SAFE CITIES*—TAX EQUITY ADJUSTMENTS AND CUTTING CORPORATE WELFARE

A Progressive package of a modest $14-billion annual expenditure for aiding America's cities does not stand or fall on the MetroBall national lottery proposal. The entire $14 billion Safe Streets, Safe Cities policy package could, if necessary, be more than adequately supported by one or more of a combination of relatively modest changes in the current American national tax structure. It is important to emphasize that eleven of the tax changes suggested in this section are not tax increases but *tax equity adjustments*— necessary and desirable modifications to change the aging tax code to make taxes more fair and less regressive, and to better connect the relationship between *who pays taxes* in the United States and *who benefits* from such tax payments. In fact, as we indicate below, one simple tax adjustment— placing a modest 5.8 percent increase in the effective tax rate on America's wealthiest individuals (*a group that received a 22 percent tax decrease in 1986 while average wage-earners saw their own tax rates rise 3 percent from 28 to 31 percent, as a result of the same Reagan-era tax "reform" package*)—would not only produce the $14 billion necessary to fight the crisis in America's cities but, according to General Accounting Office estimates, using 1993 as a base year, it would produce $32.6 billion annually; more than enough to fund Safe Streets, Safe Cities, with billions left over to finance deficit and debt reduction, as well as provide additional funding to shore up the financially troubled Medicare and Social Security programs. A good argument can be made that this one simple tax equity adjustment is the best single means of stabilizing the finances of both American metropolitan areas, and of the American national government. We turn now to an examination of not only this tax equity adjustment, but several others that might prove useful to a nation wishing to be of real assistance to America's cities, and to the children and the poor, which, in atypically high numbers, have crowded together to ride out the storm in America's metro ghettos, *kill zone* neighborhoods, and stressed-out *adrenaline cities*.

Despite the politically unpalatable nature of tax equity adjustments— which will inevitably be portrayed in some quarters as new taxes or tax increases (bear in mind that the key tax adjustment advocated by this author merely reinstitutes a tax rate on the rich that they have transferred to the poor, the elderly, and the middle class since 1986)—we include a brief discussion

TABLE 6.1

Revenue-Sharing Allocations for American Cities

Cities Ranked by 1992 Population	RS Allocation (in $ millions)	Percentage of person below poverty level, 1989		Percent of housing units built 1939 or earlier, 1990	
		Percent	Rank	Percent	Rank
Type A Cities					
New York	285.6	19.3	31	40.9	15
Los Angeles	142.8	18.9	34	17.4	35
Chicago	285.6	21.6	21	44.6	12
Houston	142.8	20.7	25	6.0	63
Philadelphia	285.6	20.3	27	51.6	09
San Diego	142.8	13.4	57	8.6	51
Dallas	142.8	18.0	40	6.8	61
Phoenix	142.8	14.2	53	2.9	70
Detroit	285.6	32.4	01	35.8	23
San Antonio	142.8	22.6	16	8.6	51
Type B Cities					
San Jose	35.7	9.3	72	5.5	65
Indianapolis	35.7	12.5	62	20.2	31
San Francisco	71.4	12.7	60	55.1	06
Baltimore	71.4	21.9	20	41.2	14
Jacksonville	35.7	13.0	59	06.9	60
Columbus	35.7	17.2	43	17.5	34
Milwaukee	35.7	22.2	19	38.4	17
Memphis	71.4	23.0	15	11.0	45
Washington, D.C.	35.7	16.9	46	37.7	19
Boston	71.4	18.7	37	57.6	03
El Paso	71.4	25.3	09	07.4	56
Seattle	35.7	12.4	64	36.2	22
Cleveland	71.4	28.7	04	52.6	08
Nashville-Davidson	35.7	13.4	57	09.3	50
Austin	35.7	17.9	41	05.0	67
New Orleans	71.4	31.6	02	33.2	26
Denver	35.7	17.1	45	25.7	30
Fort Worth	35.7	17.4	42	10.9	46
Oklahoma City	35.7	15.9	49	10.5	47
Portland	35.7	14.5	52	39.4	16
Long Beach	35.7	16.8	47	19.3	32
Kansas City	35.7	15.3	50	27.7	28
Virginia Beach	35.7	05.9	77	01.1	72
Charlotte	35.7	10.8	69	5.9	64
Tucson	35.7	20.2	28	05.3	66
Albuquerque	35.7	14.0	55	04.5	69
Atlanta	71.4	27.3	05	18.9	33
St. Louis	71.4	24.6	11	55.7	04
Sacramento	35.7	17.2	43	14.5	39

Fresno	71.4	24.0	13	08.1	54
Tulsa	35.7	15.0	51	10.4	48
Oakland	35.7	18.8	36	37.8	18
Honolulu CDP	35.7	08.4	73	07.6	55
Miami	71.4	31.2	03	11.6	42
Pittsburgh	71.4	21.4	22	55.3	05
Cincinnati	71.4	24.3	12	43.1	13
Minneapolis	71.4	18.5	38	53.2	07
Omaha	35.7	12.6	61	27.0	29
Toledo	35.7	19.1	33	35.1	24
Buffalo	71.4	25.6	08	68.1	01
Wichita	35.7	12.5	62	14.9	37
Type C Cities					
Mesa	15.6	09.5	71	01.1	72
Colorado Springs	15.6	10.9	68	08.5	53
Las Vegas	15.6	11.5	67	00.8	75
Santa Ana	15.6	18.1	39	06.1	62
Tampa	15.6	19.4	30	12.6	40
Arlington	15.6	08.2	74	00.6	76
Anaheim	15.6	10.6	70	02.3	71
Louisville	15.6	22.6	16	36.9	20
St. Paul	31.2	16.7	48	46.9	11
Newark	31.2	26.3	06	35.1	24
Corpus Christi	15.6	20.0	29	05.0	67
Birmingham	31.2	24.8	10	17.0	36
Norfolk	15.6	19.3	31	14.9	37
Anchorage	15.6	07.1	76	00.6	76
Aurora	15.6	07.4	75	00.9	74
Riverside	15.6	11.9	65	07.4	56
St. Petersburg	15.6	13.6	56	11.4	44
Rochester	31.2	23.5	14	58.7	02
Lexington-Fayette	15.6	14.1	54	11.6	42
Jersey City	31.2	18.9	34	50.8	10
Baton Rouge	31.2	26.2	07	07.3	58
Akron	15.6	20.5	26	36.8	21
Raleigh	15.6	11.8	66	07.0	59
Stockton	15.6	21.4	22	11.7	41
Richmond	15.6	20.9	24	30.0	27
Mobile	15.6	22.4	18	10.0	49
Type D Cities					
900 Cities with population 25,000–196,000	**$500,000 grant to each city.**				
Type E Areas					
Indian Reservations and Rural Areas	**$50 million RS funding pool; allocation to be determined by Congress or HUD.**				

Source: This Table is a modification of Table 3: "Cities With 200,000 or More Population Ranked," U.S. Census Bureau, 1996, Poverty and Housing Challenge Analysis. Available on the Internet as: ww.census.gov/ftp/pub/dstatab/ccdb/ccdb312.txt.

of such measures at this point in order to illustrate that, however politically unattractive, in hard policy terms, such tax equity adjustments are possible, they are modest in scope, and they would generate far more than the modest $14 billion increase in annual funding needed for the proposed Safe Streets, Safe Cities policy package.

The first tax equity adjustments to consider would be the elimination of the more than $85 billion in annual tax breaks for business corporations—corporate welfare subsidies paid for by American taxpayers for the benefit of narrow economic interests. We turn next to an examination of the possibility of ending all or part of the annual corporate welfare federal subsidies to American business, expenditures referred to by some critics as "Aid to Dependent Corporations" (Albelda & Folbre, 1996: 20), the corporate equivalent to the recently revised Aid to Families with Dependent Children (AFDC) program.

Taking a Look at Corporate Tax Breaks: Should Congress End "Corporate Welfare as We Know It"?

Consider, for a moment, that if corporations paid the same federal income tax today as the effective rate paid by corporations in the 1950s, the Federal Treasury would generate an additional $250 billion each year—an amount capable of not only providing the modest $14 billion needed annually for Safe Streets, Safe Cities, but also enough, as a recent projection has shown, to single-handedly eliminate the entire federal budget deficit (Albelda & Folbre, 1996: 20–21). After the craze for institutionalizing a balanced budget subsides and, in all likelihood, a constitutional amendment is passed mandating a balanced budget, corporate welfare and the artificially low post-1950 corporate tax environment created to favor America corporations may need to be one of the first revenue avenues to search by a Congress and president that collectively will have taken, as New Hampshire residents are wont to say, "the Pledge," regarding a balanced budget and new taxes. Instead of new taxes, cutting existing corporate tax breaks may be precisely where Congress will need to steer its budgetary ship of state.

Corporate welfare, federal subsidies to corporations, businesses, and individuals in business in America, currently amounts to annual federal expenditures ranging from $85 billion—"a sum that amounts to about a third of the annual federal budget deficit" (Albelda & Folbre, 1996: 20–21), that is, to $100 billion (Bagby, 1996: 20). The Clinton administration and Congress have, with the Welfare Reform Act of 1996, limited the duration of AFDC and welfare for America's poor to "two years and you're off," and a total lifetime allowance of five years in welfare assistance, thus, as President Clinton and welfare reform advocates insist, having "ended welfare as we know it." Perhaps it is also time to end corporate welfare as we know it; ending it immediately for corporations and businesses that have already received five or more years in subsidies, and allowing no more than two years for any new recipients of corporate welfare. Such thinking would, at least, have the benefit of applying the same rules of the road to American business and corporations that Congress has applied in 1995 and 1996 to the American poor and to American agriculture—which, with only a few exceptions, has seen the end of subsidies to farmers and agribusiness—and apply these same rules to all other large and small American businesses. As General Colin Powell said in his address in San Diego to the GOP National Convention in August 1996: "We must make sure that reduced government spending does not single out just the poor and the middle class. Corporate welfare, and welfare for the wealthy, must be first in line for elimination."

Good corporate welfare candidates for reduction include—and this concentrates on the narrow generally agreed-upon area of corporate welfare and not the larger umbrella of tax breaks to wealthy corporations and individuals, which, using a 1996 base year, the Congressional Budget Office has estimated at $440 billion dollars, a figure that is *over seventeen times greater than the combined state and federal spending on AFDC* (Albelda & Folbre, 1996: 20) the following: (1) the corporate tax rate that in 1996 averaged only 24 percent of profits, compared with corporate tax levels of approximately 45 percent in the 1950s, marking a sharp reduction in the corporate share of funding American government, down to 10 percent of federal revenues in 1995, compared with 23 percent in 1960 (Albelda & Folbre, 1996: 21); (2) corporate advertising— in 1991, the federal government spent $2.9 million in taxpayer-supported advertising for Pillsbury muffins; $10 million for Sunkist oranges; $465,000 for advertising McDonald's Chicken McNuggets; $1.2 million for American Legend mink coats; and $2.5 million advertising prunes, nuts, and pineapples for Dole (Bagley, 1996: 13); (3) add to this, $2 billion in Rural Electrification Administration and the Federal Power Marketing Administration support for highly profitable electric utility corporations, in two cases resulting in subsidizing electricity costs for such crucial national objectives as "ski resorts in Aspen, Colorado, five-star hotels in Hilton Head, South Carolina, and gambling casinos in Las Vegas, Nevada" (Bagley, 1996: 13)—all, like the electric utility cooperatives, highly profitable large-scale corporate businesses. Add to the foregoing the small but, in the aggregate, significant corporate ripoff abuses discovered by a House of Representatives investigative team in 1995 (e.g., the Martin-Marietta Corporation, which billed the Pentagon $260,000 for a Smokey Robinson concert, another $20,000 for golf balls, and $7,500 for a Christmas party; exceeded in hubris only by "Ecology and Environment of Lancaster, New York, [which] spent $243,000 of funds on 'employee morale' and $37,000 on tennis lessons, bike races, golf tournaments, and entertainment" [Bagley, 1996: 13]).

Bipartisan Support for the Elimination of Corporate Welfare

Eliminating corporate welfare is not a partisan political issue. General Colin Powell argued forcefully for the idea in a keynote address to the GOP National Convention in San Diego in 1996. In the same year, the Democratic

Leadership Council, a lynch-pin of support for the "New Democrat" approach of President Clinton, released a report denouncing thirty "tax subsidies" totaling a loss of over $133 billion to the federal treasury annually. Perhaps, in the name of fairness and in the interests of American's cities facing the seemingly permanent crisis of the 1990s, Congress and the president could begin to subsidize America's children with some small portion of the current federal corporate welfare payroll that instead subsidizes America's corporations. It would be necessary to trim corporate welfare by only $14 billion to achieve adequate funding for the Safe Streets, Safe Cities program—such a cut would leave more than $80 billion in business/corporate welfare federal financial assistance in place, a proposal that would not end corporate welfare as we know it, but merely put some wealthy corporations on a free enterprise "diet"; a diet not dissimilar to the one that Congress has recently adopted for AFDC recipients, farmers, and other less-privileged constituencies.

We should try the idea of a national lottery, which should prove workable, but in the event that it fails to be implemented, or if the president and Congress would rather leave aside the lottery option—perhaps in deference to state and local lotteries that produce needed revenues for sub-national jurisdictions—then a modest trim in the corporate welfare budget of $14 billion (a corporate welfare tax cut of only 14 percent) would produce sufficient funding for the Safe Streets, Safe Cities progressive policy package advanced in this chapter. Failing agreement on a national lottery or reductions in corporate welfare as funding sources for Safe Streets, Safe Cities, there are still modest tax equity adjustments—modifications in the current tax laws to make American taxes more fair and more equitable for the average American taxpayer—that in whole or part would not only fund the "Safe Streets, Safe Cities" programs; but, it should not noted, would also greatly aid in cutting the deficit, paying down on the nation's current debt load, balancing the national budget, and stabilizing both the Medicare and Social Security programs. We turn now to an examination of such tax equity modifications.

Potential Tax Equity Adjustments

The VAT-MAT Tax Proposal   Taxes that are programmatically, if less politically, feasible, include first, a specially earmarked *value-added tax* (VAT), a sales tax on all goods and services in the United States. Following the example of most European countries, Congress could create a value-added tax, known as the *Metro Areas Tax* (*or* VAT-MAT *tax*), a 1-percent tax on all goods and services produced in the United States. A 1-percent VAT-MAT tax on the 1991 gross national product of $5.673 trillion, for example, would generate a MAT tax metro fund of $56.73 billion (more than enough, it should be noted, to pursue the most ambitious plans set forward by groups such as the U.S. Conference of Mayors or the Eisenhower Foundation—and far more than the Safe Streets, Safe Cities plan would require).

The FLAT-MAT Tax   Second, a less equitable and less financially ad-equate *flat tax* (FLAT-MAT) of 1 percent on all taxable personal income in the United States would generate, again using 1991 as a base year, a FLAT-MAT fund of $6.16 billion in funding. While a relatively low yield and $12 billion short of the Safe Streets, Safe Cities program, it would be a good start, and a revenue-neutral start at that, toward addressing the permanent crisis in America's metro regions.

A MAT-TOP Tax   Third, there are several reasons to aim a metro tax or MAT tax at the wealthiest 1 percent of the American population. It would be a perverse logic to suggest that the burden of helping the American poor should fall equally on the rich and poor alike. It would be an equal folly to ignore the fact that, as Senator Jim Sasser of Tennessee has noted, the 1981 Reagan tax cut "not only cost the Federal Treasury $2 trillion to date, it also distributed its benefits disproportionately among the rich and very rich" (Sasser, 1993). If taxes on the wealthiest 1 percent of the U.S. population (call this a *MAT-TOP* tax) were increased by an effective rate of 5.3 percent—bear in mind that we are speaking of single individuals making $161,364, couples making $206,492, and families of four making $324,083—the Congressional Budget Office estimates, using 1993 as a base year, that a 1 percent MAT-TOP tax would have generated $32.6 billion in 1993 revenue. Over five years such a tax could be expected to produce "roughly $181 billion more in revenue" (Sasser, 1993). Not only would such a program fund the Safe Streets, Safe Cities program, it would significantly reduce the national debt and the overall budget deficit.

Perhaps a Congress that has reduced welfare benefits to the poorest Americans in the 1996 Welfare Reform Act, and reduced virtually all existing agricultural and crop subsidies to American farmers, can see the equity in also assessing a modest 1 percent "wealth flat tax"—an annual flat fee of 1 percent charged to the very persons most benefiting from American government and the American economy. If any tax equity adjustments are eventually enacted by Congress, the flat tax on America's super rich is, by far, the most equitable place to fund the Safe Streets, Safe Cities program, and to begin serious efforts to balance the budget and to reduce America's debt load.

Note that such a flat tax on the super rich is the political and economic opposite of the *wage-only*, falsely-named *flat tax* advanced in the 1996 Pres-idential campaign. The latter proposal, it should be emphasized, would have hit hardest the average-wage-earning Americans earning $30,000 a year or less, while not taxing the investment income of America's wealthiest families and investors. In fact, most journalists on the campaign trail noted the irony for the flat tax's leading proponent, who invested millions of his personal wealth in a failed presidential bid but who would have recouped his entire multi million-dollar election expenditure in a single year, had the 1996 wages-only flat tax aimed squarely at the average American wage earner actually have been enacted.

Unlike a tax aimed at the American working class, a wealth flat tax of 1% makes eminent economic and political sense. During the negotiations for the 1986 tax revision, rates for the American poor were reduced in exchange for a tax break that reduced the taxes on the wealthiest Americans from 50 percent (a rate that earlier had been pegged at 70 percent) to 28 percent, the same effective tax rate as the American middle class; a group that actually saw a tax increase to approximately 31 percent due to the elimination of several previously allowable deductions, and a new 1986 tax placed on Social Security for America's middle-income elderly (Lilly, 1990). A flat tax on America's wealthiest taxpayers would merely *increase by 1 percent* the taxes of a group of wealthy individuals and families who *decreased their income taxes by 22 percent annually beginning in 1987.* As such, the wealth flat tax is a prime candidate for tax equity tax adjustments, a modest tax increment that, indeed, America's super rich should be willing to endorse lest some populist tax crusader eventually explain to the American working and taxpaying public the net effect of the 1986 tax code changes; a tax deal in Congress that produced a tax increase from 28 percent to 31 percent for the average taxpayer and a decrease from 50 percent to 28 percent for America's wealthiest individuals and families is hardly the stuff that the average voter is likely to want to hear in the midst of a congressional or presidential election campaign. A 1 percent reversal of this tide is a meager price to fund America's cities, and to prevent a populist tax uprising that, once adequately explained to the average American taxpayer, would make the 1970s Proposition 13 Taxpayer's Revolt pale in comparison, since the average wage-earners might be persuaded in this latter-day tax revolt to simultaneously solve the deficit, debt, and federal funding for the cities problem by one simple gesture—namely, simply by restoring pre-1986 taxes levels, and thereby granting the average taxpayer a 4 percent tax cut, and the wealthiest Americans a 22 percent tax increase.

There are, of course, other tax equity adjustments that are within the reality of economic and political possibility. One, a consumption adjustment as well as an equity adjustment, would be to more directly charge gasoline consumers for the side costs associated with the high levels of gasoline consumption in the United States. We turn to that discussion now.

GAS-MAT and the Mortgage Deduction for Second Homes A fourth source of potential revenue, particularly appropriate for funding metro mass-transit systems, would be modest increases in the federal gasoline tax. In California, for example, without any significant protests from motorists, the market prices for gasoline in 1992–93 increased by about a third or even half in some places. Prices increased from roughly a dollar or less a gallon for regular gas to between $1.34 and $1.52 a gallon, depending on octane and self- or full-serve service. One analyst, using 1992 as a base year, calculated that the same increase set aside as a national gas tax (call this the *GAS-MAT tax*) would have generated between $50 and $75 billion in 1992 alone (Johnson, 1995).

Americans import approximately seven million barrels of oil a day, a figure that adds almost $50 billion to the United States trade deficit annually. A modest increase in the gasoline tax, encouraging a reduction in gasoline consumption, would help reduce this annual trade deficit. Americans might do well to bear in mind that the average price of gasoline in Europe is $4 a gallon, about $2.75 higher than in the United States. One analyst, noting this disparity, has suggested decreasing gasoline consumption, raising revenue, and decreasing the trade deficit by gradually escalating the current gasoline tax 25 cents a year for ten years (Johnson, 1995).

It is worth noting that Ross Perot's single boldest stroke during his memorable 1992 independent candidacy for the presidency was his endorsement of a plan to boost the gasoline tax to 50 cents a gallon over a ten-year period. Perot was correct, if not half bold enough to have an impact on either the deficit or gas consumption patterns in the United States. A recent estimate projects that an immediate $1 per gallon excise tax on gasoline would raise over $100 billion annually, and, because the inflationary shock would be a one-time event rather than phased-in over a number of years, it would actually fuel inflation far less than a similar or smaller increase phased in over a ten-year period (Fitch, 1992). With Italians, for example, typically paying $5 a gallon for gas, and most Europeans paying at least $4 per gallon, it is probably well past time for Americans to pay at the pump for aiding metro areas, for helping to rebuild America's decaying transportation infrastructure, and to give a shot in the arm to federal revenues and deficit reduction. Adoption in the near term of both a $1 a gallon gasoline tax increase *and* a .53 percent effective tax increase on America's wealthiest individuals and families would produce over $132 billion in federal revenues annually—probably more than enough to aid American cities, to retire the deficit and debt, and to render solvent Medicare and Social Security. Not the least of the attractions of such a tax increase would be to stave off, for at least another generation, the emerging debate over whether the United States should adopt a European-style value-added tax.

Fifth, and a final source of increased tax revenue, is the potential elimination of the income tax deduction for interest paid on home mortgages for *a second home*. It is difficult, either in rhetorical or *real politick* terms to continue to argue that a second home is, in fact, a "middle-class tax break" for average homeowners. In fact, owning more than one home is statistically rare for members of the U.S. population at large. As of 1991, only 9,672,000 U.S. households (less than 12 percent of the total number of U.S. households, using 1991 as a base year [HUD 1991]) own more than one house. Elimination of 12 percent of the 1991 base year of over $40 billion dollars in home mortgage deductions would generate approximately $4.8 billion dollars, a figure equal to over 19 percent of HUD's $25 billion annual operating budget.

IT'S GOING TO TAKE MORE THAN DOLLARS: PROCESS AND STRUCTURAL CHANGES IN PROGRESSIVE POLICIES FOR AMERICA'S CITIES

In addition to the Safe Streets, Safe Cities progressive policy package—Head Start and Jump Start programs, a revised Crime Bill, a fully funded Police Corps, funding for Second Harvest anti-hunger efforts, and better classrooms through investments in the Teacher Credential Corps Endowment Fund—two other doses of medicine are worth considering for America's cities. As noted in Chapter 3, despite housing a majority of America's residents, cities are far from constituting a majority of the influence in American national politics. Again, as noted earlier, in the words of Senator Daniel Patrick Moynihan (D-NY), cities, at present, need to wait for the periodic appearance of "our old friend, the urban crisis,"—often in the form of an urban riot or related catastrophes—before metro issues and metro police forces are addressed in national political circles. What would it take to rework this scenario, to bring cities back into national politics?

BRINGING CITIES BACK INTO AMERICAN NATIONAL POLITICS

This section explores stronger medicine for cities, medicine designed to mobilize more metropolitan-area voters, and to attack the decidedly anti-urban and rural bias in the present presidential primary election system. While the proposed medicine is admittedly strong, it will take strong medicine to bring metro regions and cities back into the mainstream of American national politics. Either of the two remedies proposed would help to produce a more level playing field for metro residents. Taken collectively, they would produce a fairer, more democratic, more equitable American political system—a system in which cities could no longer be "virtually ignored" (Fainstein & Fainstein, 1995) by the federal government for decades at a time. The remedies, in increasing order of political difficulty to obtain, are (1) enactment of a *Letter Voter Law* by Congress encouraging the use of mail-ballot elections by state and local jurisdictions, and (2) a same-day or same-week presidential primary. We turn, next, to a consideration of both of these proposals.

Mail Ballot Elections and Letter Voter Legislation: Replacing *Motor Voter* with a *Letter Voter Act*

Motor Voter was a good first cut at increasing voter mobilization among the urban/metropolitan electorate. Since taking effect in January 1995, almost one million new voters a month have either newly registered to vote or updated their voting addresses, a registration pace that is double the pre-Motor Voter registration rate (Ganz, 1996). Some states such as California and New York have lagged markedly behind this national average. In California, a partisan Republican Governor, Pete Wilson, waged an unsuccessful legal battle attempting to block increased voter registration. In New York State, which had the same gubernatorial motives for blocking increased voter registration, the case of poor implementation is a mixture of gubernatorial resistance and the fact that New York City is uniquely unsuited to a Motor Voter-linked registration drive. New York City, for example, has 67 percent of the state's welfare caseload but only 44 percent of newly registered public-aid recipients. New York state as a whole had, by January of 1996, registered only 11 percent of public-aid recipients statewide, compared, for example, with Kentucky at 18 percent, and Missouri at 31 percent.

It should be emphasized, however, that the Big Apple is not a particularly good place to look for strong impacts from the Motor Voter registration law, since only 50 percent of New York City adults possess a driver's license compared to 90 percent of adults statewide (Green, 1996). In short, in the number-one metropolitan region in the country, Motor Voter is less than an overwhelming success at producing large numbers of new voters from the previously eligible but non-participating public. As Ganz (1996) has shown, Motor Voter, while a modest success at increasing voter registration, is not and was not expected to be significantly effective at increasing voter mobilization, or at inspiring newly registered voters to actually vote at election time. There is, however, a better way.

The most recent studies reported in Ganz (1996: 48–49) indicate that only 17 percent of the 45 million unregistered voters in states covered by Motor Voter were registered under the new law. (Six states and the District of Columbia are unaffected by Motor Voter, since they have either same-day registration or no organized voter registration procedures at all.) Of those newly registered, approximately nine million persons were actually new voters, with another eleven million reregistering with a change of address, a change of party, etc. (Ganz, 1996). Of those who registered under Motor Voter, almost a quarter—approximately 24 percent—registered via the mail (Human Service Study, 1996). This use of the mail—for both registration and balloting—is the single greatest opportunity to continue registering, mobilizing, and encouraging new voters to actually *participate* in elections.

As a number of state and local jurisdictions—ranging from the states of California and Oregon, the cities of Berkeley, San Diego, and Rochester (N.Y.)—have demonstrated, use of the mail for elections—and here we move beyond motor registration to mail balloting—not only mobilizes in the range of 30-to-50-percent more voters in a given locale, it generally decreases the cost of local elections by a similar 30-to-50-percent range. While states constitutionally have the dominant role of determining state and local election procedures—subject to Civil Rights review by the U.S. Attorney General's Civil Rights Division under the Voting Rights Act of 1965—Congress should move quickly to encourage state and local jurisdictions (many of who can do so now without state enabling legislation) to adopt Mail Ballot election procedures, both for reasons of increased participation and for reasons of the cost savings involved. Further, Congress should enact a *Letter Voter Act*, encouraging the use of Letter Voter procedures by guaranteeing to reimburse 80 percent of the costs to state and local jurisdictions for any elections conducted using the mail ballot procedure as the *primary means* for voters to cast ballots in a state or local election.

Thus, a Letter Voter Bill would provide material financial incentives to subnational jurisdictions to engage in mail balloting procedures, while simultaneously respecting the constitutional right of states to determine the appropriate election procedures to be used within their own state's geographical limits. A final incentive to state and local jurisdictions is the example of Stanislaus County in California, which in 1994 ran an election with virtually no possibility of election irregularities since the return envelopes were barcoded to automatically pull up the signatures of voters and instantly verify the ballot as belonging to the voter in question. As one political commentator noted at the time, this innovation alone may prove the strongest incentive of all for states and local jurisdictions to promote the Letter Voter approach. As William Endicott put it at the time, "When was the last time anybody verified your signature when you signed at a polling place?" (Endicott, 1993). Letter Voter saves money, increases voter turnout, decreases the possibility of illegal election irregularities, increases the confidence of voters in the legitimacy of the electoral process, and greatly improves on the Motor Voter legislation of 1995. Congress should pass Letter Voter, and do so soon.

Modifying Letter Voter to Promote Same-Day, Same-Week Presidential Primaries

There is a second electoral reform that would help bring metropolitan voters and American voters in general back into the mainstream of American politics. More metro voters, via a Letter Voter Bill, will not help metropolitan residents if presidential primaries continue to be front-loaded with early primaries in rural states such as Iowa and New Hampshire, states that had a combined 1990 population of 3,886,007—1.6 percent of the U.S. population, roughly the same as Los Angeles (3,485,398—1990 population; 3,489,779—1992 population) or roughly half the size of New York City (7,322,564—1990 population; 7,311,966—1992 population). To say that an Iowa/New Hampshire front-loaded presidential primary system favors rural over metropolitan interests, and the interests of two of America smallest states over the collective interests of the other forty-eight states—not to mention the interests of Americans as a nation—is indisputable. There is, fortunately, in the Letter Voter Bill, the outlines of a cure.

New Hampshire and Iowa have proved impervious to the requests of other states that they alter their position of first in the nation primary status. States have begun to collapse or compress the primary season by scheduling regional primaries with the electoral votes of several large states within a region up for grabs on a single day. This has not, however, deterred Iowa and New Hampshire from playing the spoiler in terms of eliminating most of the candidates in the presidential "pack" in the first two primaries.

Congress should build on the incremental progress of the other forty-eight states that have moved toward a more compressed, shorter primary season by bunching their primaries into large, multi-state regional blocks; that is, Super-Tuesday in the South, in the New England States, in the West, etc. Congress should modify Letter Voter to provide funding for presidential primary elections *if and only if* such elections are scheduled on either the same day or same week nationally. Given the financial incentive, and the fact that most states would probably opt for the funding (and, thus, the required scheduling), state and local jurisdictions should have little internal incentives for resisting a primary election schedule that would collapse all of the primaries in the nation into a *same day, same week* framework. Finally, the week or day in question should be designated by the Letter Voter Bill to be no later than a publicly announced primary election scheduled in either Iowa or New Hampshire, and preferably earlier. As an incentive to Iowa and New Hampshire, the Letter Voter legislation should contain a stipulation that, in the event that Iowa or New Hampshire (or any other state) should elect to hold out for dates other than the nationally designated same-day, same-week time period, or in any other significant way sabotage the same-day, same-week primary election effort, the state or states in question (and, remember, this is not limited only to New Hampshire or Iowa) would *automatically* lose federal election funding for four years, as well as all federal revenue sharing and all ISTEA federal highway and transportation funding for a four-year period.

Same-day, same-week primaries would have the benefits of condensing the primary election season, increasing the influence of states beyond Iowa and New Hampshire in the presidential selection process, and bringing metro voters and American voters in general back into the mainstream of the presidential primary election process.

CHAPTER SUMMARY AND CONCLUSION

The *Safe Streets, Safe Cities* progressive policy package advocated in this chapter is a $14 billion annual program to aid America's troubled cities. If adopted by Congress, the MetroBall national lottery will raise approximately $14 billion in revenue-neutral funds annually. Of this amount, we have suggested a Safe Streets, Safe Cities Progressive policy package for combating the permanent crisis in America's cities, allocating annually: (1) $4 billion to the current Head Start and a new Jump Start early childhood education program; (2) $1.1 billion for a reconfigured Crime Bill that would place 50,000 new police officers—2,000 new officers in each of the top twenty-five crime cities in the United States over a four-year period; (3) $2.72 billion for a revitalized Police Corps envisioned in the original Crime Bill but currently inoperative, which would provide 80,000 Police Corps scholarships annually to college students obligated in return to serve a fixed term in state or

metropolitan police forces; (4) a $.2 billion annual allocation to the Second
Harvest hunger relief agency in an effort to help create the access to at least
one decent meal a day as a basic American right; and (5) an annual investment
of almost $1 billion a year (.98 billion) to be paid into a national Teacher
Credential Corps Endowment Fund, to help create a fund of money that
eventually will allow every certificated K–12 teacher in America to raise their
pay beyond the level of the prevailing union wages in their teaching district,
producing a "supply side" solution to the crisis of under-credentialed teachers
working in America's classrooms.

These five Safe Streets, Safe Cities program expenditures would total
$9 billion in MetroBall-generated funds annually. The remaining $5 billion
annual earnings in MetroBall funding would be allocated for a round of
unrestricted New Revenue Sharing, annual funding to be awarded to local
jurisdictions on the basis of population size and local needs. A New Revenue
Sharing distribution formula is suggested that avoids the pitfalls of the Nixon-
to-Reagan era Revenue Sharing program by (a) avoiding a simple population
or per-capita formula that assumes that all jurisdictions have equal needs and
require equal levels of support and (b) further building on this distinction
between city size and needs by including a needs-based element that calculates
the poverty level and older housing stocks of cities in the United States, and
allows for "augmented shares" to be awarded to high-poverty cities with
high numbers of aging pre-World War II housing. Finally, we have proposed
Letter Voter legislation to extend efforts to register and mobilize American
voters beyond the level made possible by the Motor Voter Bill, by providing
financial assistance to state and local jurisdictions employing the Letter Voter
methodology, and by designing such financial assistance in primary election
years to encourage the transition to a condensed national "same day, same
week" presidential primary election system.

Some readers will find these proposals promising and supportable, believing (with the present author) that a modest series of broad federal level
programs aimed at indirectly assisting cities coupled with a round of New
Revenue Sharing in which locals can rely on multi-year federal funding and
are encouraged to determine locally how such funds should be spent may
eventually lead to stronger, healthy, and *Independent Cities*.[7] Others will
find the Safe Streets, Safe Cities proposal too progressive, favoring instead
(as opposed to this author) a continuation of the federal-local policy legacy
reviewed in Chapter 4; a legacy that this author portrayed as failed policies
creating not independent cities, but dependent cities—neocolonial jurisdictions best described as *Washington's Cities*. Still others will reject both the
status quo policies described in Chapters 4 and 5, and the Safe Streets, Safe
Cities and Letter Voter progressive policies endorsed in this chapter. For such
observers, nothing short of far more radical medicine will cure the ills of
American cities. We turn next to a consideration of these views, and the policy
recommendations that flow from a more radical view of city problems, and
metro solutions.

7

Cities in Flames
Radical Policies for American Cities

This country is in a perpetual civil war.

> ANDREW HACKER, author of *Two Nations* (1992), interview
> in *New York Times* (Wilkerson, 1992)

This Great Urban Crisis is just as much a threat to our society
as the Great Depression. Our second-largest city would not
have exploded in burning and insurrection if something was
not profoundly wrong. In community after community, the
intolerable conditions are worsening: burnt-out buildings, rubble
strewn about as small children play nearby, homeless lying in
doorways . . . The specter of "Blade Runner" haunts our cities as
global trade and technology separate the professionals at the top
from the growing third world of welfare and poverty wages at the
bottom. It is ripping apart our social and civic fabric.

> JERRY BROWN, former Governor of California, former Presi-
> dential candidate, and current candidate for Mayor of
> Oakland, op-ed editorial in *New York Times* (1992)

Let us hope and pray that the vast intelligence, imagination,
humor, and courage of Americans will not fail us. Either we learn
a new language of compassion, or the fire this time will consume
us all.

> CORNEL WEST, *Race Matters* (1994: 13)

LOOKING OVER THE EDGE OF THE URBAN PRECIPICE: CITIES IN FLAMES AND POLICIES TO EXTINGUISH THE FLAMES

Writing with the benefit of hindsight, Jean Paul Sartre once argued that France
in the late 1920s and early 1930s was not at peace but, rather, "between

wars" (Sartre, 1947–1949).[1] Much the same may be said of America's cities in the 1990s. Urban America was less "at peace" in the 1970s, 80s, and early 90s than it was "between riots." American metropolitan areas were not at peace between the Watts riot of 1965 and the South Central riot of 1992; instead, the poorest and least fortunate residents of America's vast "urban reservations" were "between riots" (Waste, 1995a, 1993b). They are still *between riots* in the late 1990s. The question in the latter part of the 1990s, and as American metro areas prepare to walk across the "bridge to the twenty-first century," is not *whether* American cities will riot again, but *when*, and whether the riot activity in metro areas can finally, mercifully, end?

America's cities are not quiet but slowly simmering—engaged in a "quiet riot" (Wilson, 1996), a "slow riot" (Wilson, 1996), a riot that will not abate until the nation learns either to speak and act with "a new language of compassion" or to wait yet again for a new round of urban riots that all-too-grimly carry with them the possibility that "the fire this time will consume us all" (West, 1994: 13).

Regrettably, over a half-century of federal-local policies by the federal government has not prevented the creation of neo-colonial dependent local jurisdictions—*Washington's cities*—cities all too prone to violence and characterized by "separate societies" (Goldsmith & Blakeley, 1992), "savage inequalities" (Kozol, 1991), and a latter-day "American apartheid" (Massey & Denton, 1994), in which the Kerner Commission findings—the 1968 report by the National Commission on Civil Disorders established to investigate the 1960s urban riots—appear to have come true for many American cities. In 1968 the Kerner Commission warned that the country was

> rapidly moving toward two increasingly separate Americas . . . [a] white society principally located in the suburbs . . . and a Negro society largely concentrated within large central cities . . . [and warned that] within two decades [by 1988] this division could be so deep that it would be almost impossible to reunite. (1968: 407)

FOUR STRATEGIES TO REUNITE AMERICA AND REVITALIZE AMERICA'S CITIES

As a nation we have tried two strategies to reunite America's "separate societies," and to revitalize America's cities. The *first approach*, the fifty-year legacy of Washington, D.C.-based national urban policy, has experienced, at best, limited successes in a small number of programs such as Head Start and revenue sharing. In the aggregate, over a half-century of federal urban policies has led to the creation of weak and dependent metro areas—Washington's cities—and, at a minimum, national urban policy did not prevent the violent riots typified by Watts in 1965 or in South Central Los Angeles in 1992; nor did these policies prevent the "quiet riots" and "slow riots" of contemporary urban America. In short, Washington's policies, like Washington's cities, are failures in need of reform.

Sub-national jurisdictions, *Jefferson's cities*, have been marginally more effective as a *second approach* to reuniting suburban and center-city metro American and revitalizing America's cities, but these efforts have been inadequately funded, micro-managed from Washington, D.C., and they, too, ultimately, proved unable to prevent (though they may have forestalled) the violent riot in Los Angeles and the "slow, quiet riots" in the rest of America's large urban areas.

This book has suggested a *third approach* to America's cities and the problem of reuniting and unifying the populations of opportunity with the less fortunate populations of concentrated poverty, joblessness, and concentrated human misery—populations that are disproportionately metro residents of color, women, and children. We have proposed a *Safe Streets, Safe Cities* program, funded with a reliable and revenue-neutral annual revenue stream of $14 billion to revitalize America's metro areas.

Will the Safe Streets, Safe Cities, progressive policy package actually be more successful than earlier federal-local policy efforts? The experience of sub-national jurisdictions in the Jefferson's cities programs described in Chapter 5 suggests grounds for optimism. Clearly, this author feels that such an approach can work. It is revenue-neutral, it is substantially funded, and it is bipartisan in orientation—the Head Start element owing much to the liberal legacy of the New Frontier, the Great Society, and the War on Poverty; the Revenue Sharing element owing much to the conservative legacy of the New Federalism of the Nixon administration. The *Second Harvest*, Crime Bill, Police Corps, and Teacher Credential Corps elements are inherently bipartisan efforts that are cost-effective, avoid large federal bureaucracies where possible, and provide needed resources to cities to use as the elected leadership and community members of those cities see fit.

Will the Safe Streets, Safe Cities policy package work to quell the "quiet riot," to prevent outbreaks of future violent riots, and to revitalize America's cities? I believe so. Others can, and will, disagree. In the latter view, $14 billion—no matter how carefully targeted—is simply insufficient to the true costs of the task ahead. For these critics, metro areas will not be saved without a level of spending at least twice that proposed in the present book. For a second set of advocates of this *fourth approach*, American metro areas will not be saved unless radical changes are made in both the structure and process of American politics. We turn next to an examination of this view, that the loud and quiet riots will continue unless America contemplates far more radical— or, at least, far more expensive—medicine than we have been willing to so far prescribe for America's cities. We will examine some of these prescriptions in descending order of the likelihood of their potential adoption by both a reluctant American electorate and an equally reluctant national policymaking mechanism in Washington, D.C.

PRECURSORS TO A RADICAL FRINGE SOLUTION: THINKING LARGER AND SPENDING MORE

It should be emphasized that the first set of "thinking larger, spending more" proposals is hardly radical in nature. Two qualities of these proposals mitigate against labeling them as radical. First, many of these proposals and advocates are the essence of political centerism and mainstream political and university policy scholarship. Indeed, most of these proposals call for a level of spending only twice that of the Progressive Safe Streets, Safe Cities policy and build on the Great Depression–era Works Progress Administration (WPA) programs and similar "alphabet soup" programs of FDR and the New Deal, programs once widely popular and widely supported in American politics. As such, to label these proposals genuinely radical is inherently inaccurate.

Second, the proposals reviewed in this "thinking larger, spending more" section include programs advocated by leading New Democrats (Wilson, 1987, 1988, 1990, 1992, 1996), vociferous critics of the New Democrat position (Brown, 1992; Kaus, 1995, 1996a), high-ranking former Democratic (Bane, 1996; Ellwood in DeParle, 1994a) and Republican (Nathan, 1987, 1989, 1993, 1994) administration officials, mainstream bodies of elected officials such as the U.S. Conference of Mayors (O'Rourke, 1992; Welch, 1992a, 1992b), and equally mainstream nonpartisan philanthropic foundations such as the Eisenhower Foundation (Keating, 1994a:4).

Large Urban Aid Programs

In 1993, in a report criticizing the enterprise zone/empowerment zone approach to revitalizing cities and ghetto poverty neighborhoods, the Eisenhower Foundation called for a ten-year program, spending $30 billion annually. Half of these funds was to be targeted for a mix of programs aimed at reconstructing inner-city neighborhoods, and half was to be earmarked for programs aimed at disadvantaged children, and teens living in high-risk and/or high-poverty neighborhoods (Keating, 1994: 4). In spending levels and programs proposed, the 1993 Eisenhower Foundation report is quite similar to a $35-billion 1992 urban aid Marshall Plan for Cities program championed by Rep. John Conyers (D-Michigan) and called for by the U.S. Conference of Mayors in the wake of the South Central Los Angeles riots (Welch, 1992). The call for the immediate multi-billion-dollar direct aid program to U.S. cities by the Mayor's Conference was met by the Bush administration and Congress with a $1 billion post-riot aid and summer employment program.

More recently, calls for large-scale efforts to aid America's cities have been repeated—first, by former California governor Jerry Brown in November 1992, following his electoral loss to Bill Clinton in the race for the Democratic nomination for the presidency. Brown advocated an extension of WPA-era projects such as the WPA, the Civilian Conservation Corps, and a national youth administration, combined with community service jobs and the Clinton administration's Youth Opportunity Corps—a $20 billion "Help Cities First" proposal that, in the first year alone, was targeted to recruit as many participants as were mustered out of the armed services in the same year (Brown, 1992).

A GI Bill for American Families and the American Worker?

In the fall of 1996, perhaps in the then-certain knowledge that President Clinton would embrace some form of time-limited welfare "reform" enacted by Congress that fall, Harvard policy scholar Theda Skocpol called for a GI Bill for families—an idea supportive of but different in kind from the GI Bill for working Americans advanced in 1995 by Peter Plastrik in the Democratic Leadership Council magazine *New Democrat*, which advocated federal vouchers for job seekers and job training, and credit lines for skill training to pay the unemployed and employed workers for training or retraining for a better job in skill workshops, apprentice programs, community colleges, and universities (Plastrik, 1995: 00).[2]

Arguing that the American social benefits system is "skewed" in favor of benefits for retirees and seniors over working-age parents, Skocpol (1996: 71) suggested that expanding such programs to include working-age adults (particularly parents) is not only good policy—providing benefits to a broader segment of the tax-paying public instead of continuing to narrowly aid the elderly at the expense of middle-aged working singles and parents—but also good politics. The American Association of Retired Persons (AARP), successful in the early 1990s at stopping modest efforts to means-test and tax Social Security and Medicare benefits, might do well, Skocpol suggested, to join their issues of generational assistance to seniors and the elderly with targeted benefits for working-age parents in need of assistance, coalescing around a larger family-parent "GI Bill of Rights" type of policy package, including child care, retraining, unemployment support, and educational benefits.

Reforming the 1996 Welfare Reform Act

Marginal Changes Following the passage of the 1996 Welfare Reform Act, with the support and signature of President Bill Clinton, three top Clinton administration U.S. Department of Health and Human Services (HHS) aides resigned in protest,[3] citing an HHS study indicating that the "reform" legislation could possibly "push more than a million children into poverty" (Bane, 1996). One of the three former aides, Mary Jo Bane, the Assistant Secretary for Children and Families in HHS, went public on the Op-Ed Page of the *New York Times* with a criticism of the president, and a plan advocating softening the impact of the 1996 Welfare Bill. Bane advocated the adoption of optional vouchers that states could provide to the families of children losing benefits under the Welfare Reform Act. Vouchers for families cut from the welfare rolls but with children in poverty, or for families cut prior to the five-year lifetime eligibility language contained in the Welfare Reform Act, would put back in place a thin social safety net to children, if not to their families.

Bane also advocated other incremental changes to the Welfare Reform Act, including federally provided economic counter-cyclical funding—contingency funding from Congress in the event that economic downturns create large numbers of the poor, numbers not planned for in the annual levels of welfare assistance funding provided to the states under the new law. Bane acknowledged that genuine welfare reform discouraging multiyear welfare dependency is necessary but advocated putting in place a system that does not penalize children in poverty for the life choices and circumstances of their parents. Like Skocpol, Bane has suggested only the barest outlines of what such a plan would look like. Pressing the case that genuine welfare reform must involve stringent work requirements for welfare recipients, Bane also acknowledged that some will still be long-term recipients, whose children could be assisted if the families in question were required to work, received vouchers instead of cash assistance, and were required to complete educational objectives and/or community service.

Not-So-Marginal Changes   A second top Clinton official who resigned after the passage of the 1996 Welfare Reform Act, David Ellwood, former Harvard policy scholar and Clinton administration Assistant Secretary of HHS, has estimated that the federal government will have to create a jobs program for approximately 500,000 to 1 million former aid recipients who, due either to the five-year lifetime limit for welfare or the "two years and you're off" requirement, are off the welfare rolls but are not placed in jobs in the private sector after two years (DeParle, 1994a: 1; 1993).

Former Under Secretary of Health, Education, and Welfare, and State University of New York at Albany policy scholar, Richard Nathan, has advocated a more limited work employment program, helping high-risk but employable mothers—a targeted group of approximately 213,000 16-to-20-year-old heads of welfare families with one child—a group that historically stays on welfare longer than any other public assistance subgroup (Nathan, 1993, 1994).

These calls by Bane, Ellwood, and Nathan for incremental modifications in the Welfare Reform Act may prove successful. Others, however, advocate much larger-scale support programs for the unemployed working-age metro resident, programs modeled on the Depression era WPA program.

Latter-Day WPA Approaches: Mickey Kaus and William Julius Wilson

In a recent article (Kaus, 1996) and in his optimistically entitled book, *The End of Inequality* (1995), *New Republic* writer Mickey Kaus argued that the

1996 Welfare Reform Act, funded in grants to each of the states, amounts to equal what traditional AFDC grants would have been in each of these states otherwise (excepting large cuts in food stamps and aid to legal immigrants). As such, the Act is neither a "reform," nor is it much of a budgetary savings, since the 1996 legislation provides $3 billion more over the authorization period than traditional AFDC grants were projected to provide over the same period (Kaus, 1996a). Kaus argues that the welfare reform itself will need reforms and suggests "WPA-style jobs, but also the ambitious training efforts that the Clinton administration has so far failed to advance" (Kaus, 1996a). Exactly what finances and program dimensions this would involve, again beyond the barest outlines, is not provided by Kaus.

In a bold new work, *When Work Disappears: The World of the New Urban Poor* (1996b), one of the foremost experts on concentrated ghetto poverty in America, Harvard's William Julius Wilson, comes down hard on the 1996 Welfare Reform Act, arguing that the Act will do little good because it ignores the root cause of center-city ghetto poverty—in Wilson's view, the steadily decreasing number of liveable-wage/low-tech (low job-skill/low educational attainment–required) jobs in America's inner city. Lacking the provision of new jobs to center cities, Wilson expects many ghetto behaviors to continue unabated, including, in the words of one reviewer:

> Many ghetto dwellers will probably continue to do pretty much what they did before; get drunk, hang out on street corners, drift aimlessly from one low-paid job to the next, engage in petty crime, sell and abuse drugs and move ever further away from the much-vaunted "work ethic" that conservatives—and some liberals—claim has been eroded by the U.S. welfare system. (Wallace, 1996b)

Wilson advances several proposals to improve the life of American cities and inner-city residents including (1) mandatory academic standards for secondary schools in the United States; (2) equity in school funding so that inner-city schools receive resources more nearly matching the resources automatically available to suburban schools at present; (3) improved child care, "children's allowances," and public-assistance payments to poverty-level single mothers (such as a program currently in place in France, or those proposed in the United States by Mary Jo Bane, Richard Nathan, or Theda Skocpol),[4] and stepped-up child support payment enforcement; (4) "city-suburban partnerships" such as the Minneapolis–St. Paul tax-base sharing formula and improved inner-to-outer-city public transit to help ease the "spatial mismatch" between the location of inner-city workers and edge-city jobs; (5) and, finally (agreeing with Mickey Kaus), a "neo-WPA program of employment, for every American citizen over 18 who wants it" in the form of below minimum wage public sector jobs.

Unlike the 1996 Welfare Reform Act, the Wilson-Kaus WPA program would make public sector jobs available to persons leaving the welfare rolls and provide child-care service for single parents working at such jobs. The problem for Wilson is not welfare per se but "jobless ghettos" (Wilson, 1996a: 54). The WPA proposal "will not be cheap," admits Wilson, who estimates that a neo-WPA program might cost $12,000 per job created, a cost of $12 billion for every $1 million new WPA-style jobs created. However, Kaus and Wilson make a forceful argument that such jobs would be useful, perhaps literally rebuilding the vital center of cities in the later 1990s and early twenty-first century. Indeed, if the list provided by Kaus, and cited again by Wilson, is any indication, that is exactly what such a program could provide. As Wilson, quoting Kaus, noted:

> In it's eight-year existence, according to official records, the W.P.A. built or improved 651,000 miles of roads, 953 airports, 124,000 culverts, 8,000 parks, 18,000 playgrounds and athletic fields, and 2,000 swimming pools. It constructed 40,000 buildings (including 8,000 schools) and repaired 85,000 more. Much of New York City—including La Guardia Airport, F.D.R. Drive, plus hundreds of parks and libraries—was built by the W.P.A. (Wilson, 1996a: 52)

Neo-WPA employment programs may or may not be adopted, following experience with the "reformed" Welfare Act. The case that such employment would be useful for cities and crucially connected to revitalizing city centers, as well as aiding impoverished neighborhoods, parks, schools, and public infrastructure, is a compelling one. It is too early to tell if the Wilson-Kaus neo-WPA jobs argument will find congressional and presidential level political support. In the meantime, attempts to turn around the troubled status of public education in large American cities have found support and appear to be showing early signs of success, as well as troubling side effects.

Wilson focuses much attention on the failure of inner-city schools to prepare inner-city youth for employment, and for failing to connect students with neighborhood employers in a well-articulated school-to-work formal and informal employment network that might not only better connect high school graduates with employment but might also help to reinforce a "culture of work" in center cities in which job-seeking and job-holding are the norm rather than the exception; a norm that is, as Wilson notes, impossible to nurture "when work disappears" and when schools fail to train students for and place graduates in employment at liveable wages. Wilson, a professor of sociology and social policy at the University of Chicago for twenty-four years prior to joining the faculty at Harvard, might well applaud recent developments in public education in both Chicago and New York City; developments that are, also, not without the potential for troubling side effects.

Saving the Schools: The Big Apple and the Windy City as Role Models?

The 1990s have demonstrated two truisms about large city public schools. First, most large city school districts are plagued by inadequate financing, high drop-out rates, low academic standards, and high rates of juvenile delinquency.

Second, strong leadership by a committed and talented school-system chief executive *can* turn such school districts around. New York City and Chicago are recent examples of just such leadership. In the early 1990s, under the direction of city school chief Raymond Cortines, New York City made impressive strides forward, implementing a *Regent's Plan* for city high schools in which *all* high school students were expected to take the courses required for admission to the New York State university system. Students failing such classes were required to attend make-up courses over the summer. Early studies indicated a failure rate of only 30 percent, mitigated in many instances with the required summer make-up and remedial course work. Unfortunately, as in the case of community policing under strong leadership by a talented and able police chief in New York City, success resulted in divided ownership of the direction of the school programs and the political credit for such success between the day-to-day administrator in charge and the city's chief executive, the mayor. Ultimately, both the successful police chief and school director were removed by the mayor's office.

Chicago has a similar record of initial success with schools under a talented, powerful, and innovative schools chief. Whether the success of the city schools will be treated by Mayor Richard Daley, Jr., as a resource for his administration and one to be supported, or a challenge whose leadership needs to be removed, remains to be seen. In the meantime, Chicago's public schools, lambasted by the U.S. Department of Education in the 1980s as the worst in the nation, is experiencing a comeback. A 1970s-to-1980s era of experimental decentralization was abandoned in 1995, when the state legislature gave the mayor's office the power to control the school system, including appointing the chief executive officer, the mayor's former budget director, Paul Vallas (Alter, 1996b).

Vallas accomplished much in his first sixteen months in office. The newly reorganized Chicago public schools (CPS) system, reconfigured to resemble more a business corporation than a traditional public school district, has (1) implemented a new core curriculum; (2) put in place tough assessment standards; and (3) placed 122 schools on probation; (4) instituted remedial summer-school course work for eighth graders not ready for high school; (5) made peace with the powerful teacher's unions in exchange for salary stability overtime—preventing a repeat of earlier prolonged teacher strikes— laying off over 300 CPS central staff employees and establishing new accountability standards for principals and supervisors (Alter, 1996b). Vallas's hands-on innovative management style has borne results. As Jonathan Alter noted recently: "98 percent of the parents whose children were forced to attend summer school signed contracts committing them to helping the students complete the remedial work" (Alter 1996b).

These developments in New York City and Chicago are both encouraging and discouraging. They are encouraging for the obvious reasons: large, slow, strike-ridden, and ossified school systems are demanding and receiving excellent performance from their staff and students. They are discouraging because these laudable results are achieved at the expense of eviscerating the traditional decentralized elected school boards characteristic of American public schools and replacing them with strong, centralized, highly politicized executive leadership. The legacy of such a transition is noteworthy, both for its initial success against formidable odds and because it may signal a change in American education in which city schools are increasingly characterized by strong centralized administration at the city, and perhaps state, levels. This may be a necessary and desirable change. It is also a sharp and noteworthy departure from past practices, and a departure that bears further scrutiny as large city school systems continue to the struggle to make the changes necessary to "build a bridge to the twenty-first century."

The centralization of public school decision making and administration, the possible modification of the 1996 Welfare Reform Act including support for single parents, or the institutionalization of a neo-WPA jobs program, as well as the other "large problems, larger spending" proposals discussed in this chapter, represent policy, process, and structure changes advocated by many analysts recommending a more forceful approach to the permanent crisis in American cities. Since the early 1990s, with the rise of this permanent crisis—and particularly, since the dust has settled from the most costly urban riot in America's history in South Central Los Angeles in 1992—policies and programs to aid urban America have been advanced with increasing zeal and advocacy. One proposal, long thought to be a dead issue but that received a new lease on life in 1993, is the issue of statehood for the District of Columbia.

Statehood for Washington, D.C.

Statehood for the district, were it eventually enacted, would aid metro politics at the national level by introducing two additional metro-resident senators into a Senate already structurally biased in favor of rural areas. Additionally, the 600,000 D.C. residents would presumably be allocated at least two members of the House of Representatives. The proposal to give statehood to D.C.—to creating a state dubbed "New Columbia"—rejected on a floor vote of 277 to 153 in the House of Representatives in November 1993—is neither radical nor new. However, it is timely. The first year that the statehood issue was allowed to reach the floor for a vote in the House was 1993. The issue, now squarely raised, will continue to plague members of Congress with future floor votes until it has been successfully accommodated. Statehood for D.C. in the near future is not only desirable to remedy inequities for metro voters nationally, it is far more likely politically than ever before.

Even the most optimistic supporters of statehood, such as Eleanor Holmes Norton, D.C.'s nonvoting delegate to Congress, had estimated that the measure had only 150 supporters in the House. On the day of the vote (November 22, 1993), Holmes and a house gallery "packed with District residents—erupted into cheers when the vote board rolled past 150 'ayes' " (Associated Press, 1993). With an already strong bloc of supporters in the

House favoring passage, New Columbia may be an idea with enough critical mass to pass in the foreseeable future.

Even leaving aside the traditional debate about taxation for D.C. residents without representation versus the unconstitutionality of redrawing the boundaries of the nation's capital, the objective demographic case in favor of statehood is strong. Three states each currently have smaller populations than the 606,900 population of D.C.: these are Vermont (562,758), Alaska (550,043), and Wyoming (453,588). In terms of population density, D.C. has the second highest population density in the nation, with a 1990 density per square mile of 9,882.8—exceeded only by New Jersey (1042.0), followed by Rhode Island (960.3), and, trailing significantly, are Massachusetts (767.6) and Connecticut (678.4) (U.S. Bureau of the Census, 1990). Given the partisan Democratic voting patterns of D.C. residents, the debate on statehood will probably come down to Democrats versus Republicans in Congress, but the fact that statehood for D.C. would help inject metro issues back into national politics, and help to combat the parochial rural structural bias of the U.S. Senate, is not open to reasonable dispute. Statehood for D.C. would help bring metro politics back in. Conversely, a vote against statehood for D.C. is a vote to keep metro politics, and metro voters, in their place in American politics. Adopting statehood would provide a stronger public space in both the Senate and House for introducing metro issues into the national policymaking process.

WHEN ALL ELSE FAILS, TINKER WITH THE CONSTITUTION: A PROPOSAL FOR A NATIONAL INITIATIVE, REFERENDUM, AND RECALL

Chapter 6 set forth a Safe Streets, Safe Cities program involving $14 billion in revenue-neutral, annual expenditures to attack the seemingly permanent crisis facing American cities. While this author believes that this modest and revenue-neutral policy package has the potential to reverse the permanent crisis, to decrease stress in America's adrenaline cities, and to begin the necessary revitalization of poverty neighborhoods, schools, and workplaces, a number of critics—many of whom can present persuasive and plausible arguments—will argue that more needs to be done; that aiding cities requires thinking larger and spending more.

Perhaps the Safe Streets, Safe Cities policy package will be enough to turn the tide in America's cities. Perhaps it will not prove to be enough, and, if so, we will surely need to take the next turn of the wheel: a step involving modifying the 1996 Welfare Reform Act by establishing a works/jobs program for those who are not employed in the private sector after two years of assistance, a move that may eventually require the adoption of a neo-WPA jobs program for millions of displaced but work-worthy and work-willing American workers. These are large programs, carrying multi-billion dollar and multi-year national costs. These costs, if eventually needed, *may prove*—should the national political/policy mechanism in Washington, D.C., fail to recommend policies such as Safe Streets, Safe Cities, the amended Welfare Reform Act, or the neo-WPA jobs program—*far less expensive* to American government and politics, to the traditional American way of life, than will structural changes that may meet with popular political approval should politicians in Washington continue to treat American cities as political stepchildren, and the problems of cities as somehow less important than the grander political issues of foreign policy, Medicare, Social Security, or the reigning *issue du jour* occupying the attention of the political intelligentsia inside the capitol beltway of Washington, D.C.

While it is not clear that the national political process will continue to treat American cities and metropolitan problems as issues to be relegated to the backwaters of American national politics, it is clear that if this trend continues, pressures for changing the prevailing rules of the game are likely to increase as Americans prepare to cross the "bridge to the twenty-first century." If so, changes as we collectively cross the bridge may include rewriting the U.S. Constitution to include the application of a national initiative, referendum, and recall to the national legislative process. Initiative elections, introduced in 1898 in South Dakota, legally force a vote on public issues if a specified number of voters—usually in the range of 5-to-10 percent of the number of voters casting ballots in the previous election—sign a petition to place the measure on the ballot.[5] The District of Columbia and twenty-one states allow initiative elections at either the state or local level.

Public issues of law and/or public policy are placed before voters by a state or local legislative body in referendum elections in an attempt to determine the will of the electorate, which may be legally binding or merely advisory depending on the state or local jurisdiction and the applicable laws governing the referendum in question. Thirty-seven states allow referendum elections. Many state and local jurisdictions also allow for recall elections in which, as with initiatives following the submission of a required number of registered voters, an election is forced in order to determine whether an elected official should be removed from office.

While it is sheer speculation to suggest in the late 1990s the Constitution *needs* the addition of a provision for the initiative, referendum, or recall at the national governmental level, it is also difficult *not to speculate* that a national Washington, D.C.-based policy apparatus that continues to fail to provide relief from the permanent crisis, that continues to treat the metro regions where the vast majority of Americans live as largely invisible political stepchildren, is surely courting a rewriting of the rules of the road, a leveling of the political playing field for American cities and American politics. If so, the Constitutional "tinkering" is not likely to stop with traditionally accepted remedies such as the initiative, referendum, and recall—remedies at the state level already familiar to the residents of over thirty states, and which may strike such residents as too tame, as insufficiently radical. In such a case, metro residents may be willing to rethink the fundamentals of constitutional legislative process. Were they to do so, future radical change might include a call for revising the current configuration of the U.S. Senate. Let's examine such an argument, an argument that, one hopes, is at the water's edge of what may emerge as the radical demand for more inclusion of urban/metro concerns into the national policymaking process increasingly making itself heard in the late 1990s and the early twenty-first century.

Metro Senators: If Wyoming, Alaska, and Vermont Have Senators— Why Not New York City, Los Angeles, and Chicago?

Much has changed since the signing of the U.S. Constitution in 1787. One of the most obvious changes is that the population of the United States is overwhelmingly urban and metropolitan, with over 80 percent of Americans living on only 2 percent of the nation's land surface. Let's assume, for purposes of discussion, that the Constitution should reflect the highly urbanized nature of the U.S. population. How might this be reflected?

Consider—again, for purposes of discussion—a *Metro-Senator Constitutional Amendment*. Such an Amendment would attempt to restore a reasonable influence for urban/metro residents now denied to them, specifically in the Senate, where a voting majority of the fifty states may, in theory, be obtained by lining up a voting coalition comprised of the senators of the twenty-six smallest states—which, using the 1990 Census as a base, need not represent more than 20 percent of the total 1990 U.S. population.

The original Constitutional compromise that allowed representation of two senators for each of the states, a necessary concession in the late 1700s to the political power of the smaller states such as Delaware and Rhode Island, confronts a different demographic reality in the 1990s. The three smallest states in terms of population are Wyoming, Alaska, and Vermont—with a total population, using the 1990 Census, of 1,566,389 residents; roughly 20,000 less residents than Philadelphia (1990 pop. 1,585,577), the birthplace of the Constitution. Thus, rather ironically, the city that is the birthplace of the Constitution *and* the three least populated states both share total populations of almost 1 percent of the overall U.S. population. Each of the three states has two votes in the United States Senate; Philadelphia, of course, has none.

The Metro-Senator Constitutional Amendment would change this representational formula in the U.S. Senate. There are several ways to potentially make representation in the Senate more proportional to the actual population patterns of the United States. One could, for instance, allow one to two additional Senators for each U.S. city with a population *larger* than the smallest state (Wyoming, 1990 pop. 453,588). While perhaps more equitable than the present system, this formula would result in allowing an additional one or two metro-senators for twenty-seven cities, all of which exceed the population of Wyoming. This would result in the following Metro-Senate electorate cities: New York City, Los Angeles, Chicago, Houston, Philadelphia, San Diego,

Dallas, Phoenix, Detroit, San Antonio, San Jose, Indianapolis, San Francisco, Baltimore, Jacksonville, Columbus, Milwaukee, Memphis, Washington, D.C., Boston, El Paso, Seattle, Cleveland, Nashville-Davidson, Austin, New Orleans, and Denver.

An alternative would be to allow one to two additional metro-senators for each city with a population base that is *double* the population of Wyoming (2 × 453,588 = 907,176 residents). This would result in ten Metro-Senate electorates: New York City, Los Angeles, Chicago, Houston, Philadelphia, San Diego, Dallas, Phoenix, Detroit, and San Antonio.

A third alternative, and the one that would appear to interfere least with the size and the work structure of the Senate and, yet, introduce a measure of fairness and metro representation to the Senate, is to argue for the introduction of two additional metro-senators for each American city with a *population larger than the combined population of the three smallest states* (combined 1990 pop. of Wyoming, Alaska, and Vermont = 1,566,389). This would add ten metro-senators, two each from: New York City (1990 pop. 7,322, 564), Los Angeles (1990 pop. 3,485,398), Chicago (1990 pop. 2,783,726), Houston (1990 pop.1,630,553), and Philadelphia (1990 pop. 1,585,577).

While such a proposal, even the limited proposal for only a total of ten metro-senators, may seem unworkable, unrealistic, or utopian, it is, however, quite the opposite. These five cities represent *over 11 percent* of the total U.S. population. Allowing them each two voting members in the U.S. Senate is, on its face, far less inequitable than continuing to insist in the face of the changed demographics of the highly urbanized late 1990s, that rural states such as Wyoming, Alaska, and Vermont, with a combined total population of *only 1 percent* should continue to have six times the representation of not only Philadelphia but of four other metro areas representing over 11 percent of the total population of the United States.

THE GROWING THREAT OF URBAN RADICALISM: CONCLUSION

Such a Metro-Senator Constitutional Amendment may seem ethereal, otherworldly, and farfetched in terms of the political realities of the late 1990s, as Americans prepare to make whatever changes we will need collectively to transition across the "bridge to the twenty-first century." I would, however, suggest that the reverse is the case. A nation whose political leaders and national policy machinery in Washington, D.C., witnessed the grim misery of the South Central Los Angeles riots in 1992, which, in the wake of those riots, heard the pleas of the U.S. Conference of Mayors for a $35 billion Marshall Plan for cities, and which responded with a $2-billion aid plan eventually whittled-down by Congress and the president to a mere $1-billion band-aid package of watered-down summer jobs and temporary programs, had better, as Ann Landers is fond of saying, wake up and smell the coffee.

The response of Washington, D.C.-based policymakers to the South Central riots in 1992—a decision to allocate a little more than $1 billion after a deadly riot in America's second-largest city, a riot that was the most costly in American history—is not a policy designed to forestall the possibility of future urban cataclysms. Nor, unfortunately, is the Clinton administration's underfinanced and poorly designed urban empowerment zone program a guarantee against continued metro poverty and episodic urban rioting. Neither the Bush administration denial of the significance of the riots in Los Angeles, nor the Clinton administration's attempt to revive the failed enterprise zone policy of earlier days, will materially aid in fighting the epidemic-level permanent crisis in American cities.

Until the permanent crisis in American cities is genuinely confronted by the Washington, D.C.-based national political machinery, we are not only a nation *between riots*, we are also, in all probability, a nation *between Constitutions*. If, as a nation, in the afterglow from the fires of the next urban riot, we are forced to hastily rewrite our collective national political covenant, surely Cornel West's admonishment will be correct when he warns that either it contain "a new language of compassion, or the fire this time will consume us all."

APPENDIX

HOW IS HUNGER MEASURED IN THE UNITED STATES?

Unfortunately, there is no widely-accepted national procedure for determining the exact number of people at risk of experiencing hunger in the United States. There have been several attempts to estimate the extent of hunger in America including the Food Research and Action Center Report (1983), the Physician Task Force on Hunger in America Report (1985), and more recent reports by the U.S. Conference of Mayors (1994, 1995), as well as pioneering attempts by individual scholars and researchers, including Cohen and Burt (1989), Ashman et al. (1993), Curtis (1994), and Dehavenon (1995).

Collectively, these best estimates of Americans at risk of homelessness suggest that approximately 25 to 30 million people are at risk of hunger in America. The best recent study of who the hungry are and where they go to find assistance is the Second Harvest Study (1996). Second Harvest, the largest domestic hunger relief organization in the United States, estimated in 1996 that 25 million people are at risk of hunger in America. This estimate is drawn from a path-breaking eighteen-month study of hunger released by Second Harvest in 1996.

Here is how Second Harvest describes their study: "An ambitious national research study was undertaken and the compelling results of the study illustrate that hunger is a much more serious problem than most people realize. The study revealed that 10.4% of the population, or a staggering 25,970,319 Americans rely on food pantries, soup kitchens, homeless shelters, and other emergency feeding programs served by the Second Harvest network. That is one in ten people.

"The study confirmed that economics is the primary reason why people need charitable assistance, with 73% of the households receiving less than $10,000 in annual income.

Academic Profile: Well over half of the network clients have a high school diploma or have completed higher education. A startling number are unemployed professionals. Of 44.1% that are currently unemployed, 31.4% were last employed in technical, management, professional, clerical, and secretarial positions.

Age Profile: A significant percentage of those needing assistance are children, with 42.9% of network clients aged 17 and younger. This is well above the 25.9% figure of the overall population.

Ethnic Profile: Although African-Americans [32.8%] and Hispanics [11.4%] are disproportionately represented, white Americans [50.7%] comprise the largest group of food recipients.

About the Study: The 18-month study was conducted by the VanAmburg group, a marketing research consultant firm, and funded by a grant from Kraft Foods. A nationwide sampling of 34 food banks, 3,182 agencies, and 8,596 network clients participated. Results are statistically valid, with a 1.4% sampling error and a 95% confidence level. The overall goals of this study were to quantify the impact of the food distributed, to develop profiles of the food recipients, and to create a benchmark study that can be effectively replicated in subsequent years to pinpoint trends."[1]

HOW IS POVERTY MEASURED IN THE UNITED STATES?

Poverty in the United States is currently estimated using a rule-of-thumb formula developed by Mollie Orshansky, an economist with the Social Security Administration in 1963. At that time, Orshansky estimated that a family of four was poor if they had less cash income (before taxes) than three times the amount necessary to purchase a "minimum diet" for family meals. The minimum diet was premised on the Department of Agriculture's Economy Plan for family meal planning, a plan which the Department of Agriculture warned was only meant for use on a temporary, emergency basis. The original formula allowed an annual income providing 23 cents per meal per person. Although this poverty line has been moved up from time to time to account for inflation, the figure has never been adjusted to consider regional differences in the cost of living or housing costs in contemporary urban areas, which even in poverty neighborhoods may easily exceed two to three times the monthly cost of purchasing the ingredients for a "minimum diet" meal for a family of four.

The poverty definition used by the federal government for statistical purposes was $15,141 for a family of four in 1994. A four-person family with cash income below this threshold would be counted as poor. The figures for three-person, two-person and one-person households are: $11,821, $9,661, and $7,547, respectively. The figures vary slightly depending on whether the family members are aged 65 or older, or younger than age 65. The U.S. Census Bureau determines the overall number of persons in poverty each decade in the census, and between decades via the Census Bureau SIPP (Survey of Income and Program Participation) Survey. The most recent 1993–95 SIPP survey sampled over 20,000 households, in an elaborate four-rotation, eight-wave

---

[1]*Source:* Second Harvest, "Research Study Findings," available on the Internet at the Second Harvest web site (www.secondharvest.org/websecha/d_resrch.htm).

survey design format, producing the most accurate estimate of number and trends in poverty in the United States.[2]

HOW *SHOULD* POVERTY BE MEASURED IN THE UNITED STATES?

The measure of poverty developed by Mollie Orshansky in 1963, while useful in producing a national estimate of poor persons in the United States, is seriously out-of-tune with the financial and dietary realities of life in the United States in the 1990s.

The original figure has been adjusted from time to time to account for inflation but further adjustments are necessary. For example, regional differences in the cost of living are not accounted for in the formula. Second, the Orshansky formula assumed (correctly for the late 1950s) that an average family spent one-third of their income on food, and that the remainder of nonfood expenses (including housing) was arrived by multiplying the total food budget by its percentage of the overall family budget—resulting in a multiplier of three (family needs = three × minimum food budget expenses).

In today's market, several things have happened to weaken the original Orshansky poverty formula. Food is only one-fifth of the budget of American families and housing is far more expensive than in earlier times. The cost of living, even in inexpensive rentals in poverty neighborhoods, may easily exceed two to three times the monthly cost of purchasing the ingredients for a "minimum diet" meal for a family of four. As Deborah Stone has observed: "Food now constitutes only one-fifth of non-poor families' budgets but no agencies have been willing to use a multiplier of five. To do so would create political pressure for dramatic increases in poverty spending" (Stone, 1994: 88). Note, for example, if Orshansky's original formula were updated for current housing costs (family needs = five × minimum food budget expenses), the 1989 national poverty rate would have more than doubled, rising from 12 percent to 25.6 percent.

The National Research Council recently issued a report by Constance Citro and Robert Michael (*Measuring Poverty: A New Approach*, Washington, D.C.: National Academy Press, 1995) suggesting new poverty measures that take account of the changed nature of modern housing expenses, vary such expenses by differences in regional costs, and analyze the after-tax resources of families as those families are affected by benefits from social programs such as food stamps that would otherwise require cash outlays on the part of poor families. Such an approach has much to recommend it. See, for example

[2] *Source:* U.S. Bureau of the Census CD-ROM, Income and Poverty: 1993. See also, Gordon Fisher, "The Development and History of Poverty Thresholds," *Social Security Bulletin* (Winter 1992); and Deborah Stone, "Making the Poor Count," *The American Prospect* (Spring 1994): 84–88.

the discussions in Fisher (1996, 1992), Schwartz and Volgy (1992), Roggles (1990), and Osberg (1984).

A far simpler approach, however, would be to simply change the multi-plier, as Stone (1994: 88) suggests, by five (family needs = five × minimum food budget expenses). Since the politics of such a change are likely to be bitter and protracted, I suggest admitting that the 1963 multiplier is faulty by *at least 25 percent*. If so, the true figures for poverty in the United States are best captured by setting the poverty level at 125 percent of the current figure. While even this recalculated poverty rate would, in all probability underestimate the true number of poor persons in America at any given moment, it would result in a far more accurate picture of poverty than the snapshot suggested by the current minimally-revised 1963 Orshansky poverty formula. Using the 125 percent poverty formula I have suggested (family needs = three × minimum food budget expenses + 25 percent) would result in recalculated poverty rates from 1959 to 1994 presented in Table A.1.

Neighorhoods of Despair

Severely distressed neighborhoods have at least four of five characteristics: poverty rate about 25.7 percent; at least 39.6 percent of families headed by women; high-school dropout rate above 23.3 percent; more than 46.5 percent of men out of labor force; more than 17 percent of families on welfare. Table A.2 show the percentage of children living in such neighborhoods state by state.

HOW IS CRIME MEASURED IN THE UNITED STATES?

There are two key measures of crime in the United States, the National Crime Victimization Survey (NCVS) and the Uniform Crime Reporting (UCR) Program—both are administered by the U.S. Department of Justice. The definitions of crime and data collection techniques differ in the two studies so the data reported in the two reports frequently contain discrepancies and are not, strictly speaking, statistically comparable.

The NCVS is administered by the Bureau of Justice Statistics, which has collected information on crimes suffered by individuals and households since 1973—whether or not the crimes in question were reported to law enforcement authorities. The emphasis on all crimes (versus the focus on only reported crimes as found in the UCR methodology) is laudable; however, the NCVS excludes arson, white collar or commercial crimes, crimes against children under the age of twelve years, and homicide. Given the lack of coverage of homicide, this author and many scholars in the field prefer to use the UCR statistics for analyzing metro or urban crime rates.

The UCR Program has been supervised by the FBI since 1929 and collects information on aggravated assault, arson, burglary, homicide, larceny-theft,

TABLE A.1
Percent of U.S. Population Below Poverty Line

Line Year	Old Formula	New
1959	22.4	31.1
1960	22.2	30.4
1965	17.3	24.1
1966	14.7	21.3
1967	14.2	20.0
1968	12.8	18.2
1969	12.1	17.4
1970	12.6	17.6
1971	12.5	17.8
1972	11.9	16.8
1973	11.1	15.8
1974	11.4	16.1
1975	12.3	17.6
1976	11.8	16.7
1977	11.6	16.7
1978	11.4	15.8
1979	11.7	16.4
1980	13.0	18.1
1981	14.0	19.3
1982	14.7	20.3
1983	15.2	20.3
1984	14.4	19.4
1985	14.0	18.7
1986	13.6	18.2
1987	13.4	17.9
1988	13.1	17.5
1989	12.8	17.3
1990	13.5	18.0
1991	14.2	18.9
1992	14.5	19.7
1993	15.1	20.0
1994	14.5	19.3

Source: U.S. Bureau of the Census,1996 (census.gov/hhes/poverty/hstpov6).

motor vehicle theft, rape, and robbery. The figures used in the UCR are submitted voluntarily by over 16,000 law enforcement agencies throughout the United States, covering more than 95 percent of the U.S. population.[3]

Urbanists pay particular attention to reported changes in violent crime in the million-plus cities of Chicago, Dallas, Houston, Los Angeles, New York,

[3] *Data Source:* Students and researchers seeking UCR crime data may find a wealth of information by contacting the FBI Internet Web Page at: www.fbi.gov/ucr.

TABLE A.2
Neighborhoods of Despair

State	%	State	%	State	%
Ala.	9.6	Ky.	7.1	N.D.	2.1
Alaska	0.5	La.	17.2	Ohio	8.1
Ariz	5.2	Md.	6.2	Okla.	3.1
Ark.	7.6	Maine	0.6	Ore.	1.1
Calif.	5.1	Mass.	5.1	Pa.	6.9
Colo.	2.5	Mich.	11.5	R.I.	5.1
Conn.	5.7	Minn.	2.0	S.C.	4.4
Del.	1.7	Miss.	17.4	S.D.	3.6
D.C.	25.2	Mo.	5.2	Texas	4.8
Fla.	4.6	Mont.	2.3	Tenn.	7.3
Ga.	6.2	Neb.	1.3	Utah	0.3
Hawaii	0.5	Nev.	3.3	Vt.	0.6
Idaho	0.0	N.H.	0.1	Va.	2.8
Ill.	9.5	N.J.	4.9	Wash.	2.4
Ind.	3.0	N.M.	4.5	W. Va.	2.9
Iowa	1.0	N.Y.	12.8	Wis.	5.4
Kan.	2.0	N.C.	2.6	Wyo.	0.2

Source: 1994 Kids Count Data Book (Annie E. Casey Foundation). It should be noted that the *Kids Count* study shows that children in severely distressed neighborhoods tend to cluster into three specific geographic groups. Almost half of the children in deeply troubled neighborhoods live in six large urbanized states, including: California, Illinois, Michigan, New York, Ohio, and Texas. Second, Washington, D.C., has the highest percentage of children in the nation (25.2 percent) in "neighborhoods of despair." Third, several rural deep South states have, as a region (excluding Washington, D.C.), the highest percentages of children in distressed neighborhoods in America, including: Arkansas 7.6 percent, Georgia 6.2 percent, Louisiana 17.2 percent, Mississippi 17.4 percent, and Tennessee 7.3 percent.

Philadelphia, Phoenix, and San Diego. For example, nationally the number of violent crimes in 1995 dropped by 3 percent, a drop fueled in large measure by a drop of 8 percent in violent crime in the million-plus cities in the same year. New York City alone is responsible for one third of the decrease in violent crime in 1995.

Notes

CHAPTER 1

1. The government price tag for bailing out the failed Savings-and-Loan associations over a ten-year period is expected to cost the federal taxpayers almost $200 billion. See Nancy Folbre and the Center for Popular Economics (1995), *The New Field Guide to the U.S. Economy* (New York: The New Press), pp. 9, 12. The *Independent Cities* metro revitalization plan proposed in this book would involve expenditures ranging from $18 billion (see Chapter 3, the "Cheap Fixes" section) to an additional $50 billion (see Chapter 4, the "Expensive Fixes" section). This dollar amount differs from the S&L bailout amount in that (1) it ranges from 10 percent to 32 percent of the amount of funding required to bail out the failed thrifts; and (2) the Independent Cities metro revitalization plan is *revenue-neutral*—meaning that the plan would not add one cent to the deficit or reduce allocations for other important national objectives such as social security, health care, national defense, or deficit reduction. Financing mechanisms are explained in detail in Chapters 3 and 4.

2. Estimates of this figure differ, but only marginally. Ames et al., (1992) put the true proportion of the metropolitan poor in 1990 at 77 percent, while my own calculation of 73 percent in 1990 and 74 percent in 1995 agrees with figures provided via the Internet by the Census Bureau Housing and Economics Statistics Division. This is, however, a minor mathematical quibble. The trend line in both calculations is a *major increase*—in the range of a 17-to-20 percent increase—in the number of persons in poverty in American metropolitan areas from 1979 to 1992–95. It should also be emphasized that both calculations accept and rely on the official U.S. poverty line (a line at least 25 percent below a figure that might more accurately depict the true level of poverty in the United States—see the discussion in the Appendix of "How Should Poverty be Measured in the United States?"), a measure that artificially deflates the overall U.S. poverty figure by, at least, 25 percent. See D. Ames, N. Brown, M. H. Callahan, S. Cummings, S. M. Smock, and J. Zeigler (1992), "Rethinking American Urban Policy," *Journal of Urban Affairs*, Vol. 14: 197–217; and U.S. Department of Housing and Urban Development (1995), "Empowerment: A New Covenant with America's Communities: President Clinton's National Urban Policy Report, July 1995" (Washington, D.C.; hereafter cited as HUD/NUPR, 1995). See also, P. A. Jargowsky and M. J. Bane (1991), "Ghetto Poverty in the United States, 1970–1980" in C. Jencks and P. E. Peterson (eds.), *The Urban Underclass* (Washington, D.C.: Brookings Institution); William J. Wilson (1991), "Public Policy Research and the Truly Disadvantaged," in C. Jencks and P. E. Peterson (1991), pp. 460–81; R. Anglin and B. Holcomb (1993), "Poverty in Urban America," *Journal of Urban Affairs*, Vol. 14: 447–68; D. S. Massey

and N. A. Denton (1994), *American Apartheid* (Cambridge, Mass.: Harvard University Press); D. Rusk (1993), *Cities without Suburbs* (Baltimore: Johns-Hopkins University Press), "Bend or Die: Inflexible State Laws and Policies Are Dooming Some of the County's Central Cities" (1994), *State Government News* (February): 6–10, and "Inelastic Cities" (1994), Lecture delivered at the Maxine Goodman Levin College of Urban Affairs, Cleveland State University, Cleveland, Ohio (September 23); and Robert Waste (1995), "Urban Poverty and the City as Reservation," *Journal of Urban Affairs*, Vol. 17. For further documentation, see the following reports: U.S. Bureau of the Census, 1991a, 1991b, 1992, and 1993.

3. This estimate of Americans at-risk of hunger is drawn from a ground-breaking 1996 baseline survey conducted by the VanAmburg Group, a marketing research consulting firm, funded by a grant from Kraft Foods, for Second Harvest, the largest domestic hunger relief organization in the United States. The 18-month study surveyed a sample of 34 food banks nationally, 3,182 agencies, and a total of 8,596 Second Harvest network clients. The results, with a 1.4 percent sampling error and a 95 percent confidence level, establish the best state-of-the-art estimates of hunger and emergency feeding programs available to date. (Research findings and methodology are available from Second Harvest via Internet at www.secondharvest.org.)

4. U.S. Bureau of the Census (1996), "1996 Survey of Income and Program Participation" (Washington, D.C.: August, 1996). The SIPP Study analyzed the income patterns of 2,000 families from 1992 to 1993. The year-long survey tracked 2,000 families and concluded that 5 percent of the American public is chronically poor, while a larger total of 14-to-15 percent of the public at-large may be poor at any given time during the year. The chronically poor differ from the more transitory poor (who have a "spell" of poverty lasting typically about five months) in that they are far more difficult to integrate into the labor market because, as Elizabeth Sawhill of the Urban Institute has noted: "other studies have shown that nearly two-thirds of the [adult] chronically poor never graduated from high school" (Ramon McLeod [1996], "Majority of Poor Recover Quickly, U.S. Study says," *San Francisco Chronicle*, August 19, p. A3). For a more detailed overview of the Census Bureau SIPP Survey, see Appendix A.

5. The Annie E. Casey Foundation, *1994 Kids Count Data Book*, analyzes "severely distressed neighborhoods," defined as census tracts with "high levels of (1) poverty; (2) female-headed families; (3) high school drop-outs; (4) unemployment; and (5) reliance on welfare. For our purposes, 'high levels' were defined as rates at least one standard deviation above the mean" (p. 9). High levels included a poverty rate above 27.5 percent, number of female-headed families at 39.6 percent or higher, a high school drop-out rate above 23.3 percent, number of males unattached to the labor force at above 46.5 percent, and families receiving public assistance at 17.0 percent and above (p. 16). See also John D. Kasarda (1993), "Inner-City Concentrated Poverty and Neighborhood Distress: 1970–1990," *Housing Policy Debate*, Vol. 4, No. 3, pp. 253–302.

6. Preliminary 1995 FBI figures for violent crime indicate a small 2.9 percent decrease in the rate of arrest of young people for violent crimes. The arrest rate for homicide was 11.2 per 1,000, down from 13.2 in 1994. The 1995 combined juvenile arrest rate—a figure combining arrests for homicide, rape, robbery, and aggravated assault—was 511.9 per 1,000, down from a 1994 level of 527.4. See the "1995 Annual Crime Report: Preliminary Release,"

(http://www.fbi.gov/ucr/95prepl.htm); and Fox Butterfield (1996), "Adult Homicides Decrease by Half, a Data Study says," *New York Times* August 19, p. 1.

While the comparatively small decline in violent crime in 1995 is cause for guarded optimism, two authorities cite significant caveats. Attorney General Reno cautioned, at the press conference releasing the new figures, that: "What is so important is that we not relax . . . because the number of young people is going to increase significantly in the next fifteen years. So the actual number of crimes, unless we work real hard, is going to go up" (*Bee* News Services [1996], "U.S. Youths Commit Less Violent Crime," *Sacramento Bee*, August 9, p. 1). Additionally, as Professor Alfred Blumstein of Carnegie-Mellon University has noted: "New York [City] is about 8 percent of the national total, so a drop of 25 percent in New York City would take two percentage points off the national rate" (Associated Press [1996], "Violent Crime Arrests Down Among Teens," *San Francisco Chronicle*, August 9, p. 1). In fact, that is exactly what happened in New York City under the "community policing" leadership of former Police Commissioner William J. Bratton; the New York City homicide count declined from a record high in 1960 of 2,245 to 1,182 in 1995. Even at that level, a *permanent crisis* of public safety exists in New York City and elsewhere. As Clifford Krauss (1966) noted: "compared to the 390 murders [in New York City] in 1960, or even the 986 in 1968, the murder rate in 1995 still conjures images of Dodge City." "1966 Data Show Crime Rates Are Still Falling in New York," *New York Times*, January 28, 1995, pp. 1 and E5. Put in more academic terms, renowned legal scholar Lawrence M. Friedman of Stanford University Law School observed that: Everybody is crowing about what is going on in New York but we remain at a very high plateau."

7. These figures are drawn from the Children's Defense Fund's *1996 Yearbook* (Washington, D.C.). Also included in the report is the finding that each day 2,833 teens drop out of school, and 2,700 unmarried girls get pregnant.

8. See also, Bank of America (1995), "Beyond Sprawl: New Patterns of Growth to Fit the New America," Pamphlet; and HUD/NUPR 1995: 19.

9. See also, E. J. Blakeley and D. L. Ames (1992), "Changing Places: American Planning Policy for the 1990s," *Journal of Urban Affairs*, Vol. 14: 423–46; Neal Peirce (1993), "Cities Blight Now Extends into Suburbia," *Sacramento Bee*, October 11; and R. Kling, S. Olin, and M. Poster (eds.) (1991), *Postsuburban California: The Transformation of Orange County since World War II* (Berkeley: University of California Press).

10. Harvard political scientist Robert Putnam has advanced an important argument that voter participation and civic participation in general—"social capital," in Putnam's terms—is declining rapidly in American life. Putnam's data suggests that Americans vote less, join civic organizations such as the PTA the Scouts less, and associate less with each other than ever before in modern times—a phenomenon Putnam calls "bowling alone," following the curious argument that American bowling-league play has declined sharply in the last few decades despite the paradoxical increase in the numbers of individual bowlers in so-called "singleton leagues." Putnam advances a strong case for increased investments in social capital-building infrastructure such as better schools, economic development, and increased voter participation mechanisms. This argument anticipates and runs parallel to arguments advanced in Chapters 3 and 4. See Putnam (1993), "The Prosperous Community: Social Capital and Public Life," *American Prospect*,

Vol. 13 (Spring); and (1995) "Bowling Alone: America's Declining Social Capital," *The American Prospect*; 65–76.

11. See, especially, Massey and Denton (1993); HUD/NUPR 1995; and Henry G. Cisneros (1993), *Interwoven Destinies: Cities and the Nation* (New York: W. W. Norton).

12. Excellent studies arguing that 1990s-era center-city problems are inherently metropolitan-wide problems requiring metro-wide solutions, support, and funding include: Larry C. Ledebur and William R. Barnes (1993), *All in it Together—Cities, Suburbs, and Local Economic Regions* (Washington, D.C.: National League of Cities); Henry G. Cisneros (1995), "Regionalism: The New Geography of Opportunity" (Washington, D.C.: U.S. Department of Housing and Urban Development); Neal Peirce, with Curtis W. Johnson and John Stuart Hall (1993), *Citistates: Does the American City Have a Future? How Urban America Can Prosper in a Competitive World* (Washington, D.C.: Seven Locks Press); Myron Orfield (1994), *Metropolitics: A Regional Agenda for Community and Stability* (Minneapolis: unpublished manuscript); Neal Peirce (1994), *Citistates*; David Rusk (1995), *Baltimore Unbound* (Baltimore: Johns-Hopkins University Press), as well as Rusk (1993), *Cities without Suburbs* (Baltimore: Johns-Hopkins University Press). 2nd. Edition, revised, 1995; and William Barnes and Larry Ledebur (1997), *The U.S. Economy of Metropolitan Regions* (Thousand Oaks, Calif.: Sage Publications).

See also, Peirce (1993d) and (1993b) "Blueprint to Put Cities Back Together Again," (*Sacramento Bee*, December 21, p. B7); H. V. Savitch, David Collins, Daniel Sanders, and John P. Markham (1993), "Ties that Bind: Central Cities, Suburbs, and the New Metropolitan Region," *Economic Development Quarterly*, 7: 341–58; and, finally, Edward W. Hill, Harold L. Wolman, and Coit Cook Ford III (1994), "Can Suburbs Survive without Their Central Cities? Examining the Suburban Dependence Hypothesis," paper presented at a U.S. Department of Housing and Urban Development Roundtable, December 1994.

13. In fairness, it should be noted several of these poverty neighborhoods prominently feature public housing projects and that the Chicago public housing authority has made substantial progress addressing many of the issues of substandard high-rise public housing and violence on Housing Authority grounds under the leadership of the new director, Joseph Shuldinger, a former HUD Assistant Secretary for Indian and Public Housing in the Clinton administration.

14. As high as these unemployment figures are, they are probably still dramatically (and inaccurately) low. This discrepancy results from the fact that the official report on joblessness compiled by the U.S. Department of Labor counts only persons eligible for unemployment benefits and simultaneously searching for work. This decision-rule on who to count as "jobless" ignores people with disabilities, people who have given up their job search, and persons who might like to find work but are unable to match the skill level, hours, location, or difficulty of the potential job in question.

A recent (September 1996) survey of 2,310 Californians was taken by the Field Institute in California, and sponsored by the HealthCare Forum, The Institute for the Future, and the Institute for Health Policy Studies at the University of California at San Francisco. The survey is the largest privately sponsored statewide survey of work and health ever conducted in the United States, and has a margin of error of two percentage points. This poll found that the official California jobless figure of 1.1 million people or a jobless rate of 7.1 percent for July 1996 actually undercounted the unemployed by 2.8 million people who would like "unconditionally" to find work, and another 1.8 million people who would take employment if the hours, location, skill or job difficulty level were within their means, and thus, "would accept a job under the right circumstances." If the official state jobless figure of 1.8 million and 7.1 percent were combined with the 2.8 million Californians seeking work "unconditionally," the actual number of job seekers in California would read 3.9 million persons or a state jobless rate of 20 percent. If these discrepancies hold true nationally, it seems reasonable to assume that national unemployment figures may underestimate the true extent of joblessness and job-seeking by a margin of error ranging from 50 to 150 percent. For an excellent journalistic account of the study, see Cathleen Ferraro (1996), "Millions More Want Jobs Than Stats Show," *Sacramento Bee*, September 2, p. 1.

15. I have conservatively estimated the cost of the permanent crisis in American cities annually to be $585.3 billion. The key components of this follow (Note that the metro "share" of each of the first 9 annual figures was set at 80% (the percent of the U.S. population currently living in the 72 largest Metropolitan Statistical Areas (MSAs). Eighty percent of the annual expenses of the 9 components is $477.3 billion. To this I added 100 percent of the annual cost of each of components 10 and 11.):

> 1. The annual cost of drug abuse, $58.3 billion a year (Meredith E. Bagby 1996), *Annual Report of the United States of America, 1996*, (New York: HarperBusiness), p. 31.
> 2. The total medical cost of violence in the United States, $13.5 billion (*1994 Futures Report* [Washington, D.C.: National League of Cities, p. 9]).
> 3. Federal local expenditures on the homeless annually, $2 billion (Bagby, 1995, p. 30; A. S. Baum and D. W. Burnes [1993], *A Nation in Denial: The Truth about Homelessness* [Boulder, Colo.: Westview Press, p. 183]).
> 4. State and local government welfare expenditures annually, $154.2 billion (Bagby, pp. 66–67).
> 5. State and local police expenditures annually, $34.6 billion (Bagby, pp. 66–67).
> 6. State and local transit system expenditures annually, $21.9 billion (Bagby, pp. 66–67).
> 7. U.S. federal expenditures in penal corrections, $20.1 billion (Bagby, p. 31).
> 8. U.S. federal aggregated welfare costs, $54.9 billion annually (Bagby, p. 27).
> 9. U.S. federal community development expenditures annually, $9.2 billion (Bagby, p. 8).
> 10. Metro crime, is $50 billion annually (HUD/NUPR, 1995).
> 11. Job productivity loss due to traffic congestion, $58 billion annually (HUD/NUPR, 1995).

The resulting figure—$585.3 billion—is a conservative estimate of the annual cost of the permanent crisis in American cities. This figure is 9% of the 1996 (Quarter 1) Gross Domestic Product figure of $6.87 trillion, a per capita cost annually of over $2,000 to every man, woman, and chld in America. While some of these categories double count the expenses associated with crime, it should be noted that the cost of metro hunger, child abuse, voter alienation, racial and economic balkanization, and the lost opportunities associated with the deplorable conditions of many metro public schools is not included in the current cost projection.

Undoubtedly, the components used in this study understate the true cost of the permanent crisis in American cities because the annual figure does not include the cost of educational components, nor does the figure attempt to estimate the federal costs associated with traffic congestion, rapid transit, or—more tragically— the estimated dollar value of lost lives and lost opportunities associated with the everyday pathologies of American cities. Importantly, the present cost figure is intended as point of departure for discussing the larger permanent crisis issue, and not as a definitive econometric estimate of the hard dollar costs. The permanent crisis is, in large part, a moral or ethical as well as a financial crisis for American policy and politics. As such, a key point to remember is that the sheer presence of the crisis itself represents a mortal danger to American democracy, to American cities, and to the uniquely American way of life. In the end it is this threat as much as the hard dollar costs associated with the crisis that represent the greatest threat associated with the permanent crisis in American cities. In this respect, it is worth remembering that Alexis de Tocqueville once sagely observed that: "America is great because it is good, and if it ever ceases to be good, it will also cease to be great." Tocqueville's warning is more timely than ever. For children trapped within the permanent crisis in America's cities, America has long ago "ceased to be good."

CHAPTER 2

1. I am indebted to an Associated Press news article, which pointed out the derivation of "stress" from the Latin, and which, in a collateral finding, noted that the American Medical Association recently estimated that "up to 70% of all patients seen by general practice physicians come with symptoms directly related to unrelieved stress. Stress is among the top reasons Americans miss work, according to the Occupational Safety and Health Administration." While I did not attempt to calculate the number of days of missed work and the cost of this absenteeism for the permanent crisis costs estimated in Chapter 1, such costs could be reasonably be assumed to be a major cost variable associated with the permanent crisis in American cities. At the anecdotal level, this finding by the AMA suggests that residents of adrenaline cities are experiencing very real stress-adrenaline maladies associated at least in part with the permanent crisis. (Associated Press [1996]), "Stress Levels are Soaring: 70% of American Patients Now Showing Symptoms," *San Francisco Chronicle*, August 17, p. A6. At the non-anecdotal level, National Public Radio's "Morning Edition" newscast (November 11, 1996) carried a report of a 1996 study that estimated that stress costs the U.S. economy $200 billion annually.

2. David Rusk is a former New Mexico state legislator and mayor of Albuquerque, and now a Washington, D.C.-based author, speaker, and consultant on urban issues. Rusk's argument that "inelastic cities"—cities that aggressively annex surrounding territory and that, then, administer local problems and resources

from a more metropolitan or regional perspective, is presented in several recent and important publications, including: (1993) *Cities without Suburbs*; (1994) *Baltimore Unbound*; and (1994) "Bend or Die: Inflexible State laws and Policies Are Dooming Some of the Country's Central Cities."

3. The term *urban reservation* dates back to the neo-classical urban scholar Norton E. Long (1971), "The City as Reservation," *The Public Interest* Vol. 25: 22–32. I have operationalized this concept statistically elsewhere. See, for example, Robert Waste (1995), "Urban Poverty and the City as Reservation," *Journal of Urban Affairs*, Vol. 17: 3.

4. NUPR, 1995, pp. 13–15. See also, John D. Kasarda (1992 and 1993), *Urban Underclass Database Machine Readable Files*, Social Science Research Council, New York. See also, John Kasarda (1990, 1993), cited in R. Anglin and B. Holcomb, "Poverty in Urban America," *Journal of Urban Affairs*, Vol. 14: 451. These urban reservation five-city statistics—staggeringly high as they are—may actually understate the true level of poverty, both in the five-city sample and nationally. See, for example, the discussion in Chapter 3, "Worse Than We Think."

   Two indications of this are (1) William Julius Wilson, formerly Chair of the Sociology Department at the University of Chicago and now a professor at Harvard University, has reported the increase in extreme poverty neighborhoods citywide for the five cities (versus the narrow measure used in the current study of center-city extreme poverty neighborhoods) to be 161 percent from 1970 to 1980 alone (William J. Wilson (1987), *The Truly Disadvantaged: The Inner City, the Underclass, and Public Policy* (Chicago: University of Chicago Press, p. 46). (2) Even Wilson's figures may be an underestimate, since the official poverty-estimating formula developed in 1963 is fatally flawed in terms of accurately estimating contemporary housing costs, a flaw that skews the federal poverty formula, producing a significant undercount of the true number of the poor, both nationally and in cities.

   James Schwarz and Thomas Vogly (1992) and Deborah Store (1994) have argued that the true poverty rate in the U.S. may be twice that of the official Census Bureau reported figures.

5. See David Rusk (1994), "Bend or Die": 9–10.

6. See P. Applebome (1993), "C.D.C.'s New Chief Worries as Much About Bullets as About Bacteria," *New York Times*, September 26, p. E7. An epidemic is not too strong a term to use in referring to handgun violence alone. Dr. Katherine Kayfner, a pediatrician who founded the national HELP Network in 1992, an organization attempting to deal with the monumental public health consequences of gun violence, estimates that more than 5,000 juveniles and 33,000 adults die annually from gunshot wounds alone. As Police Officer Michael Robbins, the Director of HELP, has noted: "This is an epidemic that is 10 times as big, in terms of lives lost, as the great polio epidemic in the first half of this century. This new scourge paralyzes as many people as polio did at its worst. It needs to be stopped" (Bob Herbert [1996], *New York Times*, August 26, Op-Ed Page).

7. Scholarly studies include: C. R. Block (1990), "Hot Spots and Isocrimes in Law Enforcement Decision Making," Conference on Police and Community Response to Drugs: Frontline Strategies in the Drug War, University of Illinois at Chicago (December); C. R. Block and R. Block (1992), "Homicide Syndromes and Vulnerability: Violence in Chicago's Community Areas Over 25 Years," *Studies on Crime and Crime Prevention*, Vol. 1: 61–85; R. C. Block, L. Higgins,

and L. Green (1994), *The GeoArchive Handbook* (Chicago: Illinois Criminal Justice Information Authority); R. C. Block. C. Vates, and T. Fuechtman (1995), "The Loyola Community Safety Project: Liquor Licenses and Criminal Activity," Paper presented at the Loyola GeoArchive Conference, Chicago (February 24). See also, M. B. Gulak (1995), "Homicide and the Physical Environment," Paper presented at the Annual Meeting of the Urban Affairs Association, Portland, Oregon (May 3–6). Particularly well-written journalistic accounts include: Carla Marinucci and Jim Zamora (1995), "The Kill Zone," *San Francisco Chronicle*, May 19, p. A5; and, Alan Finder (1995), "New York Pledge to House Poor Works a Rare, Quiet Revolution," *New York Times*, April 30, p. 1.

8. See Marinucci and Zamora (1995), "The Kill Zone."

9. Finder, "Quiet Revolution."

CHAPTER 4

1. This paragraph draws heavily from the richly detailed discussion of types of federal grants in Bernard H. Ross, Myron A. Levine, and Murray Stedman (1991), *Urban Politics: Power in Metropolitan America*, 4th edition (Itasca, Ill.: F. E. Peacock Publishers, Inc.), pp. 338–40. For a detailed discussion of federal-local aid issues and the discussion of New Federalism raised in this chapter, see also Michael Reagan and John Sanzone (1991), *The New Federalism*, 2nd edition (New York: Oxford University Press) 1981; and Deil S. Wright (1988), *Understanding Inter-governmental Relations*, 3rd edition (Monterey, Calif.: Brooks-Cole Publishing Company).

   For a finely drawn portrait of one of the ironic paradoxes of the New Federalism program, see William Hudson (1980), The New Federalism Paradox, *Policy Studies*, 8, 900–905.

2. For a trenchant and accurate account of the counter-productive effects of the FHA program, see Edward C. Banfield (1974), *The Unheavenly City, Revisited* (Boston: Little, Brown), pp. 16–17, 32–33. See also Lawrence J. R. Herson and John M. Bolland (1990), *The Urban Web: Politics, Policy, and Theory* (Chicago: Nelson-Hall Publishers) p. 293; Ross, Levine, and Stedman (1991), pp. 17–18; and Bernard H. Ross and Myron A. Levine (1996), *Urban Politics: Power in Metropolitan America*. 5th edition (Itasca, Ill.: F. E. Peacock), pp. 34–36.

3. For a discussion of the contemporary "resonance" of the GI Bill, see Theda Skocpol (1996), Delivering for Young Families: The Resonance of the GI Bill," *The American Prospect*, Vol. 28 (September–October): 66–72; and Skocpol (1994), *Protecting Soldiers and Mothers: The Political Origins of Social Policy in the United States*, (Cambridge, Mass.: Harvard University Press).

4. One well-documented—arguably infamous—example of such failed attempts to direct city and neighborhood revitalization from Washington is a multi-million-dollar effort attempted in the City of Oakland by the Small Business Administration (SBA) in the 1960s. The SBA economic revitalization program, a program designed to turn-around an American city clearly in crisis and in danger of outbreaks of urban rioting and unrest (which later did break out in Oakland) resulted in a small number of temporary jobs after a federal expenditure of several million dollars. The episode is described well in Jeffrey Pressman and Aaron Wildavsky

(1973), *Implementation: How Great Expectations in Washington are Dashed in Oakland* (Berkeley: University of California Press). For a more sanguine account of later federal-local aid programs in Oakland and the San Francisco Bay Area, see Rufus Browning, David Tabb, and Dale Rogers Marshall (1984), *Protest Is Not Enough: The Struggle of Blacks and Hispanics for Equality in Urban Politics* (Berkeley: University of California Press).

5. The discussion by Heller of how a post-Vietnam budgetary surplus might be plowed back into domestic issues and programs to aid the cities should sound familiar to contemporary ears. A similar discussion of how to spend the "peace dividend" that presumably flowed from the end of the Cold War, circa 1987–88, briefly sparked a number of issues and proposals to aid America's cities. Virtually all of these proposals fell prey to the Congressional budget accord of 1990—the Budget Enforcement Act of 1990—that held that all new expenditures must be balanced either by cuts in existing federal programs or new taxes, or both.

6. There is another political or tactical irony in proposing the revival of revenue sharing. If, as is often said of President Nixon's diplomatic recognition of China, "only Nixon could go to China," perhaps the domestic policy analog to this is that "only Clinton (or another card-carrying fiscally conservative New Democrat" such as Vice President Al Gore) could revive revenue sharing.

7. This discussion of Reagan-era federal-local program relies in part on an earlier analysis of New Federalism II policymaking in Roger Caves and Robert Waste (1987), "New Federalism, Reaganomics and Western Cities: The View of Western Officials," a paper presented at the Annual Meeting of the Western Political Science Association, Anaheim, California (March 1987).

8. Buttressing this argument that the recent creation of *urban villages* or *edge cities*, with increased office space of no genuine benefit to the poorest residents of America's center-city poverty neighborhood residents, is the grim finding that from 1970 to 1991—the latest figures available at the time of this writing—of the twenty cities with the highest rate of new office construction, the inner-city unemployment rate has remained steady at 26 percent, while the average family income has declined by 4 percent. See Robert Wood (1991), "Cities in Trouble," *Domestic Affairs*, Vol. 1 (Summer): 232.

9. For a rigorous attempt to prove that the numbers of homeless are lower than these estimates, see Christopher Jencks (1994), *The Homeless* (Cambridge, Mass.: Harvard University Press) pp. 1–7. Part of the frustration in fashioning a coherent intervention policy to address the homeless issue is the lack of clarity on the exact size and service needs of the homeless population in the United States. Government estimates have ranged from the 1990 Census estimate of 600,000 homeless persons—a figure so low that the Bureau of the Census, itself, rejects the figure in favor of an adjustment developed by Martha Burt of the Urban Institute—to the finding by Culhane, Link and others that, as reported in 1994 by HUD, 7,000,000 Americans were homeless at some point during the second half of the 1980s.

A recent, and disturbing, trend is the rise of the number of veterans—particularly Vietnam vets—in the population of single men using homeless shelters in the late 1990s. A survey conducted by the International Union of Gospel Missions, a nondenominational shelter organization, which has conducted the survey annually since 1988, found that between 1991 and 1993 the number of vets in the single homeless male population remained steady at 29%. More recently, the number of vets in the homeless population has increased to 34%, an increase of 15 percent since 1993. The Veterans Administration (VA) estimates a lower figure for homeless vets of 250,000 annually in 1996 but admits that whatever the true figure, the needs of homeless veterans greatly exceed the ability of the VA and the federal government to deal with the problem. For a summary of the findings from the 1996 annual survey, see John Diamond (1996), "Survey Says High Ratio of Homeless Men Are Veterans," *Sacramento Bee*, November 10, p A11.

10. See also, Don Norris and Lyke Thompson (eds.) (1995), *The Politics of Welfare Reform* (Newbury Park, Calif.: Sage Publications); Barbara Goldman, Daniel Friedlander, Judith Gueron, and David Long (1985), *Findings from the San Diego Job Search and Work Experience Demonstration Program* (New York: Manpower Demonstration Research Corporation) (March); State of California, Legislature, Legislative Analyst Office (1985), *An Analysis of Findings from the San Diego Work Experience Demonstration Program* (Sacramento: LAO) (May); Judith Gueron (1986), *Work Initiatives for Welfare Recipients: Lessons from a Multi-State Experiment* (New York: Manpower Demonstration Research Corporation) (March); and, John Wallace and David Long (1987), *GAIN: Planning and Early Implementation* (New York: Manpower Demonstration Research Corporation) (April). For a contrary, albeit empirically largely unsubstantiated, view, see Charles Murray (1984), *Losing Ground: American Social Policy, 1950–1980* (New York: Basic Books).

11. While $30 billion a year, the recommended figure contained in the 1989 Ford Foundation Report, sounds at first blush to be an astronomically high federal expenditure level, it should be noted that, by way of contrast, the Savings and Loan crisis absorbed $500 billion during this same time period, an amount that would have funded the Ford Foundation–recommended program for 16.67 program years. Or note, again for purposes of comparison, that the "Operation Desert Storm" Gulf War pursued by the Bush Administration cost in excess of $2 billion a day. Thus, fifteen days of the Desert Storm operation would have funded an entire year of social deficit spending.

12. For a lively exchange between three knowledgeable urban policy insiders on the possibility and desirability of a coherent national urban policy, see Robert C. Wood (1995), "People versus Places: The Dream Will Never Die," in Roger W. Caves, *Exploring Urban America: An Introductory Reader* (Newbury Park, Calif: Sage Publications), pp. 137–43; and Marshall Kaplan and Franklin James (eds.) (1990), *The Future of National Urban Policy* (Durham, N.C.: Duke University Press). Franklin argues that "the era of national largess concerning city problems appears to the writers in this book to be over. Urban initiatives no longer appeal" (Kaplan & James, 1990: 351). Kaplan, in turn, argues that since "the federal government does not have a theory of city development and city decay . . . None of the models put forth to explain urban problems and/or city trends stands up well under sustained scrutiny . . . [Thus urban scholars and urban policy advocates should] figure out how non-urban policies that are likely to win favor in the Congress— welfare reform, infrastructure assistance, education help—could best benefit the

cities . . . [and] guarantee cities a fair shake or favored position" (Kaplan & James, 1990: 181–84; cited in Wood, 1995).

Wood throughly disagrees with the ultimate conclusion of Kaplan and James that: "renewed efforts to establish a national urban policy . . . [would] be futile" (Kaplan & James, 1990: 234).

This position is consistent with Professor Hal Wolman of Wayne State University, who has long argued at Urban Affairs Annual Meetings that contemporary Administrations from the Reagan Administration to the Clinton Administration have found it far easier to aid cities indirectly rather than directly, urging adoption of social programs, reforms, or national economic goals that, then, rebound, into the more localized urban arena. Myron Levine has gone further, arguing, in a memorable phrase that such policies and programs, notably in the first term of the Clinton Administration, amounted to "stealth urban policy." See Bernard Ross and Myron Levine (1996).

Lawrence Herson and John Bolland summed up the societal dilemma in fashioning a national urban policy quite well when they noted that: "As to the realization of a comprehensive national urban policy, its realization seems remotest of all . . . [At least in part, because] Our vision of cities is clouded by an ambivalent regard: We see them as symbols of accomplishment and as creators of culture and wealth, but we also see them as places of violence and evil that are merely to be endured. Side by side, both visions work to constrain our policy options." See Lawrence Herson and John Bolland (1990), *The Urban Web*.

13. It is worth emphasizing that the hostility or cynicism that has evolved since the Reagan/Bush Administration to the Clinton Administration that now constitutes a conventional wisdom among even some liberal advocates of aid to cities has been widespread. Even the central congressional architect of much recent social welfare policy, Senator Daniel Patrick Moynihan (D-NY), who has acknowledged that the " 'breakdown in family structure and the rise of welfare dependency,' along with [the] 'geographic isolation' of inner cities lies at the heart of America's problems of race, poverty and crime," has concluded in a recent book that: "No one has a clue as to what it would take [to address the problems of welfare dependency, poverty, and America's cities] . . . Expect little of government, especially national government" (Daniel Patrick Moynihan [1996], *Miles to Go: A Personal History of Social Policy* [Cambridge, Mass.: Harvard University Press]; cited in Mickey Kaus [1996], "Moynihan on Moynihan: The Senator says what he thinks, and what he thinks of what he used to think," *New York Times Book Review*, November 10, p. 14).

We will argue in Chapter 6 that Moynihan is correct on both points, but that rather than this being an argument *against* aiding cities from Washington, it is, instead, an excellent rationale for providing cities with significant but revenue-neutral funds and encouraging cities to use their own local judgment in selecting from successful intervention strategies already locally implemented in a number of local jurisdictions throughout the United States.

14. Assuming, for purposes of argument, that the American Revolutionary War and the establishment of the present Constitution in 1787 constitutes the First American Revolution, which created the federal government, while the Second Revolution on the Civil War and the Lincoln Presidency saved the federal government from dissolution and clarified the significant but secondary role of the states and sub-national partners. The Third American Revolution—the

restructuring of American national political institutions and policies to reflect the fact that the vast majority of the U.S. population lives in America's cities and metropolitan areas, in other words, the "reinventing of American urban politics," remains unaccomplished. A president or presidents that succeed in facilitating the transition to the Third American Revolution would, if successful, rightly be viewed as members of the small pantheon of founders along-side Washington, Jefferson, Adams, Madison, and Lincoln.

15. A full explanation of the Clinton Administration efforts to expand and improve Head Start is contained in U.S. Congress, Senate (1995), Senate Committee on Labor and Human Resources, Subcommittee on Children, Family, Drugs, and Alcoholism, *The Administration Proposal for Head Start Reauthorization*, 103rd Congress, Second Session.

16. One measure of the centrality of urban problems and urban policy for the Clinton Administration, at least in the first term of his administration, is the fact that for at least the first two years of the Administration, according to HUD Secretary Henry Cisneros, Vice President Al Gore set aside one morning a week for in-depth briefings on urban problems facing the nation (Peirce, 1993b).

17. The first minimum wage was established by the federal government in 1938, at 25 cents an hour. In recent times, the minimum wage has been increased by each of the past seven presidents running for reelection. The 1996 minimum wage legislation, enacted in August 1996, also included a $10-billion, five-year package of tax cuts for small businesses, although riders and language in the bill also extended special tax benefits to several of the largest companies in the country, including: Domino's Pizza, Hewlett-Packard, Johnson & Johnson, and Microsoft, Also included in the bill were elimination of state barriers to interracial adoptions, and a $5,000 tax credit for adopting a child. See the summary of the new legislation in Leo Rennert (1996), "Clinton signs increase in minimum wage," *Sacramento Bee*, August 21, p. A1.

18. As Ross and Levine note (1996: 443); nine states were granted waivers for health care experiments, while over thirty states received waivers for welfare service delivery innovations.

19. Bear in mind, however, that when speaking of down-sizing the federal work force, that in terms of general trends, the federal civilian employment workforce has *decreased* as a percentage of the civilian employment figure since 1950. See the Advisory Commission on Intergovernmental Relations (1992), *Significant Features of Fiscal Federalism*, Vol. 2 (Washington, D.C.; cited as ACIR).

20. Churchill fans will instantly recognize the reference to Churchill's famous quotation when, after seeing action in the Boer War in Africa, Churchill remarked: "Nothing so concentrates the mind as being shot at to no effect."

21. It should be emphasized that although HUD has stood out as a politically attractive target for down-sizing and "reinvention" from the time of the Reagan administration onward, the scale of administrative malfeasance at HUD—leaving aside, if one can, the personal malfeasance and corruption associated with Sam Peirce's turn at the helm of HUD—is slight when contrasted with older line departments such as Defense, Agriculture, and the Internal Revenue Service. As a recent Heritage Foundation *meta-analysis*—a large study analyzing and combining the results of previous studies, in this case reports from government watchdog agencies such as the General Accounting Office (GAO) and the Inspector General (IG) office of several federal agencies—documented several large scale

nominees for reinvention. These include a finding by the IG at the Department of Agriculture of $7 billion dollars worth of equipment misused as a result of inadequate management, material control, and record-keeping. The Department of Defense reported "problem disbursements or untraceable spending" exceeding $27 billion. The IRS, when audited by the GAO, had record-keeping errors so profound that the GAO concluded that an audit of IRS was, due to the magnitude of its financial mismanagement and inadequate record-keeping, actually impossible, a plea that the IRS would surely find unacceptable if attempted by a citizen undergoing one of the infamous audits of tax records it regularly inflicts on the tax-paying population at large. For a description of the Heritage Foundation study findings by the chief architect of the study, see the op-ed piece by Scott Hodge (1996), "Reinventing Government Effort Needs Some Reinventing, *Sacramento Bee*, November 11, p. F6.

22. For purposes of comparison, current work programs employ about 3,000 adult welfare recipients nationwide. As DeParle (1994:1) notes: "The only modern parallel [to the Clinton welfare/jobs program] comes from the Comprehensive Employment and Training Act, which created about 750,000 jobs at its peak. But the program, begun by President Richard M. Nixon, was widely viewed as an exercise in make-work, and it was abolished by President Ronald Reagan."

23. The influence of "soccer moms" was almost certainly exaggerated by political pundits during the 1996 presidential campaign. Married suburban mothers with children at home never exceeded 6% of the presidential electorate. ABC exit polls indicated that Dole won a slim (44% to 43%) majority of the male vote, while women voted 54% to 37% for the President. See Ellen Goodman (1996), "Women's Issues Carried the Day," *San Francisco Chronicle*, November 12 p. A21.

CHAPTER 5

1. For a justification of current Head Start efforts, and Clinton administration plans to expand and improve Head Start, see U.S. Congress, Senate (1995), Senate Committee on Labor and Human Resources, Subcommittee on Children, Family, Drugs, and Alcoholism, *The Administration Proposal for Head Start Reauthorization*, 103rd Congress, Second Session.

2. A recent summary of Head Start research and research design strategies for future study of Head Start may be found in Deborah A. Phillips and Natasha J. Cabarera (eds.) (1996), "Beyond the Blueprint: Directions for Research on Head Start," *Roundtable on Head Start Research*, Board on Children, Youth and Families, Commission on Behavioral and Social Sciences and Education, National Research Council, Institute of Medicine (Washington, D.C.: National Academy Press).

3. Specifically, I advocate the "targeting within universalism" approach suggested by Harvard policy scholar, Theda Skocpol (1990a), "Targeting within Universalism: Politically Viable Policies to Combat Poverty in the U.S.," a paper presented at the Annual Meeting of the American Political Science Association, San Francisco, August 30–September 2; and, Skocpol (1990b), "Sustainable Social Policy: Fighting Poverty without Poverty Programs," *The American Prospect* (Summer): 58–70.

4. Although the "reinvented HUD" advocated in this chapter would involve a reduction in the scope and scale of the present-day HUD organization and activities, I would argue that the suggested changes are more a "reconfiguration" than a "reduction," more an attempt at "right-sizing" than "down-sizing." In addition to the national clearinghouse function suggested in this chapter, I would also advocate retaining the HUD Section 8 housing and rental assistance program, which has made notable progress with Move to Opportunity (MTO) programs, and also retain the HUD oversight of continuing McKinney Act funding for homeless programs and CHAS compliance by local jurisdictions.

This reconceptualization of HUD is a major modification of the role of HUD, from that of a Washington, D.C.-based monitor, to that of a collaborative and facilitative change agent.

5. Admittedly, encouragement for community policing and additional staffing are both provided to local jurisdictions by the Crime Bill, and, to that extent, this assistance is crucial in helping to lower the level of violence in American cities.

6. The literature on community policing is extensive. The key scholars associated with the development of the community policing approach are Robert Trojanowicz and Bonnie Bucqueroux. See, for example, Trojanowicz and Bucqueroux (1990), *Community Policing: A Contemporary Perspective* (Cincinnati: Anderson Publishing Company); Trojanowicz (1991), *Community Policing and the Challenge of Diversity.* (East Lansing, Mich.: Michigan State University, National Center for Community Policing); Trojanowicz and David Carter (1988), *The Philosophy and Role of Community Policing* (East Lansing, Mich.: Michigan State University, The National Neighborhood Foot Patrol Center); Trojanowicz and Mark Moore (1988), *The Meaning of Community in Community Policing* (East Lansing, Mich.: Michigan State University, The National Neighborhood Foot Patrol Center). See also, Sidney Verba, Kay Schlozman, Henry Brady, and Norman Nie (1993), "Citizen Activity: Who Participates? What Do They Say?" *American Political Science Review*, Vol. 87 (2): 303–18; Samuel Walker (1997), "Answers to 10 Key Questions About Civilian Review," *Law Enforcement News*, Vol. 18 (355): 8–10.

Approximately 100 metropolitan police departments have Community Policing Mission Statements listed on the Internet, under the heading, "Community Policing." Additional informative sources of information on community policing, include: (1) Dennis P. Rosenbaum (ed.) (1994), *The Challenge of Community Policing: Testing the Promises.* (Newbury Park, Calif.: Sage Publications); (2) U.S. Department of Justice, National Institute of Justice (1995), *Community Policing in Chicago.* (Washington, D.C.: U.S. Department of Justice); (3) U.S. Department of Justice, Office of Justice Programs, Bureau of Justice Assistance (1993), *The Systems Approach to Crime and Drug Prevention: A Path to Community Policing.* (Washington: U.S. Department of Justice); and (4) U.S. Department of Justice, Office of Justice Programs, National Institute of Justice (1992), *Community Policing in Seattle: A Model Partnership Between Citizens and Police* (Washington, D.C.: U.S. Department of Justice).

7. Court Watch is a neighborhood-based program increasingly popular in neighborhoods facing serious crime threats. In a typical Court Watch program, neighborhood residents use a number of strategies, including meeting with local police to inform them of neighborhood problem spots and enforcement priorities, writing letters to judges expressing the desire of neighborhood residents to see maximum allowable sentences given to criminals convicted of serious neighborhood crimes, attendance in large numbers at the trials and, particularly, at the sentencing, of convicted neighborhood perpetrators. Other activities include the identification of neighborhood crack houses, and working with CDCs to purchase, rehab, and transfer ownership of such houses to working families in the neighborhood, families committed to the eradication of crime and the increasing safety of their given neighborhood area.

I had the pleasure of working with community groups from the Ohio City, West Side of Cleveland during a brief tenure in 1994–1995 as the Albert A. Levin Chair of Urban Studies and Public Service at the Maxine Goodman Levin College of Urban Affairs at Cleveland State University. The West Side Cleveland Court Watch program in that city, working with the Cleveland State University Law School Community Law Clinic under the direction of Professor Alan Weinstein, is a remarkably effective Court Watch program, one deserving replication in crime-troubled neighborhoods elsewhere.

8. For an account of the failure of city-county consolidation to be be successful when placed on the ballot as a referendum, see Timothy Mead (1997), "Who Killed Cock Robin?" a paper presented at the Annual Meeting of the Urban Affairs Association, Toronto (March).

9. A repeated theme of several panels at the 1995 Annual Meeting of the Urban Affairs Association, Portland, April, 1995 was exactly this point. There is widespread consensus among urban scholars that Portland represents, in David Rusk's words, "a model structure for multi county regional governance." See David Rusk (1993), *Cities without Suburbs*, p. 104.

10. Personal communication with the author. Professor Krumholz, former planning director for the City of Cleveland and professor of planning at the Levin College of Urban Affairs at Cleveland State University, is very much "on the record" with this positive assessment of Gautreaux. For more on Krumholz and the "equity planning" movement seeking to explicitly and systematically include social capital needs and the needs of poorer inner-city neighborhoods into the everyday planning protocols and procedures of American city planning, see Norman Krumholz and Pierre Clavel (1984), *Reinventing Cities: Equity Planners Tell Their Stories* (Philadelphia: Temple University Press). The phrase "reinventing" in the title of that book and in the text of this book are purposely meant to overlap, in terms of emphases, research interests, and normative prescriptions. As Krumholz once remarked when introducing David Rusk at a Levin College Symposium in Cleveland, "we're all working on the same book on cities . . . only our last chapters are different" (Krumholz, Levin College Rusk Symposium and Retreat, October 1994).

11. For an excellent accounts of Chicago politics and urban issues generally, see William J. Grimshaw (1992), *Bitter Fruit: Black Politics and the Chicago Machine, 1931–1991*, (Chicago: University of Chicago Press).

12. It should be emphasized that more recently under the new CHA leadership of Joseph Shuldinger, former Clinton Administration Assistant HUD Under Secretary for Housing and Indian Affairs, the Chicago Housing Authority has embarked on an ambitious program of reform and renovation. It is far too early at this writing to forecast the probability of Shuldinger being successful at turning around the most troubled large-city public housing authority in America.

The crime and safety challenges facing CHA management are almost impossible to overstate. Bear in mind, as described in Chapter 2, 300 shootings were reported in one *two-week period* during the summer of 1994 at the Robert Taylor low-income housing project in Chicago.

13. Critics charge that the prominent center-city development projects by planner James Rouse, such as Boston's Quincy Market/Faunal Hall, Baltimore's Harbor-front, or San Antonio's Riverwalk, have a uniform homogenized yuppie shopping theme-mall flavor that further deteriorated a declining center-city area; defenders argue that the theme shopping centers have produced vitally needed jobs and development anchors for problematic city areas.

14. For a powerful argument against the degenerative aspects of cultural nationalism among leading African-American spokespersons, see Manning Marble (1992), *The Crisis of Color and Democracy: Essays on Race, Class and Power* (Monroe, Maine: Common Courage Press); and Cornel West (1994), *Race Matters* (New York: Vintage Books).

    Marble argues: "Our challenge is not to be become part of the system but to transform it for everyone. We must struggle to make economic and racial equality for all" (Marble, 1992: 19). West, in a passage both apocalyptic and optimistic, argues that: "In these downbeat times, we need as much hope and courage as we do vision and analysis; we must accent the best of each other even as we point out the vicious effects of our racial divide and the pernicious consequences of our maldistribution of wealth and power. We simply cannot enter the twenty-first century at each other's throats, even as we acknowledge the weighty forces of racism, patriarchy, economic inequality, homophobia, and ecological abuse on our necks. We are at a crucial crossroad in the history of this nation—and we can either hang together by combating these forces that divide and degrade us or we hang separately" (West, 1994: 159).

15. For a sensitive analysis of a complex and literally inflammatory issue, see Raphael Sonenshein (1996), "The Battle Over Liquor Stores in South Central Los Angeles: The Management of Interminority Conflict," *Urban Affairs Review*, Vol. 31 (July): 710–37, which contains a careful analysis of conflict between the African-American community and Korean liquor-store owners in South Central Los Angeles.

16. See Steven P. Erie (1988), *Rainbow's End: Irish-Americans and the Dilemmas of Urban Machine Politics, 1840–1985* (Berkeley: University of California Press).

17. For a detailed and methodologically sophisticated recent comparative study of income inequality in American cities, see Sanjoy Chakravorty (1996), "Urban Inequality Revisited: The Determinants of Income Distribution in U.S. Metropolitan Areas," *Urban Affairs Review*, Vol. 31 (6) (July): 759–77. See also Martin Carnoy (1996), *Faded Dreams: The Politics and Economics of Race in America* (New York and London: Cambridge University Press), for an extensive analysis of racial and ethnic income differences.

18. An equally effective metaphor, and equally apocalyptic view, is the image of Los Angeles depicted in Mike Davis (1992), *City of Quartz*. New York: Vintage Books.

19. Race matters greatly. For what is, perhaps, the most effective argument supporting this contention, see the argument by Professor Manning Marble (1992), *The Crisis of Color and Democracy*.

20. For a well-written, if polemical, argument that Jefferson's legacy—both halves—should be abandoned, but the Jeffersonian product, the Declaration of Independence, retained, see Connor Cruise O'Brien (1996), "Thomas Jefferson: Radical

and Racist," *Atlantic Monthly* (October): 53–72; and the larger, book-length argument in O'Brien (1996), *The Long Affair: Thomas Jefferson and the French Revolution* (Chicago: University of Chicago Press).

CHAPTER 6

1. Nor is there a legal barrier to the national government entering the lucrative lottery market to produce funding for aiding America's metropolitan areas. An early-1820s U.S. Supreme Court case, *Champion v. Ames*, resolved the question of whether Congress could pass an Act prohibiting the carrying of a lottery ticket across state lines in favor of Congress; finding that Congress could do so in that the action in question involved commerce between the states over which Congress has complete power due to the Commerce Clause of the U.S. Constitution.

   The Supreme Court held that lotteries per se were not a tax but commerce, and bolstered this decision with later opinions reflecting the same federal sovereignty over lotteries as commerce in cases involving the land lotteries that accompanied the settlement of the Western reserve, and at the Oklahoma and Oregon territories. Some of these properties were "land rushed," but others were lotteries, a system again used in a different context for issuing radio frequencies in the early days of radio. The legitimate and dominant role of the federal government in lotteries has also been upheld in lottery cases involving the military draft, and some types of licenses, all of these examples using chance lotteries to distribute or take the good, opportunity, or service in question.

2. Figures for the Irish and U.K. National lottery obtained via Internet at www.dublin.iol.ie/resource/lottery/lott.html and www.connect.org.uk/lottery/Info/About.html.

3. This section draws heavily from an analysis of the status of American early-childhood educational programs by Irving B. Harris (1996), "Starting Small, and Thinking Big," in *The American Prospect* (September–October): 74–77.

4. This section and the collegiate Police Corps section draws from several sources. Key among these are: (1) an op-ed opinion article written by Robin Wilson, former President of California State University, Chico. See Robin Wilson (1992), "Contemplating a Collegiate Cop Corps," *Chico State University Orion*, November 11, p. 6; (2) an article by the founding figure of community policing and the Police Corps concept, Adam Walinsky (1995), "The Crisis of Public Order," *Atlantic Monthly* (July): 39–54; and (3) an article on Walinsky by Elizabeth Kolbert (1994), "Adam Walinsky: Private Lobbyist for Public Safety," *New York Times Magazine* (July): 42–45.

5. There is another aspect of the Police Corps proposal that is worth raising at this juncture. The Police Corps would greatly aid in introducing ethnic, economic, and gender diversity to America's police forces. As Walinsky acknowledges: "Our crime problem is only our race problem wearing a different face. Look, the job of the police in America, at least for the last 30 years, is to keep 'them' away from 'us.' Nobody wants to know how they do it. They just want it done" (Walinsky, 1995: 44). A Police Corps cadet program increasing the number and diversity of America's police officer ranks should, almost by definition, address the very issue that Walinsky had the courage and insight to raise in his provocative 1995 *Atlantic Monthly* article.

6. Intriguingly, the TIMSS Report found that Singapore, Korea, and Japan were among the top four countries in math scores for school children but in the lowest scores internationally for parental satisfaction with student's performance. As one newspaper editorializes about the results, it noted that: "In the United States, with its mediocre results, parents and students were pretty well satisfied. That, too, ought to tell us something." See "Schools and Consequences" (1996), Editorial, *Sacramento Bee*, November 24, p. F4. It also ought to tell us something that a survey of American school children and their teachers would probably be able to document that most American school students—and many of their teachers—cannot distinguish between mean or average and median scores on a survey such as that contained in the TIMSS Report.

7. Students of political philosophy will recognize this view of the city as that of Aristotle, who argued in *The Politics* "that the city draws its strength—and we our understanding of the city—from the family" (Waste, 1989). In turn, the family allows the city to have jurisdiction over the family because families, as individuals, reach their greatest independence and greatest degree of protection, from the city. To aid the city in this drive for self-reliance, independence (*autrikia*) [moderns are wont to call this the "sustainable city" but this latter-day abbreviation misses much of the richness of the classical point at issue] not only produces *independent cities* but also, as Aristotle recognized, is the single greatest hope for the family and the larger society in which the family is embedded to realize its full potential. I have argued this point in other writings (Robert Waste, 1989), *The Ecology of City Policymaking* (New York: Oxford University Press); and, in an essay analyzing the writings of the urban scholar and classicist most prominently associated with a neo-Aristotlean view of the "unwalled city," Norton Long, in R. Waste (1995), "Urban Poverty and the City as Reservation," *Journal of Urban Affairs*, Vol. 17: 3.

CHAPTER 7

1. See the classic postwar trilogy of novels by Jean Paul Sartre, *The Road to Freedom* (1951), published as *The Age of Reason, The Reprieve*, and *Troubled Sleep* (New York: Alfred A. Knopf).

2. See also, a similar proposal by Barry Bluestone, utilizing tax surpluses in the Social Security Trust Fund as financing for loans to students, adults, and, interestingly, mid-career currently employed adults. See B. Bluestone (1990).

3. The three are: Assistant Secretaries Bane, Edelman, and Ellwood in the U.S. Department of Health and Human Services. It is perhaps worth noting that Edelman is also the husband of Marian Wright Edelman, Director of the Washington, D.C.-based Children's Defense Fund, and a key organizer of the Washington, D.C. "Stand for Children" march and rally in the Summer of 1996.

4. The case advanced by Mary Jo Bane, Richard Nathan, and William Julius Wilson for the support of at-risk single mothers in center-cities and elsewhere may be markedly helped by a recent finding that speaks directly to the logic of the popular, if now demonstrably incorrect, view that female center-city residents choose to become mothers in order to secure welfare payments and the questionable amenities that accompany a life on public assistance. The 1996 study by the California Office of Criminal Justice and Planning attacks the "myths" that teen pregnancies

are caused by teen-age boys, noting instead that most teen pregnancies—56 percent—are caused by men over the age of 25. Stricter enforcement against statutory rape, as is currently being implemented in California under an initiative that insures that the same investigators and prosecutors stay on a case "from start to finish," would seem the appropriate policy response to protect at-risk teen females, and the interests of the large society as a whole. See an article detailing the California initiative by the Associated Press (1996), "Statutory Rape Crackdown Explodes Teen Pregnancy Myth," *Chico Enterprise-Record*, November 30, p. 5A.

Another promising policy option, one strongly recommended by William Julius Wilson, is the stepped-up child support enforcement. A 1995 study by the Public Media Center Project, funded by the Rosenberg Foundation, estimates that if all parents paid "their fair share of child support," American children would receive $34 billion more each year; enough to raise millions of children out of poverty-level family incomes. The 1995 study notes, in an ironic finding, that half of all U.S. children owed child support receive little support or nothing at all—a dollar amount that is nearly twice that suffered by all adults in a one-year period due to muggings, home burglaries, and thefts of all types. See the brief synopsis of the 1995 Report by the Public Media Center Project in an Op-Ed page description, "Can You Name the Most Common Crime Against Children?" *New York Times*, December 5, p. A19.

5. This explanation of the initiative, referendum, and recall process draws heavily from an explanation I authored in Robert Waste (1989), *The Ecology of City Policymaking* (New York: Oxford University Press): pp. 191–92.

Glossary

This glossary defines many terms used in this book. The chapter number in which the term is discussed is bracketed at the end of each definition. In many cases the name of the scholar primarily associated with the term or concept appears within parentheses following the chapter citation.*

acute versus incubatory policies: Nelson Polsby has distinguished between Type A (acute) policies, which are treated as emergencies and which require rapid action from policymakers, and Type B (incubatory) policies, which require a lengthy gestation period prior to enactment. [4,5] (Polsby)

adrenaline cities: As metropolitan statistical areas experiencing severe chronic stress due to the permanent crisis of American cities in the 1990s, these forty-four cities have—since at least 1990—been stuck in a prolonged state of acute stress. [2]

crime measures: There are two key sources of crime statistics in the United States, the National Crime Victimization Survey (NCVS) and the Uniform Crime Reporting Program—both administered by the U.S. Department of Justice. The definitions of crime and data collections techniques differ in the two studies, and therefore the data in the two reports frequently contain discrepancies and are not, strictly speaking, statistically comparable.

The NCVS is administered by the Bureau of Justice Statistics, which has collected information on crimes suffered by individuals and households since 1973, whether or not the crimes in question were reported to law enforcement authorities. The emphasis on all crimes—versus the focus on only reported crimes as found in the UCR methodology—is laudable; however, the NCVS excludes arson, white, collar or commercial crimes, crimes against children under the age of twelve, and homicide. Given the lack of coverage of homicide, this author and many scholars in the field prefer to use the Uniform Crime Reporting (UCR) statistics for analyzing metro or urban crime rates.

The UCR program has been supervised by the FBI since 1929 and collects information on aggravated assault, arson, burglary, homicide, larceny-theft, motor vehicle theft, rape, and robbery. The figures used in the UCR are submitted voluntarily by over 16,000 law-enforcement agencies throughout the United States, covering more than 95 percent of the U.S. population. [1,2,5,6, Appendix]

federalism: This refers to the division of government authority into national and subnational units, with each unit having a genuine measure of power and political authority. [4,5]

---

*Some of these terms appeared earlier in a concluding glossary section in Robert Waste (1989), *The Ecology of City Policymaking* (New York: Oxford University Press), pp. 188–97.

Frostbelt cities: *Frostbelt cities* are those located north of a line drawn, roughly, from Richmond, Virginia, to San Francisco, California. They are frequently characterized by (1) weak local economies, often due to a once-strong but now troubled heavy industrial base; (2) population emigration, resulting in a deteriorating tax base; and (3) increasingly serious infrastructure costs and problems, often associated with the age of the city itself and the severity of winter conditions. [1–3]

incremental policy: This is an approach to public policymaking that argues that policymaking involves minor additions or subtractions added-to or subtracted-from earlier programs and policies. Thus, incrementalism involves successive comparisons and an extensive reliance on past behavior as a guide to current behavior. It is characterized by pluralist politics, designed to suffice or satisfice rather than maximize services or program goals. [4,5]

initiative, referendum, and recall elections: Introduced in South Dakota in 1898, initiative elections force a vote on public issues if a specified number of voters— usually 5-to-10 percent—sign a petition to place the measure on the ballot. Twenty-one states and the District of Columbia permit initiative elections at the state or local level. All but two of these states (Maine and Mississippi) are west of the Mississippi River.

In a referendum election, a state or local legislative body may put a question of public policy on the ballot to determine the will of the electorate. Thirty-seven states, including Connecticut and New York, have provisions allowing referendum elections.

Several state and local governments also provide for recall elections in which a specified number of voters—typically 20-to-30 percent—can, by signing a petition, force an election to determine whether an elected official should be removed from office. [7]

mandated city programs: Beginning in the 1940s, cities have often been ordered to undertake certain programs—water and sewage treatment, transportation or mental health programs, or affirmative action in hiring and promotion decisions— by the county, state, or federal governments. Many of these programs are *unfunded mandates*, requiring the local jurisdiction to provide a service without providing the city any funds to help in doing so. Because local jurisdictions are ordered to provide such services, these programs are referred to as *mandated* programs, a reference to the Latin verb *mandare*, meaning 'to order'. [4]

metropolitan statistical area (MSA): The U.S. Census Bureau refers to cities and their adjacent suburban communities as *metropolitan statistical areas*. The official Census Bureau explanation of an MSA is: "A geographic area consisting of a large population nucleus together with adjacent communities which have a high degree of economic and social integration with that nucleus." To qualify as an MSA, a city must have a population of 50,000 or greater, or be part of a metro region with a population of 100,000 or greater.

The largest MSA regions in the country are designated as consolidated metropolitan statistical areas (CMSAs) when, for example in the case of New York City and New Jersey, more than one state and more than one primary metropolitan area is included in the Census population designation. New York City, Los Angeles, and Chicago are prominent examples of CMSAs.

no return cities: David Rusk described thirty-four American cities as "cities beyond the Point of No Return." Rusk used three key indicators for severely distressed *no-return* cities: no-return cities have lost population, increasingly isolated their nonwhite minority populations, and decreased the incomes of city residents vis-à-vis their suburban counterparts. [2]

permanent crisis: Since at least 1990, American cities have experienced persistently high levels of poverty, hunger, homelessness, violent crime, infrastructure deterioration, fiscal stress, and voter alienation, accompanied by correspondingly low levels of voter turnout and civic participation. The permanent crisis currently consumes over 8 percent of the gross national product of the United States annually. [1]

poverty measures: Poverty in the United States is currently estimated using a rule-of-thumb formula developed by Mollie Orshansky, an economist with the Social Security Administration in 1963. At that time, Orshansky estimated that a family of four was poor if they had less cash income (before taxes) than three times the amount necessary to purchase a "minimum diet" for family meals. The original formula allowed an annual income providing twenty-three cents per meal per person. Although this poverty line has been moved up from time to time to account for inflation, the figure has never been adjusted to consider regional differences in the cost of living or housing costs in contemporary urban areas, which even in poverty neighborhoods may easily exceed two to three times the monthly cost of purchasing the ingredients for a "minimum diet" meal for a family of four. The poverty definition used by the federal government for statistical purposes was $15,141 for a family of four in 1994. [1,2, Appendix]

privatization: This is the process of contracting out to the private sector the performance of services such as road repairs or garbage collection, services that are normally carried out by traditional city departments. [4,5]

satisfice: This term is a combination of *satisfy* and *suffice*, used to denote the fact that public policymakers must often make do with less-than-perfect options and results. [4–6]

Second Harvest: Second Harvest is the largest domestic hunger relief organization in the United States. In 1996 Second Harvest found that 25 million people are at risk of hunger in America. [6, Appendix]

severely distressed neighborhoods: According to the Annie E. Casey Foundation, severely distressed neighborhoods have at least four of five characteristics: poverty rate above 25.7 percent; at least 39.6 percent of families headed by women; high-school dropout rate above 23.3 percent; more than 46.5 percent of men out of the labor force; and more than 17 percent of families on welfare. It should be noted first, that the most recent *Kids Count* study shows that children in severely distressed neighborhoods tend to cluster into three specific geographic groups. Almost half of the children in deeply troubled neighborhoods live in six large urbanized states, including: California, Illinois, Michigan, New York, Ohio, and Texas. Second, Washington, D.C., has the highest percentage of children in the nation (25.2 percent) in severely distressed neighborhoods. Third, several rural deep-South states have, as a region (excluding Washington, D.C.), the highest percentages of children in distressed neighborhoods in America, including: Arkansas (7.6 percent), Georgia (6.2 percent), Louisiana (17.2 percent), Mississippi (17.4 percent), and Tennessee (7.3 percent). [1,2, Appendix]

shooting-gallery cities: Fourteen U.S. cities were collectively responsible for over 30 percent of all homicides in the United States annually during 1994 and 1995. [2, Appendix]

sunbelt cities: Kevin Phillips coined the term "sunbelt" to describe a region of the United States south of a line drawn, roughly, from Richmond, Virginia, to San Francisco, California. The area south of this line is generally considered more politically conservative than is the area north of the line. The northern area has also been referred to as the frostbelt or rustbelt. Sunbelt cities are characterized by political conservatism; strong local economies; many based on defense industries and military bases recently experiencing downsizing as a result of post–Cold-War military conversion programs; university and research centers located in or near them; strong population growth pressures; and a growing political unrest between residents of newer suburbs and supporters of downtown commercial or central city neighborhood revitalization. [3,4]

unanticipated consequences: Murphy's Law states that if anything can go wrong, it will. Unanticipated consequences, such as the *maximum feasible misunderstanding* accompanying community action programs (CAP) in the 1960s, are the many things, both positive and negative, that will crop up once implementation of a program or project has begun. [4]

urban reservation cities: Five U.S. cities—Chicago, Los Angeles, New York City, Philadelphia, and San Francisco are *urban reservation* cities, meaning that they have the highest concentrations of extreme-poverty neighborhoods (neighborhoods with 40 percent or more of residents below the official poverty line) in the nation. Extreme poverty neighborhoods have concentrated in these cities so heavily that from 1980 to the 1990s these five urban reservation cities have accounted for over 25 percent of the national total of extreme poverty neighborhood residents. [2]

References

Advisory Commission on Intergovernmental Relations. (1994). *Significant features of fiscal federalism, 1994.* Washington D.C.; cited as ACIR in text.

Albelda, R., & Folbre, N. (1996). *The war on the poor*; Report by the Center for Popular Economics. New York: The New Press.

Alford, R., & Lee, E. (1968). Voting turnout in American cities. *American Political Science Review,* 62, 796–813.

Alin, F., & Davila, R. D. (1993). South Central's woes still burn. *Sacramento Bee,* April 18, A1.

Alter, J. (1996a). Where real people live: Those 'small issues' Morris fashioned for Clinton aren't so small to the voters. *Newsweek,* September 9, p. 38.

———. (1996b). Setting a standard: Finally, a city and its mayor take a crippled school system head-on. *Newsweek,* November 11, p. 36.

Ames, D., Brown, N., Callahan, M. H., Cummings, S., Smock, S. M., & Zeigler, J. (1992). Rethinking American urban policy. *Journal of Urban Affairs,* 14, 197–217.

Anderson, M. (1964). *The federal bulldozer: A critical analysis of urban renewal, 1949–1962.* Cambridge, Mass.: MIT Press.

Anglin, R., & Holcomb, B. (1993). Poverty in urban America. *Journal of Urban Affairs,* 14, 447–68.

Applebome, P. (1991). Although urban blight worsens, most people don't feel its impact. *New York Times,* January 28, p. 1.

———. (1993). C.D.C.'s new chief worries as much about bullets as about bacteria. *New York Times,* September 26, p. E7.

———. (1996). Enrollments soar, leaving dilapidated school buildings frayed at the seams. *New York Times,* September 26, p. A1.

Asimov, N. (1996). National panel blasts U.S. teacher standards: Report calls for overhaul of profession. *San Francisco Chronicle,* September 12, p. A1.

Associated Press. (1992). Demos yield to pressure to cut urban aid bill. *San Francisco Chronicle,* June 18, p. A13.

Associated Press. (1993). House says no to statehood for Capital. *San Francisco Chronicle,* November 22, p. 1.

Associated Press. (1996a). Registration: 20 million 'motor voters'. *New York Times,* October 16, p. A2.

Associated Press. (1996b). FBI reports drop in violent crime. *Chico Enterprise Record,* October 13, p. A1.

Associated Press. (1996c). Clinton proposes reading aid plan: Says college students can be tutors. *Sacramento Bee,* October 26, p. A8.

Bagby, M. E. (1996). *Annual report of the United States of America.* New York: Harper Collins.

Balfour, D. L., & Smith, J. L. (1996). Transforming lease-purchase housing programs for low income families: Towards empowerment and engagement. *Journal of Urban Affairs*, 18, 173–88.

Bane, M. J. (1996). Stand by for casualties. *New York Times*, November 10, p. E13.

———., & Jargowsky, P. A. (1988). Urban poverty areas: Basic questions concerning prevalence, growth, and dynamics. Paper presented for the Committee on National Urban Policy, National Academy of Sciences, Washington, D.C.

Banfield, E. C. (1974). *The unheavenly city, revisited*. Boston: Little, Brown.

Bank of America. (1995). Beyond sprawl: New patterns of growth to fit the new America. Pamphlet.

Barnes, W. (1990). Urban policies and urban impacts after Reagan. *Urban Affairs Quarterly*, 25, 562–73. Reprinted in Caves, R. W. (ed.) (1995). *Exploring urban America*. Newbury Park, Calif.: Sage Publications, Inc., 110–18.

Barnes, W., & Ledebur, L. (1993). *All in it together—cities, suburbs, and local economic regions*. Washington, D.C.: National League of Cities.

Barnes, W., & Ledebur, L. (1997). *The new regional economies: The U.S. common market and global economy*. Newbury Park, Calif.: Sage Publications, Inc.

Barr, S. (1994). Gore sees cynicism endangering reform. *Washington Post*, July 14, A21.

Baum, A. S., & Barnes, D. W. (1993). *A nation in denial: The truth about homelessness*. Boulder: Westview Press.

Bazar, E. (1996). Teacher readiness doubted: Many new hires fail standards, study says. *Sacramento Bee*, September 13, p. A1.

Berke, R. (1994). The good son. *New York Times Magazine*, February 20, pp. 28–35.

Blakely, E. J., & Ames, D. L. (1992). Changing places: American planning policy for the 1990s. *Journal of Urban Affairs*, 14, 423–46.

Block, C. R. (1990). Hot spots and isocrimes in law enforcement decision making. Conference on police and community responses to drugs: Frontline strategies in the drug war. University of Illinois at Chicago, December.

Block, C. R., Higgins, L., & Green, L. (1994). *The geoarchive handbook*. Chicago: The Illinois Criminal Justice Information Authority.

Block, R., & Block, C. R. (1992). Homicide syndromes and vulnerability: Violence in Chicago's community areas over 25 years. *Studies on Crime and Crime Prevention*, 1, 61–85.

Block, R., Vates, C., & Fuechtman, T. (1994). The Loyola community safety project: Liquor licenses and criminal activity. Paper presented at the Loyola geoArchive conference, Chicago, February 24.

Bluestone, B. (1990). Generational alliance: Social security as a bank for education and training. *The American Prospect* (Summer).

Brown, E. G., Jr. (1992). Help the cities first. *New York Times*, November 11, p. E17.

Brown, L. D., Fossett, J. W., & Palmer, K. T. (1984). *The changing politics of federal grants*. Washington DC: Brookings Institution.

Browning, R., Marshall, D. R., and Tabb, D. (1984). *Protest is not enough*. Berkeley, Calif: University of California Press.

Burt, M. (1992). *Over the edge*. New York: Russell Sage Foundation.

Burt, M., & Cohen, B. (1989). *America's homeless: Numbers, characteristics and the programs that serve them*. Washington, D.C.: Urban Institute.

Butler, S. M. (1981). *Enterprise zones: Greenling the inner cities*. New York: Universe Books.

Caputo, D. A. (1976). *Urban America: The policy alternatives.* San Francisco: W. H. Freeman and Company.

Caputo, D. A., & Cole, R. (1973). Revenue sharing and urban services: A survey. *Tax Review*, 34 (October).

———. (1974). *The impact of citizen participation on the expediture of general revenue sharing funds.* Paper presented at the Northeast Political Science Association Meeting, Saratoga Springs, N.Y., November.

Caputo, D. A., & Cole, R. (1975). General revenue sharing expenditure decisions in cities over 50,000. *Public Administration Review*, 35, 136–42.

Annie E. Casey Foundation (1994). *Kids Count, 1994.*

Caves, R. W. (ed.) (1995). *Exploring urban America: An introductory reader.* Newbury Park, Calif.: Sage Publications, Inc., 137–43.

Chakravorty, S. (1996). Urban inequality revisited: The determinants of income distribution in U.S. metropolitan areas. *Urban Affairs Review*, 31, 759–77.

Cisneros, H. G. (ed.) (1993). *Interwoven destinies: Cities and the nation.* New York: W. W. Norton.

———. (1995a). *The university and the urban challenge.* Washington, D.C.: U.S. Department of Housing and Urban Development Report (January).

———. (1995b). *Defensible space: Detering crime and building Community.* Washington, D.C.: U.S. Department of Housing and Urban Development Report (February).

———. (1995c). *Regionalism: The new geography of opportunity.* Washington, D.C.: U.S. Department of Housing and Urban Development Report (March).

———. (1995d). *Urban entrepreneurialism and national economic growth.* Washington, D.C.: U.S. Department of Housing and Urban Development Report (September).

Clark, T. N. (1994). *Urban innovation: Creative strategies for turbulent times.* Thousand Oaks, Calif.: Sage Publications, Inc.

City of Los Angeles Mayor's Committee on Children, Youth, and Families. (1994). *LA4KIDS.* Los Angeles, CA.

Coldwell and Banker. (1990). Coldwell banker commerical real estate. *Boston Globe*, October 2, p. 29.

Cole, R., & Tachel, D. (1981). *Attitudes of local officials to President Reagan's new federalism.* Arlington, Texas: Institute of Urban Studies.

Crowe, T. (1991). *Crime prevention through environmental design.* Boston: Butterworth-Heinemann.

Culhane, D., Dejowski, E. F., & Ibanez, J., et al. (1993). Public shelter admission rates in Philadelphia and New York City. Working paper. Washington, D.C.: Fannie Mae Office of Housing Research.

Dahl, R. A. (1980). *Democracy in the United States: promise and performance*, 3rd. ed. Chicago: Rand McNally.

———. (1996). Is there a better way to deal with complex issues like health care? New Haven, Conn.: Yale University, unpublished manuscript.

Davis, B. (1996). ACIR releases report on federal manadates. *PA Times*, 19, p. 3.

DeIlulio, J., Garvey, G., & Kettel, D. F. (1993). *Improving government performance: An owner's manual.* Washington, D.C.: Brookings Institution.

DeLeon, R., & LeGates, R. (1976). Redistribution effects of special revenue sharing for community development. Working Paper #17. Berkeley: University of California, Institute of Governmental Studies.

DeParle, J. (1991). Poverty rate rose sharply last year as incomes slipped. *New York Times*, September 9, p. A1.

DeParle, J. (1993). Clinton welfare planners outline big goals financed by big saving. *New York Times*, December 3, p. A1.

———. (1994a). Change in welfare is likely to need big jobs program. *New York Times*, January 30, p. 1.

———. (1994c). Report to Clinton sees vast extent of homelessness, higher spending sought. *New York Times*, February 17, p. 1.

Derthick, M. (1978). *Uncontrollable spending*. Washington, D.C.: Brookings Institution.

Diamond, J.—Associated Press. (1996). Survey says high ratio of homeless men are veterans. *Sacramento Bee*, November 10, p. A11.

Dommel, P. R. (1980). Social targeting for community development. *Political Science Quarterly*, 95, 465–78.

Downs, A. (1985). *Tax reform: What about real estate? Urban Cond.*, August: p. 14.

Endicott, W. (1993). Stay-at-homes in Stanislaus. *Sacramento Bee*, November 30, p. A3.

Erickson, R. E., & Friedman, S. W. (1991). Comparative dimensions of state enterprise zone policies. In Green, R. E. (ed.), *Enterprise zones: new directions in economic development*. Newbury Park, Calif.: Sage Publications, 155–78.

Erie, S. (1988). *Rainbow's end: Irish-Americans and the dilemmas of urban machine politics*. Berkeley: University of California Press.

Fainstein, N. (1993a). Race, class and segregation: discourses about African Americans. *International Journal of Urban and Regional Research*, 15, 384–403.

———. (1993b). Underclass, over class, race and inequality. *Urban Affairs Quarterly*, 29, 340–47.

Ferman, B. (1996). *Challenging the growth machine: Neighborhood politics in Chicago and Pittsburgh*. Lawrence: University Press of Kansas.

Fishkin, J. S. (1991). *Democracy and deliberation: New directions for democratic reform*. New Haven, Conn.: Yale University Press.

———. (1995). *The voice of the people: Public opinion and democracy*. New Haven, Conn.: Yale University Press.

Fitch, D. (1992). A radical proposal for closing the deficit. *San Francisco Chronicle*, November 30, p. A22.

Ford Foundation. (1989). *The common good: Social welfare and the American future*. New York: Ford Foundation.

———. (1990). *Participatory democracy project*. New York. Ford Foundation.

Frederickson, H. G. (1994). Total quality politics: TOP. *Spectrum: The Journal of State Government*, 67, 13–15.

———. (1996). Comparing the reinventing government with the new public administration. *Public Administration Review*, 56, 271–80.

Frej, W., & Specht, F. (1976). The housing and community development act of 1974: Implications for policy and planning. *Social Service Review*, 50, 275–92.

Frey, W., & Speare, A. (1988). *Regional and metropolitan growth in the United States*. New York: Russell Sage Foundation.

Friedlander, D., & Burtless, G. (1996). *Five years after: The long-term effects of welfare-to-work programs*. New York: Russell Sage Foundation.

Gans, H. (1962). *The urban villagers*. New York: The Free Press.

Ganz, M. (1996). Motor voter or motivated voter? *The American Prospect*, 28, 41–48.

Garreau, J. (1991). *Edge city.* New York: Doubleday.

Geary, R. (1996). Motor voter's breakdown lane. *The American Prospect.* 28, 41–48.

Gladstein, J. (1992). *Journal of Adolescent Medicine.*

Glaser, M. A., Soskin, M. D., & Smith, M. (1996). Local government-supported community development: Community priorities and issues of autonomy. *Urban Affairs Review*, 31, 778–98.

Glover, M. (1993). U.S. defines poverty line. *Sacramento Bee*, April 4, p. B1.

Goldfield, D. R., & Brownell, B. A. (1990). *Urban America: a history* (2nd ed.). Boston: Houghton-Mifflin.

Goldman, B., Friedlander, D., Gueron, J., & Long, D. (1985). *Findings from the San Diego job search and work experience demonstration.* Program. New York: Manpower Research Corporation (March).

Goldsmith, W. W. (1982). Enterprise zones: If they work we're in trouble. *International Journal of Urban and Regional Research*, 6, 24–35.

Goldsmith, W. W., & Blakely, E. J. (1992). *Separate societies: poverty & inequality in U.S. cities.* Philadelphia: Temple University Press.

Goodman, E. (1996). Women's issues carried the day. *San Francisco Chronicle*, November 12, p. A21.

Gore, A. (1993). *The Gore report on reinventing government.* New York: Random House–Times Books.

Gottman, J. (1964). *Megaopolis.* New York: Macmillan.

Great Britain Department of the Environment. (1987). *An evaluation of the enterprise zone experiment.* PA Cambridge Economic Consultants. London: Her Majesty's Stationary Office.

Green, R. E. (ed.) (1991). *Enterprise zones: New directions in economic development.* Newbury Park, Calif.: Sage Publications.

Green, R. E., & Brintnall, M. (1991) Conclusions and lessons learned. In Green, R. E. (ed.), *Enterprise zones: New directions in economic development.* Newbury Park, Calif.: Sage Publications, Inc., 241–57.

Greenstein, R. (1991). Universal and targeted approaches to relieving poverty: An alternative view. In Jencks, C., & Peterson, P. (eds.), *The urban underclass.* Washington, D.C.: Brookings Institution.

Greer, S. (1965). *Urban renewal and American cities.* Indianapolis: Bobs-Merrill.

Gueron, J. (1986). *Work initiatives for welfare recipients: Lessons from a multi-state experiment.* New York: Manpower Demonstration Research Corporation (March).

———., Wallace, J., & Long, D. (1987). *GAIN: Planning and early implementation.* New York: Manpower Demonstration Research Corporation (April).

Gulak, M. B. (1995). *Homicide and the physical environment.* Paper presented at the Annual Meeting of the Urban Affairs Association, May 3–6, Portland, Oregon.

Haar, C. (1975). *Between the idea and the reality: A study in the origin fate, and legacy of the Model City Program.* Boston: Little, Brown and Company.

Hacker, A. (1992). *Two nations.* New York: Macmillan.

Hall, P. (1977). Green fields and grey areas. Papers of the RTPI Annual Conference, Chester. London: Royal Town Planning Institute. Reprinted in Hall, P. (1981). *The enterprise zones concept: British origins, American adaptations.* Berkeley: University of California, Institute of Urban and Regional Development, Working Paper 350.

———. (1981). Enterprise zones: A justification. *International Journal of Urban and Regional Research*, 6, 1–18.

————. (1989). *Cities of tomorrow: An intellectual history of urban planning and design in the twentieth century.* Oxford: Basil Blackwell.

————. (1991). The British enterprise zones. In Green, R. E. (ed.) (1991). *Enterprise zones: New directions in economic development.* Newbury Park, Calif.: Sage Publications, Inc., 241–57.

Hamilton, R. (1971). The municipal voter: voting and nonvoting in city elections. *American Political Science Review*, 65, 1135.

Hansen, S. B. (1991). Comparing enterprise zones to other economic development techniques. In Green, R. E. (ed.), *Enterprise zones: New directions in economic development.* Newbury Park, Calif.: Sage Publications, Inc., 7–26.

Harrington, M. (1962). *The other America.* New York: Penguin Books.

————. (1984). *The new American poverty.* New York: Penguin Books.

Harris, I. B. (1996). Starting small, and thinking big. *The American Prospect*, 28, 74–77.

Henig, J. (1985). *Public policy and federalism.* New York: St. Martin's Press.

Herbert, B. (1993). The echos of Bushwick. *New York Times*, October 6, p. A5.

Hernandez, R. (1996). Albany plans to act against failing schools. *New York Times*, July 19, p. B1.

Herson, L. J. R., & Bolland, J. M. (1990). *The urban web: Politics, policy, and theory.* Chicago: Nelson-Hall Publishers.

Hill, E. W. N., Wolman, H. L., & Ford, C. C. III. (1995). Can suburbs succeed without their central cities? Examining the suburban dependance hypothesis. *Urban Affairs Review*, 31, 147–74.

Hirsch, A. R. (1983). *The making of the second ghetto: Race and housing in Chicago, 1940–1960.* New York: Cambridge University Press.

Hochschild, J. (1989). Equal opportunity and the estranged poor. In Wilson, W. J., (ed.) (1989).The ghetto underclass: social science perspectives. *Annals of the American Academy of Political and Social Science*, 501 (January), 26–47.

Hodge, S. A. (1996). Reinventing government effort needs some reinventing. *Sacramento Bee*, November 11, p. F6.

Hudson, W. (1980). The new federalism paradox. *Policy Studies*, 8, 900–905.

Human Relations Commissions. (1985). Joint report of the Human Relations Commissions, City and County of Los Angeles. Los Angeles (January).

Jackson K. (1985). *Crabgrass frontier: The suburbanization of the United States.* New York: Oxford University Press.

Jacobs, J. (1961). *The death and life of great American cities.* New York: Random House.

Jargowsky, P. (1996). *Poverty and place: Ghettos, barrios and the American city.* New York: Russell Sage Foundation.

Jargowsky, P. A., & Bane, M. J. (1991). Ghetto poverty in the United States, 1970–1980. In Jencks, C., & Peterson, P. E. (eds.), *The urban underclass*, Washington, D.C.: Brookings Institution.

James, F. J. (1991). The evaluation of enterprise zone programs. In Green, R. E. (ed.), *Enterprise zones: New directions in economic development.* Newbury Park, Calif.: Sage Publications, 225–40.

Jencks, C. (1992). *Rethinking social policy: Race, poverty and the underclass.* Cambridge, Mass.: Harvard University Press.

————. (1994). *The homeless.* Cambridge, Mass.: Harvard University Press.

Jencks, C., & Peterson, P. E. (1991). *The urban underclass.* Washington, D.C.: Brookings Institution.

Johnson. C. E. (1995). We can erase deficit with a gasoline tax. Letter to the Editor. *New York Times*, May 30, p. A10.

Judd, D. (1988). *The politics of American cities.* 3rd ed. Boston: Little, Brown and Company.

Judd, D. (1994). In Memorium. *Urban Affairs Quarterly*, 29, 496.

Juster, F. T. (ed.) (1976). *The economic and political impact of general revenue sharing.* Washington, D.C.: Government Printing Office.

Kaplan, M., & James, F. (eds.) (1990). *The future of national urban policy.* Durham, N.C.: Duke University Press.

Kasarda, J. D. (1985). Urban change and minority opportunities. In Peterson, P. E. (ed.) (1985). *The new urban reality.* Washington, D.C.: Brookings Institution, 33–68.

————. (1988). Jobs, migration, and emerging urban mismatches. In McGeary, M. H. G., & Lynn, Jr., L. E. (eds.), *Urban change and poverty.* Washington, D.C.: National Academy of Sciences, 227–54.

Kasarda, J. (1989). Urban industrial transition and the underclass. In Wilson, W. J. (ed.), *The ghetto underclass: Social science perspectives.* The Annals of the American Academy of Political and Social Science, 26–47.

————. (1990). Structural factors affecting the location and timing of urban underclass growth. *Urban Geography*, 11, 234–64.

————. (1995). *The end of inequality.* New York: Basic Books.

Kaus, M. (1996a). How welfare bill may help Democrats revive liberalism. *Sacramento Bee*, August 12, p. B5.

————.(1996b). Moynihan on Moynihan: The Senator says what he thinks, and what he thinks of what he used to think. *New York Times Book Review*, November 10, 14–15.

Keating, D. (1976). Report to the Ford Foundation on CDBG program evaluation in California. Draft # 2. Berkeley, Calif., October 18.

————. (1994a). Guilding the ghetto: The debate revisited. Paper presented at the American Collegiate Schools of Planning Annual Meeting, Tempe, Arizona, November 5.

————. (1994b). *The suburban racial dilemma: Housing and neighborhoods.* Philadelphia: Temple University Press.

————., Krumholz, N., and Starr, P. (eds.) (1996). *Revitalizing urban neighborhoods.* Lawrence: University Press of Kansas.

Kell, G. (1992). Counting Tenderloin's children. *Sacramento Bee*, June 22, p. A3.

Kern, P. (1989). Suburbs and a blighted city foresee a future in common. *New York Times*, September 7, p. A1.

Kerner Commission. (1968). Report of the national advisory commission on civil disorders. New York: Bantam.

Kerr, P. (1989). Suburbs and a blighted city foresee a future in common. *New York Times*, September 7, p. A1.

Kling, R., Olin, S., & Poster, M. (eds.) (1991). *Postsuburban California: The transformation of Orange County since World War II.* Berkeley: University of California Press.

Kolbert, E. (1994). Adam Walinsky: Private lobbyist for public safety. *New York Times Magazine*, October 30, 42–45.

Kozol, J. (1991). *Savage inequalities: Children in America's schools.* New York: Crown
     Publishers.
Krumholz, N., & Clavel, P. (1994). *Reinventing cities: Equity planners tell their stories.*
     Philadelphia: Temple University Press.
Langie, C.—Associated Press. (1996). 'Connecting the dots' in riot-torn LA: Drawing
     black money into black community vital to rejuvenation. *Chico Enterprise-Record,*
     November 11, p. A6.
Ledebur, L., & Barnes, W. (1992). *Metropolitan disparities and economic growth.*
     Washington, D.C.: National League of Cities.
———. (1993). *All in it together: Cities, suburbs, and local economic regions.* Washing-
     ton, D.C.: National League of Cities.
———. (1997). *Local economies: The U.S. common market of local economic regions.*
     Thousand Oaks, Calif.: Sage Publications.
Leinberger, C., & Lockwood, C. (1986). How business is reshaping America. *Atlantic
     Monthly,* 258, October: 34–38.
Lemann, N. (1994). The myth of community development. *New York Times Maga-
     zine.* January, 26–31, 53–60.
———. (1996). Notes and comments: Kicking in groups. *Atlantic Monthly,* April 27,
     22–26.
Lilly, B. (1990). To fix the budget mess, restore pre-'86 taxes. Letter to the Editor.
     New York Times, October 19, p. A10.
Link, B., Susser, E., & Stueve, A., et al. (1993). Life-time and five-year prevalence of
     homelessness in the United States. Manuscript. New York: Columbia University
     and New York State Psychiatric Institute.
Listokin, D., & Casey, S. (1979). *Mortgage lending and race: Conceptual and analyti-
     cal perspectives of the urban financing problem.* Piscataway, N.J.: Center for Urban
     Policy Research.
Lockhart, C. (1986). *Gaining Ground.* Berkeley: University of California Press.
Loh, J.—Associated Press. (1995). Fort Worth model of community policing. *Cleve-
     land Plain Dealer,* April 16, p. A13.
Long, N. E. (1962). Power and Administration. In Long, *The Polity.* Chicago: Rand
     McNally, pp. 50–63.
———. (1971). The city as reservation. *The Public Interest,* 25, 22–32.
———. (1972). *The unwalled city: reconstituting the urban community.* New York:
     Basic Books.
Lovell, C., & Korey, J. (1975). The effects of general revenue sharing on ninety-seven
     cities in Southern California. In *General revenue sharing utilization project,* Vol. 2.
     Washington, D.C.: National Science Foundation, Research Applied to National
     Needs.
Lowi, T. (1966). *The end of liberalism.* New York: W. W. Norton.
Marble, M. (1992). *The crisis of color and democracy: Essays on race, class and power.*
     Monroe, Maine: Common Courage Press.
Marmor, T. R., Mashaw, J. L., & Harvey, P. L. (1990). *America's misunderstood welfare
     state: Persistent myths, enduring realities.* New York: Basic Books.
Marshall, D. R., & Waste, R. J. (1977). *Large cities responses to the Community
     Development Act.* Davis: University of California, Davis Institute of Governmental
     Affairs.
Massey, D. S. (1982). Enterprise zones: A political issue. *International Journal of
     Urban and Regional Research,* 6, 61–67.

———., & Denton, N. A. (1987). Trends in the residential segregation of blacks, Hispanics, and Asians. *American Sociological Review*, 52, 802–25.

———. (1988). Suburbanization and segregation in U.S. metropolitan areas. *American Journal of Sociology*, 94, 592–626.

———. (1989). Hypersegregation in U.S. metropolitan areas. *Demography*, 26, 373–91.

———. (1994). *American apartheid: Segregation and the making of the underclass.* Cambridge, Mass.: Harvard University Press.

Massey, D. S., & Eggers, M. L. (1990). The ecology of inequality: Minorities and the concentration of poverty, 1970–1980. *American Journal of Sociology*, 95, 1153–88.

———. (1994). The spatial concentration of affluence and poverty during the 1970s. *Urban Affairs Quarterly*, 29, 299–315.

Meckler, L. (1996). Crime bill doesn't always put more cops on streets. *Sacramento Bee*, November 6: p. A6.

Meehan, E. J., & Judd, D. R. (1994). Norton E. Long. *PS: Political Science*, 284–85.

Metropolitan Council, Minneapolis, Minnesota. (1991). *Fiscal disparaties discussion paper*, April 16.

Mewman, Oscar (1971). *Defensible space.* New York: Macmillan.

Meyer, P. B., Yeager, J., & Burayidi, M. A. (1994). Institutional myopia and policy distortions: The promotion of home ownership for the poor. *Journal of Economic Issues*, 28, 567–76.

Moe, R. C. (1994). The reinventing government exercise: Misinterpreting the problem, misjudging the consequences. *Public Administration Review*, 54.

Mollenkopf, J. (1983). *The contested city.* Princeton, N.J.: Princeton University Press.

———. (1992). *A phoenix in the ashes.* Thousand Oaks, Calif.: Pine Forge Press.

Moore, M. (1988). What makes ideas so powerful? In Reich, R. (ed.) (1988). *The power of public ideas.* Cambridge, Mass.: Harvard University Press.

Morrison, H. (1987). *The regeneration of local economies.* Oxford: Oxford University Press.

Moynihan, D. P. (1969). *Maximum feasible misunderstanding: Community action in the war on poverty.* New York: The Free Press—Macmillan.

———. (1996). *Miles to go: A personal history of social policy.* Cambridge, Mass.: Harvard University Press.

Murray, C. (1984). *Losing ground: American social policy, 1950–1980.* New York: Basic Books.

Nathan, R. P. (1987). Will the underclass always be with us? *Society*, 24, 57–62.

———. (1989). Is the underclass beyond help? *New York Times*, January 6, op-ed commentary.

———. (1993). Reform welfare? What for? *New York Times*, October 7, p. A19.

———. (1994). Welfare, work and the real world. *New York Times*, January 31, p. A11.

———. (1995). Reinventing government: What does it mean? *Public Administration Review*, 55, 213–15.

———., & Adams, C. F. (1977). *Revenue-sharing: The second round.* Washington, D.C.: Brookings Institution.

Nathan, R. P., & Dommel, P. R.l (1978). Federal-local relations under block grants. *Political Science Quarterly*, 93, 421–42.

National League of Cities. (1995). *The state of America's cities.* Washington, D.C.: National League of Cities.

National Performance Review (1993a). *From red tape to results: Creating a government that works and costs less.* Washington, D.C.: U. S. Government Printing Office (September); cited in text as NPR.

Nenno, M. (1974). Housing and community development act of 1974: An interpretation. *Journal of Housing,* 31, 345–62.

Newsweek. (1996). City slickers: The 25 most dynamic mayors in America. *Newsweek,* November 11, 28–38.

New York Times. (1996). Mail-in democracy. February 2, p. A20.

Norris. D., & Thompson, L. (eds.) (1995). *The politics of welfare reform.* Newbury Park, Calif.: Sage Publications.

O'Brien, C. C. (1996a). Thomas Jefferson: radical and racist. *Atlantic Monthly,* October, 53–74.

———. (1996b). *The long affair: Thomas Jefferson and the French revolution, 1785–1800.* Chicago: University of Chicago Press.

Orfield, G., & Ashkinaze, C. (1991). *The closing door: Conservative policy and Black opportunity.* Chicago: University of Chicago Press.

Orfield, M. (1994). *Metropolitics: A regional agenda for community and stability.* Unpublished manuscript.

O'Rourke, L. M. (1992). Cities' problems on the rise, glum mayors say at meeting. *Sacramento Bee,* January 26, p. B11.

Ortiz, R. (1981). *Mail ballot election: documentation.* San Diego: Registrar of Voters, June 22.

Osborne, D., & Gaebler, T. (1992). *Reinventing government.* Reading, Mass.: Addison-Wesley.

Pape, A. M. (1990). New revenue sources. Letter to the Editor. *New York Times,* October 19, p. A10.

Pear, R. (1993). Poverty 1993: bigger, deeper, younger, getting worse. *New York Times,* October 10, p. E5.

Peirce, N. R. (1993a). Cities blight now extends into suburbia. *Sacramento Bee,* October 11, p. B15.

———. (1993b). Blueprint to put cities back together. *Sacramento Bee,* December 21, p. B7.

———. (1993c). An urban agenda for the president. *Journal of Urban Affairs,* 15, 457–67.

———. (1995). In Indianapolis, a mayor and unions work together to streamline government. *Sacramento Bee,* November 21, p. B7.

Peirce, N., with Johnson, C. W., & Hall, J. S. (1993). *Citistates: does the American city have a future? How urban America can prosper in a competitive world.* Washington, D.C.: Seven Locks Press.

Peirce, N., & Guskind, R. (1993). *Breakthroughs: Re-creating the American city.* New Brunswick, N.J.: Rugters University Press, Center for Urban Policy Research.

Perlman, E. (1988). Reagan's last budget. *City and state,* February 29: p. 1–22.

Peterson, P. E. (1981). *City Limits.* Chicago: University of Chicago Press.

———. (1992). An immodest proposal: Let's give children the vote. *Brookings Review,* 11, 18–23.

———., and Rom, M. C. (1990). *Welfare magnets: A new case for a national standard.* Washington, D.C.: Brookings Institution.

Phillips, D. A., & Cabera. N. J. (eds.) (1996). *Beyond the blueprint: Directions for research on Head Start.* Roundtable on Head Start Research, Board on Children,

Youth and Families, Commission on Behavioral and Social Sciences and Education, National Research Council, Institute of Medicine. Washington, D.C.: National Academy Press.

Phillips, K. (1969). *The emerging republican majority.* New York: Arlington House.

Phillips, K. (1990). *The politics of rich and poor: Wealth and the American electorate in the Reagan aftermath.* New York: Harper Perennial.

———. (1994). *Boiling point: Anger and middle class politics in the American suburbs.* New York: Harper Perennial.

Plastrik, P. (1995). *New Democrat* (January–February).

President's Commission for a National Agenda for the Eighties. (1980). Report of the Panel on Policies and Prospects for Metropolitan and Non-Metropolitan America. Washington, D.C.: U.S. Government Printing Office.

Polsby, N. (1984). *Political innovations in America: The politics of policy innovation.* New Haven, Conn.: Yale University Press.

Putnam, R. D. (1993). The prosperous community: Social capital and public life. *The American Prospect,* 13, (Spring).

———. (1995a). Bowling alone: America's declining social capital. *The American Prospect,* 6, 65–76.

———. (1995b). Bowling alone: An interview with Robert Putnam about America's collapsing civic life. *Bulletin of the American Association for Higher Education* (September), 3–7.

———. (1995c). The strange disappearance of civic America: The Ithiel de Sola Pool Lecture. *PS:Political Science* (Winter).

———. (1995d). The strange disappearance of civic America. *The American Prospect,* 24, [http://epn.org./prospect/24/24putn.html].

———. (1996). Robert Putnam responds. *The American Prospect,* 25, 26–28. (Http://epn.org/prospect/25/25-cnt.html#putn).

Quadagno, J. (1994). *The Color of welfare: How racism undermined the war on poverty.* New York: Oxford University Press.

Reagan, M., & Sanzone, J. (1981). *The New Federalism.* New York: Oxford University Press.

Reeves, R. (1993). Put on a gas tax. *Sacramento Bee,* January 9, p. B6.

Reich, R. (ed.) (1988). *The power of public ideas.* Cambridge, Mass.: Harvard University Press.

———. (1991). The secession of the successful. *The New York Times Magazine,* January 20, 16–17, 42–45.

Rennert, L. (1996). Clinton signs increase in minimum wage. *Sacramento Bee,* August 21, p. A1.

Rich, M. J. (1992). UDAG, economic development and the death and life of American cities. *Economic Development Quarterly,* 6, 150–72.

Ricketts, E. R., & Sawhill, I. V. (1988). Defining and measuring the underclass. *Journal of Policy Analysis and Management,* 7, 316–25.

Richmond, H. R. (1994). Rationale and program design. National Land Use Policy Institute, June 1994.

Roberts, S. (1993). 2 senators confront urban ills. *New York Times,* April 19, p. A12.

Rohe, W. M., & Stegman, M. (1990). *Public housing homeownership demonstration assessment.* Chapel Hill, N.C.: University of North Carolina; published for the U.S. Department of Housing and Urban Development.

Rosenbaum, D. P. (ed.) (1994). *The challenge of community policing: Testing the promises.* Newbury Park, Calif.: Sage Publications.

Rosenbaum, J. E. (1995). Black pioneers—Do their moves to the suburbs increase economic opportunity for mothers and children? *Housing Policy Debate*, 2, (4).

Ross, B. H., & Levine, M. A.(1996). *Urban politics: Power in metropolitan America*, 5th edition. Itasca, N.Y.: F. E. Peacock Publishers, Inc.

———., & Stedman, M. S. (1991). *Urban politics: Power in metropolitan America*, 4th edition. Itasca, N.Y.: F. E. Peacock Publishers, Inc.

Rubin, H. J. (1993). Understanding the ethos of community-based development: Ethnographic description for public administrators. *Public Administration Review*, 53, 428–37.

Rusk, D. (1993). *Cities without suburbs.* Baltimore: Johns-Hopkins University Press; 2nd. edition.

———. (1994a). Bend or die: Inflexible state laws and policies are dooming some of the country's central cities. *State Government News*, February, 6–10.

———. (1994b). Inelastic Cities. Lecture delivered at Cleveland State University, the Maxine Goodman Levin College of Urban Affairs, September 23.

———. (1996). *Baltimore unbound: A strategy for regional renewal.* Baltimore: The Abell Foundation.

———., & Mosley, J. (1994). The academic performance of public housing children—does living in middle class neighborhoods and attending middle class schools make a difference? Washington, D.C.: Urban Institute (May).

Russell, G. D. (1997). The political economy of police reform. *Police Studies*, 4 (forthcoming).

Sacramento Bee. (1996). Oregon: candidates in dead heat. January 20, p. A12.

San Francisco Chronicle News Services. (1996). Clinton reveals plan for children to have work-study tutors. *San Francisco Chronicle*, October 26, p. A3.

Sartre, J. P. (1947, 1949). *Les Chemins de la liberté.* Published in English translation in the United States as *The age of reason* (1947), *The reprieve* (1949), and *Troubled Sleep* (1951). New York: Alfred A. Kropf, 1947.

Sasser, J. (1993). Soak the rich, not the elderly. *New York Times*, February 2, p. A13.

Sauas, E. S. (1982). *Privitizing the public sector.* Chatham, N.J.: Chatham House Publishers.

Savitch, H. V., Collins, D., Sanders, D., & Markham, J. P. (1993). Ties that bind: Central cities, suburbs, and the new metropolitan region. *Economic Development Quarterly*, 7, 341–57.

Schneider, M. (1980). *Suburban growth: Policy and process.* Brunswick, Ohio: Kings Court Communications.

Schneider, W. (1992). The suburban century begins. *Atlantic* (July), 33–44.

Schwarz, J. E., & Volgy, T. J. (1992). *The forgotten Americans.* New York: W. W. Norton.

Skocpol, T. (1985). Brother can you spare a job? Work and welfare in the United States. Paper presented at the annual meeting of the American Sociological Association, Washington, D.C., August 17.

Skocpol, T. (1990a). Targeting within universalism: Politically viable policies to combat poverty in the U.S. Paper presented at the Annual Meeting of the American Political Science Association, San Francisco, August 30–September 2.

———. (1990b). Sustainable social policy: Fighting poverty without poverty programs. *The American Prospect*, 3, 58–70.

————. (1994). *Protecting soldiers and mothers: The political origins of social policy in the United States.* Cambridge, Mass.: Harvard University Press.

————. (1996). Delivering for young families: The resonance of the GI Bill. *The American Prospect, 28,* 66–72.

Skogan, W. G. (1991). *Disorder and decline: Crime and the spiral of decay in American neighborhoods.* New York: The Free Press.

Smith, T. W. (1987). That which we call welfare by any other name would smell sweeter. *Public Opinion Quarterly, 51,* 75–83.

Sonenshein, R. J. (1996). The battle over liquor stores in South Central Los Angeles: The management of an interminority conflict. *Urban Affairs Review, 31,* 710–37.

Stanley, H. (1987). *Voter mobilization and the politics of race.* New York: Praeger Publishers.

State of California, Office of the Legislative Analyst. (1985). *An analysis of findings from the San Diego job search and work experience demonstration program.* Sacramento, May.

Stegmen, M. A. (1991). *More housing, more fairly.* New York: Twentieth Century Fund Press.

Stegman, M. A., & Luger, M. I. (1993). Issues in the design of locally sponsored home ownership programs. *Journal of the American Planning Association, 59,* 417–32.

Stein, L. (1996). State income disparity tops industrialized world, nation. *Sacramento Bee,* November 17, p. F1.

Sterngold, J. (1996). Scratch 'n' spend: Muting the lotteries perfect pitch. *New York Times,* July 14, p. E1.

Sternlieb, G. (1971). The city as sandbox. *The Public Interest, 25,* 14–21.

Stone, C. (1995). School reform and the ecology of games metaphor. *Journal of Urban Affairs,* 17.

Stone, D. (1994). Making the poor count. *The American Prospect, 17,* 84–88.

Swanstrom, T. (1993). Beyond economism: Urban political economy and the postmodern challenge. *Journal of Urban Affairs* 15, 55–78.

————. (1994). The philosopher in the City: The new regionalism debate. *Journal of Urban Affairs,* 17.

Terry, D. (1995). Chicago housing agency to be taken over by U.S.: Dilapidated empire overwhelms local officials. *New York Times,* May 28, 1.

Terry, L. (1990). Leadership in the administrative state. *Public Administration Review,* 21, 395–412.

————. (1993). Why we should abandon the misconceived quest to reconcile public entrepreneurship with democracy. *Public Administration Review, 53,* 393–95.

Thompson, Frank J. (ed.) (1993). *Revitalizing state and local service.* San Francisco: Josey-Bass.

Toner, R. (1992). *Politics of welfare: focusing on the problems.* New York Times, July 5, p. 1.

Trojanowicz, R. (1991). *Community policing and the challenge of diversity.* East Lansing, Mich.: Michigan State University, National Center for Community Policing.

————., & Bucqueroux, B. (1990). *Community policing: A contemporary perspective.* Cincinnati: Anderson Publishing Company.

————., & Carter, D. (1988). *The philosophy and role of community policing.* East Lansing, Mich.: Michigan State University, The National Neighborhood Foot Patrol Center.

————., & Moore, M. (1988). *The meaning of community in community policing.*
East Lansing, Mich.: Michigan State University, The National Neighborhood
Foot Patrol Center.

Tucker, C. (1996). Women's practical vote for Clinton. *San Francisco Chronicle,*
November 11, p. A20.

Tym, R., and Partners & Weeks L. D. (1984). *Monitoring enterprise zones: Year three
report.* London: Roger Tym Associates.

U. S. Bureau of the Census. (1973). 1970 census of the population: Low income areas
in large cities, PC-2-9B. Washington, D.C.: U.S. Government Printing Office.

U. S. Bureau of the Census. (1985). 1980 census of the population: Low income areas
in large cities, PC-2-8D. Washington, D.C.: U.S. Government Printing Office.

U. S. Bureau of the Census. (1990). 1990 census of the polutation: Low income areas
in large cities, PC-2-8D. Washington, D.C.: U.S. Government Printing Office.

U. S. Bureau of the Census. (1991a). Metropolitan areas and cities, 1990 Census
Profile, No. 3 (September).

U. S. Bureau of the Census. (1991b). Poverty in the United States: 1990 Current
Population Reports. Series R60, No. 175. Washington, D.C.: U.S. Government
Printing Office.

U. S. Bureau of the Census, and U. S. Department of Housing and Urban Development, Office of Policy Development and Research (1991). Current Housing
Reports: Supplement to the American Housing Survey for the United States in
1991. Washington, D.C.: H151/91.

U. S. Bureau of the Census. (1996a). CPS Report (September). Washington, D.C.:
U.S. Government Printing Office.

U. S. Bureau of the Census. (1996b). SIPP Study. Washington, D.C.: U.S. Government Printing Office.

U. S. Congress, Senate. (1995). Senate Committee on Labor and Human Resources,
Subcommittee on Children, Family, Drugs and Alcoholism. *The administration
proposal for Head Start reauthorization.* 103rd Congress, Second Session.

U. S. Department of Health and Human Services. (1996). Annual survey of drug use
(August).

U. S. Department of Housing and Urban Development. (1996). Moving up to the
American dream. Washington, D.C.: HUD (July).

U. S. Department of Housing and Urban Development. (1994). Priority home: The
federal plan to break the cycle of homelessness. Washington, D.C., (July); cited
in text as HUD, 1994.

U. S. Department of Housing and Urban Development. (1995). Empowerment: A
new covenant with America's communities—President Clinton's national urban
policy report (July 1995). Washington, D.C.: Government Printing Office; cited
in text as HUD/NUPR, 1995.

U. S. Department of Housing and Urban Development. (1991). Supplement to the
American housing survey for the United States, 1991. Washington, D.C.: HUD.

U. S. Department of Justice. (1992). Community policing in Seattle: A model partnership between citizens and police. Washington D.C.: U. S. Department of Justice,
Office of Justice Programs, National Institute of Justice (August).

U. S. Department of Justice. (1993a). The systems approach to crime and drug
prevention: A path to community policing. Washington, D.C.: Bureau of Justice
Assistance, Vol. 1 (September).

U. S. Department of Justice. (1993b). Community policing in Chicago. Washington, D.C.: Office of Justice Programs, National Institute of Justice (October).

U. S. General Accounting Office. (1994). Homelessness: McKinney Act programs and funding through fiscal year 1993. Washington, D.C. (June); cited in text as GAO.

Varady, D. P., & Lipman, B. J. (1994). What are renters really like? Results from a national survey. *Housing Policy Debate*, 5, 491–531.

Vidal, A. (1992). *Rebuilding communities: A national study of urban community development corporations.* New York: New School for Social Research, Community Development Research Center.

Vidich, A., & Bensman, J. (1958). *Small town in mass society.* Princeton, N.J.: Princeton University Press.

Voith, R. 1992. City and suburban growth: Substitutes or complements? Federal Reserve Bank of Philadelphia. *Business Review*, 21–31.

Wagman, F. W., & Botein, H. (199–). Housing mobility and life opportunities. *Clearinghouse Review*, Vol. 27.

Walinsky, A. (1995). The crisis of public order. *Atlantic Monthly* (July), 39–54.

Walker, C. (1993). Nonprofit housing development: Status, trends, and prospects. *Housing Policy Debate*, 4, 369–414.

Walker, Thai. (1996). Housing Secretary unveils plan to aid inner-city homebuyers. *San Francisco Chronicle*, August 8, p. B1.

Wallace, B. (1996). Why reforming welfare won't force people to go to work. *San Francisco Sunday Chronicle and Examiner Book Review*, September 15, 5.

Wallis, A. D. (1994). The third wave: Current trends in regional governance. *National Civic Review* (Summer–Fall).

Waste, R. J. (1987). Innovation and the making of social welfare policy: The California workfare program. Paper presented at the Annual Meeting of the American Political Science Association, Chicago (September).

———. (1989a). *The ecology of city policymaking.* New York: Oxford University Press.

———. (1989b). Federal urban policy in the 1990s: deja vu and disaster. *Urban Resources*, 5, 21–24.

———. (1993a). City limits, pluralism, and urban political economy. *Journal of Urban Affairs*, 15, 445–55.

———. (1993b). Between riots: urban reservations and urban poverty. A paper delivered at the Annual Meeting of the Urban Affairs Association, Indianapolis (April 21–24).

———. (1994). Reinventing urban politics: Policy proposals to bring the city back into national politics. Paper delivered at the Annual Meeting of the Urban Affairs Association, New Orleans, March 2–6.

———. (1995a). Urban poverty and the city as reservation. *Journal of Urban Affairs*, 17, p. 3.

———. (1995b). California: From workfare for the poor to warfare on the poor. In Norris, D., & Thompson, L. (ed.) (1995). *The politics of welfare reform.* Newbury Park, Calif.: Sage Publications.

———., & Sparrow, G. (1985). Democracy through the mail. *Social Policy*, 58–59.

Weir, M., Orloff, A. S., & Skocpol, T. (1988). Epilogue: the future of social policy in the United States: constraints and possibilities. In Weir, M., Orloff, A. S., & Skocpol, T., *The politics of social policy in the United States.* Princeton, N.J.: Princeton University Press.

Welch, W. M.—Associated Press. (1992a). $1 Billion urban aid bill ok'd as Congress meets Bush's terms. *Sacramento Bee*, June 19, p. A4.

———. (1992b). Mayors want $35 billion for urban ills: cut foreign aid they recommend. *San Francisco Examiner*, June 21, p. A4.

West, C. (1994). *Race Matters*. New York: Vintage Books.

Westbrook, M. (1992). Connecticut's new affordable housing appeals procedure assualting the presumptive validity of land use decisions. *Connecticut Bar Journal* (June).

Wilkerson, I. (1992). The tallest fence: feelings on race in a white neighborhood. *New York Times*, June 21, p. Y12.

Will, G.—Washington Post Writers Group. (1996). Education in Harlem. *Chico Enterprise-Record*, September 15, p. A12.

Wilson, J. Q. (1994). Reinventing public administration: The John Gaus lecture. *PS: Political Science*, 27, 667–73.

Wilson, M. (1996). Hopes for shopping center soar as murder rate declines. *San Francisco Chronicle*, October 7, p. A1.

Wilson, R. (1992). Contemplating a collegiate cop corps. *Chico State Orion*, November 11, p. 6.

Wilson, W. J. (1984). The black underclass. *Wilson Quarterly*, 8, 88–99.

———. (1991a). Public policy research and the truly disadvantaged. In Jencks, C., & Peterson, P. E. (eds.), *The urban underclass*. Washington, D.C.: Brookings Institution, 460–81.

———. (1991b). Studying inner-city social dislocations: the challenge of public agenda research—1990 presidential address. *American Sociological Review*, 56, 1–14.

William, W. J. (1985). The urban underclass in advanced industrial society. In Peterson, P. E. (ed.). *The new urban reality*. Washington, D.C.: Brookings Institution.

———. (1987). *The truly disadvantaged: the inner city, the underclass, and public policy*. Chicago: University of Chicago Press.

———. (1988). American social policy and the ghetto underclass. *Dissent*, 57–64.

———. (ed.) (1989). The ghetto underclass: social science perspectives. *Annals of the American Academy of Political and Social Science*, 501, 26–47.

———. (1990). Race and the democratic coalition. *The American Prospect*, 1, 1.

———. (1992). The right message. *New York Times*, March 17, p. A15.

Wilson, W. J. (1996a). "When Work Disappears," *New York Times Sunday Magazine*, (August 18): pp. 26–33, 48–53.

———. (1996b). *When work disappears: The world of the new urban poor*. New York: Knopf.

Wolman, H., & Agius, E. (1996). *National urban policy: Problems and prospects*. Detroit: Wayne State University.

Wood, R. (1991). Cities in Trouble. *Domestic Affairs*, 1, 221–38.

———. (1995). People Versus Places: The dream will never die. In Caves, R. W. (ed.), *Exploring urban America*. Nerwbury Park, Calif.: Sage Publications, Inc., 137–43.

Zehr, M. A. (1995). Civil investing: Getting involved in civic life. (http://www.cof.org/docs/fnc496b.html).

Index

Page numbers in *italic* refer to tables.